Jaliila

ANTHROPOLOGICAL PAPERS

MUSEUM OF ANTHROPOLOGY, UNIVERSITY OF MICHIGAN

NO. 14

TELL ṬOQAAN:
A SYRIAN VILLAGE

BY

LOUISE E. SWEET

ANN ARBOR

THE UNIVERSITY OF MICHIGAN, 1974

PREFACE

SINCE FULL-LENGTH STUDIES of the villages of the Near East have been rare, in this monograph I am presenting an outline, in as broad a scope as the circumstances of my residence permitted, of the life of one Arab village in Syria, Tell Ṭoqaan. My intent is to present data that will be useful to others. Past studies and the accounts of travellers and missionaries in the Near East have concentrated on mountain villages in the Lebanon, Palestine, or Iraq areas. Owing to the position of Tell Ṭoqaan, close to the shepherd pastoral zone of northwestern Syria, material is available here from a locality which has not been extensively described in English.

Because this is the first report on a Muslim Arab village made by a woman ethnographer, since Hilma Granqvist's monographs on the Palestinian village of Artas, a few notes on the field situation seem appropriate. I lived in Tell Ṭoqaan from January 4 to May 20, 1954, but had contact with the village from mid-December, 1953. It was my good fortune to live in a peasant household and not to be separated by class residence from the village population. I did not have an interpreter and very few English-speaking Arabs of the peasant class came my way. My small command of Arabic was a serious obstacle in many ways, but it had its advantages. The villagers were unfailingly patient in helping me to understand as much as possible. And breaches of courtesy and custom which I unknowingly committed from time to time were kindly explained away on the basis of my ignorance. As the days wore on, the more I learned to understand and the more coherently I could speak, the more, they said, I became "like them."

I found it an advantage to be a woman—and to work alone—in a Muslim Arab village. I had free access to all dwellings whether or not I was escorted, and more often because I was not escorted. As a foreigner and an American I was a guest at luncheons at which no village woman of whatever class would be allowed. As a woman it was acceptable, after the first month or so of establishing acquaintance, for me to participate in some of the working activities, at least enough to learn the simple techniques.

In Tell Ṭoqaan, both Eastern (Julian) and Western (Gregorian) calendars are recognized in regard to political and economic activities. The Muslim calendar, of course, governs religious events, and is apparently synchronized with the Western calendar. The Western calendar runs thirteen days ahead of the Eastern calendar. In the text of the monograph dates are given according to the Western calendar, the basis of my observations; but in Table V (which see) the dates are cited in the Eastern Calendar, since this is the basis of the villagers' calculations in respect to the events diagrammed. The importance of maintaining the distinction as I have is illustrated in the information on the the two "accursed periods" of the musta kurdat, one for each calendar. Wherever the monetary unit "pound" is used, reference is always to the Syrian pound. In 1953-54 the exchange averaged three and one-half pounds to the American dollar.

The question whether to use an Arabic term or the English equivalent is simply not settled here. Many of the words were learned in Tell Ṭoqaan for the first time and their concrete reference is hard to get over. In other cases the Arabic term sounds just as well to me as the English and is used as a synonym to avoid repetitions (jilbaan or vetch). In still other cases the English term (e.g., mayor) is not quite the equivalent of the Arabic (e.g., muxtaar), so the Arabic is preferred. As a concession to the appearance of the printed page the convention of underlining Arabic terms is omitted. The transliteration system is given in Appendix A.

The opportunity to make this field study is owed to the Department of Near East Studies, University of Michigan, and to its Aleppo Field Session of 1953-54, of which I was a member.

I appreciate the financial support that enables me to publish this monograph. It is furnished, in part, by the Ford Foundation Near East Field Session grant to the Department of Near Eastern Studies and, in part, by the Museum of Anthropology, both of the University of Michigan.

My thanks are extended especially to Associate Professor William D. Schorger, Director of the Session, for his help, encouragement, and support during the initial experience in ethnographic field work and in the writing up the material, and for his continued interest and aid. The study was originally prepared under the Departments of Anthropology and Near Eastern Studies in partial fulfillment of the requirements for the degree of philosophy in the University of Michigan. Parts of the original text have been extensively rewritten. To Miss Katharine A. Fellows I owe thanks for patient and expert editorial help in this final form of the study.

I am also indebted to many others at the University of Michigan, without whose help and advice, teaching and encouragement, this monograph could not have been completed. I am particularly grateful to Professor Horace Miner for his extensive editorial assistance throughout the original manuscript, and for his suggestions on the chapter on Social Structure. I also thank Assistant Professor Ernest McCarus for his help on linguistic materials, Associate Professor George F. Hourani, of the Department of Near East Studies, for suggestions on the historical section, and Professor Clark Hopkins, of the Department of Classical Studies for his translation of a Seleucid inscription from Zammaar, and Mrs. Jeanne M. Plummer for maps and drawings. Interpretation of data and recording of material I take as my responsibility; they do not represent those of the persons, institutions or foundations who have supported this work.

To the people of Tell Ṭoqaan, of Saraaqab, Afess, Kuusaniyya, Zammaar, and Ras ^{l} Ain, to the many visitors from other villages, I express my gratitude for their courtesy and hospitality, and moreover, for their patience and understanding of my purpose among them. I am grateful to Mr. Ilhan Tchelebi, of Aleppo, for his concern and aid in making the field work possible, and to Mr. YaHya ṢalaaH ad Diin, of Aleppo, who arranged for me to live in Tell Ṭoqaan and extended many courtesies to me during my stay there. To YaHya ^{c}aarif, my host and chief informant, and to his family, I am grateful as only a friend and member of his household can be for their care and consideration, their daily kindness and instruction, for their encouragement and patience, for the primary needs of food, shelter, and good companionship, and for making my stay with them in Tell Ṭoqaan one I hope I may repeat.

CONTENTS

Page

I. Introduction 1

II. Tell Ṭoqaan area 7

Geography and topography 7

Topography and drainage 9

Soil types and distribution 10

Climate and seasons 11

Vegetation 12

Fauna 14

Settlements and communications 15

Ethnogeography 17

III. People of Tell Ṭoqaan 22

Population and vital statistics 22

Physical appearance 22

Pathological condition 23

Census categories 23

Urban or rural origin 26

Tribal representation 27

IV. Language in Tell Ṭoqaan 29

Local knowledge of language 29

Features of Arabic spoken in Tell Ṭoqaan 30

V. History of Tell Ṭoqaan 33

The villagers' historical concepts 33

Shayx MaHmuud and his history 36

History of Tell Ṭoqaan 37

General historical setting 41

VI Land system of Tell Ṭoqaan 48

Settlement and lands 48

Settlement pattern 51

Legal category of lands 57

Landholders in Tell Ṭoqaan 59

	Page
Division of land and the field system	61
Subtenures and contracts	65
VII. Agriculture and gardening	67
Agriculture	67
Gardening	83
VIII. Animal husbandry	89
Traditional classes of animals	89
Property in animals	91
Property marks	92
Taxes	93
Breeding	93
Care of animals	96
Herding and grazing	97
Milk and its processing	101
Other animal products	105
Poultry	107
Bees	108
IX. Buildings and compounds	110
The compound	110
Construction types	112
Construction procedures	116
Organization of labor in housebuilding	117
Interiors of dwellings	118
Other structures of the family compound	121
Other buildings in Tell Ṭoqaan	122
Ownership of buildings	123
X. Household technology and economics	125
Food	127
Cooking	129
Eating	131
Bread	132
Household work and crafts	134
A day in a peasant household	136

	Page
XI. Distribution and commerce	143
Noncommercial distribution and exchange	143
Commercial distribution	145
XII. Division of labor	148
Landlord-hired hand system	150
Tribal Shayx unit	151
Peasant system	153
Division of labor by sex	154
Division of labor by age	156
Division of labor by ethnic group	157
Division of labor for village as a unit	158
Specialists and specialization	158
XIII. Social structure	163
Kinship	163
The family	164
Lineages	169
Marriage	173
Kinship terms and usage	182
Village organization	189
Relations with the state	191
Social life and occasions	195
Clothing and its social significance	198
XIV. Ideology and ritual	205
Life-cycle ceremonies	206
Medicine and magic	216
Islam	220
XV. Conclusion	225
Tell Ṭoqaan: the local factors	225
Culture patterns in Tell Ṭoqaan	227
Tell Ṭoqaan and the urban system	228
Nature and direction of cultural change	230

Appendix

A. Phonemic symbols used in transcription of Arabic words . . . 237

B. List of families and individuals in Tell Ṭoqaan 240

C. Land divisions in Tell Ṭoqaan 249

Bibliography 250

ILLUSTRATIONS

Figures

Frontispiece Facing title

1. Northwest Syria 8

2. Tell Ṭoqaan area 19

3. Land divisions of Tell Ṭoqaan 49

4. Settlement pattern of village 53

5. A Tell Ṭoqaan lineage: Bayt Tell Haanii 171

(Numbers 6-54 follow page 256)

6. Tell Ṭoqaan

7. Shayx Nuuri's house and stable compound

8. Cemetery and camping ground

9. Shepherd family following their flocks to spring grazing

10. Qirbaat (Gypsy) tents

11. Boy with hedgehog

12. Young men playing ball

13. Young men and hunting dogs

14. Market day at Ma ᶜaret Mishriin

15. Plowing

16. Plowshare

17. Peasant's seedling bed

18. Young woman planting cotton with seed tube

19. Irrigation wheel

20. Irrigating garden beds

21. Jilbaan (vetch) harvest

Figure

22. The Haylaan (threshing machine)

23. Excavating on the village midden

24. A shayx's tomb in Tell Ṭoqaan

25. Milking sheep

26. Selling milk to cheese agent

27. Mixing mud for bricks

28. Making mud bricks

29. Mason laying a mud brick wall

30. Constructing an arch

31. Building a domed room

32. Women building a storage bin

33. Interior

34. Interior: molded shelf

35. Burden carrying

36. Girls drawing water

37. Tools and utensils

38. Making winter fuel

39. Making a tray of wheat straw

40. Washing pots and pans

41. Baking village bread

42. Portable fireplace

43. Stationary fireplace

44. Mother and children

45. Pounding wheat at Shayx Nuuri's

46. Carpenter repairing plow

47. Horseshoeing

Figure
48. Seed tubes mounted on tractor.
49. Women's clothing: Pastoralist
50. A recent bride
51. Facial tattoos
52. Forearm tattoos
53. Plow and threshing machine
54. Man smoking a water pipe

TABLES

Table		Page
I.	Phonological differences in Tell Ṭoqaan Arabic	31
II.	Landholders, landholdings, and manner of supervision in Tell Ṭoqaan	60
III.	Landholding, landholders in Quṣm Jabas division of land	63
IV.	Comparison of peasant and industrial equipment and labor in agricultural operations in Tell Ṭoqaan	68
V.	The agricultural calendar in Tell Ṭoqaan	80
VI.	Control of resources in property, tools, and labor among landlords, tribal shayx, peasants, and laborers in Tell Ṭoqaan	149
VII.	Distribution of families in Tell Ṭoqaan according to type	165
VIII.	Kinship and sociocultural segment endogamy and exogamy in 73 marriages	175
IX.	Kind of marriage and village endogamy and exogamy in 54 marriages	177
X.	The Aghaydaat-Bu Layl	180
XI.	Kinship terms	185
XII.	Phonemic symbols used in transcription of Arabic words	237
XIII.	Resident families of Tell Ṭoqaan	241
XIV.	Individuals living in Tell Ṭoqaan	248
XV.	Land divisions of Tell Ṭoqaan	249

I

INTRODUCTION

TELL ṬOQAAN is a small Muslim Arab farming, gardening, and sheep- and goat-raising village located in the plains area of northwest Syria. According to its particular features, it exemplifies the economic functions and social place of village life and villagers in the whole sociocultural system of the Levant area.[1] The ways in which the three major subsystems of traditional Levant culture are integrated are represented in Tell Ṭoqaan, as well as the ways in which they are distinct from each other, for Tell Ṭoqaan is distinguished more for its cultural and ethnic heterogenity than for its internal uniformity. Yet in its position as a small agrarian community it acts, on the whole, like a peasant village, but one in which the traditions of shepherd pastoralism are unusually strong.

The three spheres which comprise the indigenous sociocultural whole of the Levant are the urban system, the agricultural village system, and the shepherd pastoral system. In the most inclusive sense each of these may be regarded as a part of the whole of Levant culture and society, each interlocks with the others in the total scene.

In general syntheses of the cultural features of the Near East it has been the custom to map it, particularly the peak of the Fertile Crescent, in terms of dominant subsistence patterns, into three zones: the inner, eastern desert steppe of the nomadic Bedouin camel tribes, the middle zone of the "semi-sedentary" shepherd tribes, and an outer western rim devoted to sedentary agriculture and urban-based manufacturing and commerce (Bacon, 1946, 1954; Patai, 1951; Weulersse, 1946: 60-66). Such a concept tends to join or relate sociocultural units which are separate,

1. The Levant area of the Near East comprises here the areas of the present states of Lebanon, Syria, Israel, the Hashemite Kingdom of Jordan, northern Iraq, and the Hatay area of southeastern Turkey in which the city of Antioch is located. The sources on this area which I have used define its vague boundaries as much as, if not more than, the features of the area itself. It is equally difficult to be specific about the "indigenous socio-cultural whole," but in a general way it refers to those features present in the area before the fall of the Ottoman Empire (1918) which are regarded as characteristic of the Levant and Near East.

such as the two kinds of pastoralism, and to draw the arbitrary lines of classification by subsistence pattern and apparent autonomy across the real lines of regional economic and social interdependence.

The customary tri-zone concept of cultural relations in the Near East allies the shepherds culturally to the Bedouin, whereas it seems more likely that there is a greater cultural distinction between camel nomads and shepherd pastoralists than between the latter and peasant cultivators. At least, this seems to be true for the Levant area. Ashkenazi (1938: 56-57), for example, noted that in division of labor and in marriage customs, the practices of seminomad or shepherd tribes of northern Palestine are very different from those of the camel or "true" Bedouin and are more like those of the peasants. The role, or sphere, of camel pastoralism in the Near East seems to be historically more closely connected with, and dependent upon, the oasis towns of Arabia than with the continuous belt of cultivation of the Levant area.[2] Culture traits of Bedouin life which may be found among the shepherd peoples of the Levant result rather from contact, prestige of the powerful Bedouin tribes, and the political necessity of close arrangements to avoid mutual destruction.

Shepherd pastoralism in the Levant constitutes a characteristic subsystem of the whole culture of the area and is distributed continuously throughout it. The relative political independence of some Syrian shepherd tribes, such as the Mawali and the Hadiidiin, appears to be a consequence of their locus of territorial occupation, historical circumstances, and the general economic and political conditions in the Levant at different times. Political unification of the area, under indigenous or foreign control, has alternated with periods of areal disunity and local autonomy. During periods when the shepherd tribes were independent, the local sectors of the predominately agricultural area, such as the Druze territory, were equally independent political entities. Thus the tri-zone concept with its crossing of types of political units with an arbitrary drawing of subsistance zones tends to obscure a system of urban-rural relationships which,

2. Implicit here is a division of the Near East into subareas in terms of distinctive patterns of ecological adaptation: desert-oasis, exotic river basins, rain-fed plains, humid tropical or subtropical coasts, and mountains. In all cases, except the mountain areas, an economic trichotomy of urban craft and mercantile system, cultivating village system, and nomadic pastoral system could be demonstrated, but this is a topic for future synthesis and outside the present scope. Features of contact zones of occupation and the interregional routes of traditional caravan commerce add further interesting problems, some of which enter into this paper at the descriptive level.

in the Levant, link peoples of the cities, of the agrarian villages, and of nomadic sheep raising.

It is in the study of Tell Ṭoqaan that the interdependence of these spheres, from the rural point of view, becomes clear, as well as the distinctiveness of each from the others. The majority of the populations of the Near Eastern States are made up of agricultural villagers. Along with urban artisans and laborers, they constitute the bulk of the members of Near Eastern society, but in economic and social status they form a distinct and inferior class to the urban elite. In this consideration the nomad tribal pastoralists have generally been left out of the picture as numerically small and separate societies, in spite of the fact that their economic contribution is significant and their territorial dominance remains considerable. But political and economic control in the Levant states is located in the urban centers, in the hands of the urban notables—landowners in particular—and the gap between this elite and the subordinate working class is marked in every aspect of culture (Hakim, 1953; Tannous, 1955). Outside the major cities the effects of the diffusion of western industrial civilization, in terms of technological exploitation of the land, standard of living, or education, have only recently begun to affect the village system and the rural area. In Tell Ṭoqaan, as with other villages, the manner of living retains in material culture and custom much of the traditional pattern of the Near East before the fall of the Ottoman Empire.

The cities and towns of the Levant depend on their rural hinterlands for their food supplies and raw materials for local manufactures. As well as serving as market centers for both peasants and pastoralists, the urban centers secure their needs by means of control of the land and its crops through ownership and tenant contracts. Contracts with shepherds also control a considerable amount of livestock and animal products. Systems of trading also reach out from the cities into the countryside and follow various patterns. There is the itinerant peddler or artisan who, as an individual, joins a caravan of similar traders going out from his town to trade with the pastoralists in the eastern grazing zone. There is the entrepreneurial system headed by an urban merchant-capitalist who may specialize in one product. His agents and employees go out to the hinterland and buy up wool, milk, manure, and so forth. There is also the urban-based merchant who has purchaser or patron relations with clients on a formal and traditional basis. He may be a grain merchant and speculator who loans landholders or peasant farmers money on their crops. It is by such means, in times of crop failure, that many urban elite have secured land, and control of the resources of the rural hinterlands have been concentrated in the urban centers (Gibert, 1949: 152).

Outside the urban centers the countryside of the Levant is marked by a division between village agriculture and pastoralism. Most of the arable land is put to double use as cultivated fields and as pasturage. The agricultural field system is based on a two- or three-field rotation of winter crops which leaves half to two-thirds of the lands of each village fallow each year. Pastoralism is concerned chiefly with flocks of sheep and goats as the major product animals and these depend on open or "natural" grazing, rarely on forage crops or stable feeding, and not at all upon closed, fenced pastures. Fallow, field border, wasteland, and uncultivated steppe are its provinces. Whether in the mountains or plains such grazing practices require seasonal movements to open pastures at greater or smaller distances depending upon habitat conditions and size of flocks. Thus shepherd and cultivator are separated by their respective techniques. Competition for and cooperation in land usage between sedentary agriculture and pastoralism have developed between the two systems terms of contract or political relations which reflect the relative strength of one or the other in the control of the land. In the relatively well-watered and fertile areas of the west and of the mountains, agriculture predominates, and pastoralism is a secondary economic activity of specialists. Property in flocks is largely held by cultivating people and the flocks tend to be small and used primarily for household needs rather than raised for the market. The farther east into the open steppe one moves, however, the more insecure is agricultural exploitation of the dry plains by the traditional peasant cultivating techniques and economic organization. The eastern plains are thus more open to shepherd pastoralism. Here, where competition for land between cultivation and grazing is in favor of the pastoralist, the social consequences of the technological dichotomy between agriculture and livestock raising have given rise to such independent tribal societies as the Mawali and Hadiidiin. Among the pastoral people sheep are the basic property, and the way of life is elaborated around their raising, processing of milk, and marketing of animals and wool to the agricultural villagers and to the urban centers. It is not a self-sufficient economy, however, and depends on both urban center and village cultivators for material needs and services.

Both the urban populations and the pastoral peoples depend upon the products of agriculture for their staple foods, and upon the villages for their markets. These are the basic needs which link all three spheres together. The agrarian economy is the support of the whole and makes possible the development of manufacturing and trading in the towns and extensive sheep raising among the pastoralists.

The arable countryside of the Levant is characteristically divided into nucleated village communities with their attached fields, gardens, and wastelands. The antiquity of this settlement pattern is generally accepted, though its origin is not clear. Such village-land units certainly predate the Ottoman period (Preston, 1903) and long formed the basis of the traditional tax-farming system.

As the techniques of handling sheep are a specialization of the pastoralists, so the control of traditional cultivation technology and techniques of exploiting local natural resources rests with the peasants of the villages and is passed down from generation to generation within the family and the local community. But inasmuch as the peasant cultivators have been subject to taxation, tribute, and tenancy obligations, control of the land and its products lies ultimately with the urban elite or ruling power.

In the Levant area diversity of environment and diversity of the population in ethnic origin and religion give rise to many kinds of villages, but in all cases the village economy is the most self-sufficient of the three spheres of Levant life, and by its capacity to produce a surplus of crops supports the other two. The scale of the traditional economic organization is "small," based primarily upon the labor force of the extended patrilineal family and supplemented by some migratory seasonal labor at harvest and year-round availability of landless men. Different regions of the Levant produce special crops, fruits in the mountains of the Lebanon, garden vegetables along the small rivers where intensive cultivation can be practiced, and cereals in the open plains of Syria. Industrial cash crops, tobacco and cotton, are beginning to spread in the area, and citrus and banana plantations on the Lebanon coast are beginning to modify the traditional peasant farming predominance.

Tell Ṭoqaan, like other Syrian villages, takes its place in the village system as a community producing a surplus of crops for the urban markets. Unlike most villages, it is internally diverse in cultural content and structure, divided between traditional peasant and sedentarized pastoralist traditions. While the cultivation of the old summer and winter field crops and irrigated gardening form the basis of its economy, to them have been added properties in flocks of sheep and goats which are of local importance. Traditional village crafts and exploitation of natural resources play only a small part in its affairs and are not marketed outside. Cotton is becoming valuable as a cash crop. In technology, Tell Ṭoqaan is mixed; both pastoral and peasant techniques are present. The use of some industrial agricultural machinery—tractors, pumps, and harvesting combines—illustrates one manner in which industrial civilization is spreading in the Levant area.

Socially diverse, sedentarized pastoralists and peasants of different origins compose its population, and Tell Ṭoqaan is the headquarters of the shayx of a small, partly settled shepherd tribe. Most of the land is controlled by an elite composed of the shayx and a small group of urban landholders.

In undertaking this study I have sought to record as much as possible of the unique character of Tell Ṭoqaan as a culturally mixed village, but one which is involved in the interaction of the three traditional subsystems of the Levant, the urban, the pastoral, and the agrarian village. Since it also participates in the advance of industrialized agriculture into the area it is possible to suggest in a few ways from its example how a shift is taking place in the village system from small-scale traditional peasant economy and social segmentation toward larger scaled production and organization.

II

TELL ṬOQAAN AREA

GEOGRAPHY AND TOPOGRAPHY

IN NORTHWEST SYRIA the brackish marsh of Maadek spreads south of the city of Aleppo in an irregular, shallow basin about 28 kilometers long. At the southern end of the basin a prong of the marsh stretches northwest around a low headland. The village of Tell Ṭoqaan is located near the southwest edge of this portion of the big marsh. From the highest point near Tell Ṭoqaan, the top of the ancient city mound which stands next to the village, the horizon of red and gray-brown earth or blue marsh water draws a sharp flat line against the sky; only at one point to the northeast does the ridge of the Jebel Hass raise a rugged, shadowy line of low crests in the distance. Thus, Tell Ṭoqaan lies at one of the lowest points of a minor, inland drainage basin in the northwest quarter of Syria (Fig. 1). From this point to the coast of the Mediterranean Sea, 110 kilometers straight west, the Syrian terrain climbs up in a series of limestone ridges and karst formations to the north end of the Jebel Zawiyya to a height of 877 meters from there it drops down into the northern end of the cleft of the Ghaab swamp, then rises again, at the northern end of the Jebel Alowite (*ca.* 1000 meters), before it finally dips down to the sea edge near the Ras al Basiita Peninsula north of the port of Latakia. The double massif of the Jebel Zawiyya and the Jebel Alowite separates the humid Mediterranean coast of the northern Levant from the arid plains of the interior; it corresponds, although altitudes are not as high, to the Lebanon and Anti-Lebanon ranges which continue the coastal barrier south of the Tripoli-Homs Gap. The Jebel Zawiyya is about 25 kilometers west of Tell Ṭoqaan.

Eastward from Tell Ṭoqaan the terrain rises slowly across the Ma^{c}mura zone to the Jebel Hass, about 40 kilometers away and beyond which lies the northern end of the Shombol or grazing steppe of the nomads. Twenty-eight kilometers north of Tell Ṭoqaan, the Quwayk River empties into the northern end of the marsh, after passing through Aleppo from its sources beyond the Turkish border. Southward from Tell Ṭoqaan the terrain slopes gradually upward toward the vicinity of the city of Hama, 78 kilometers south southwest.

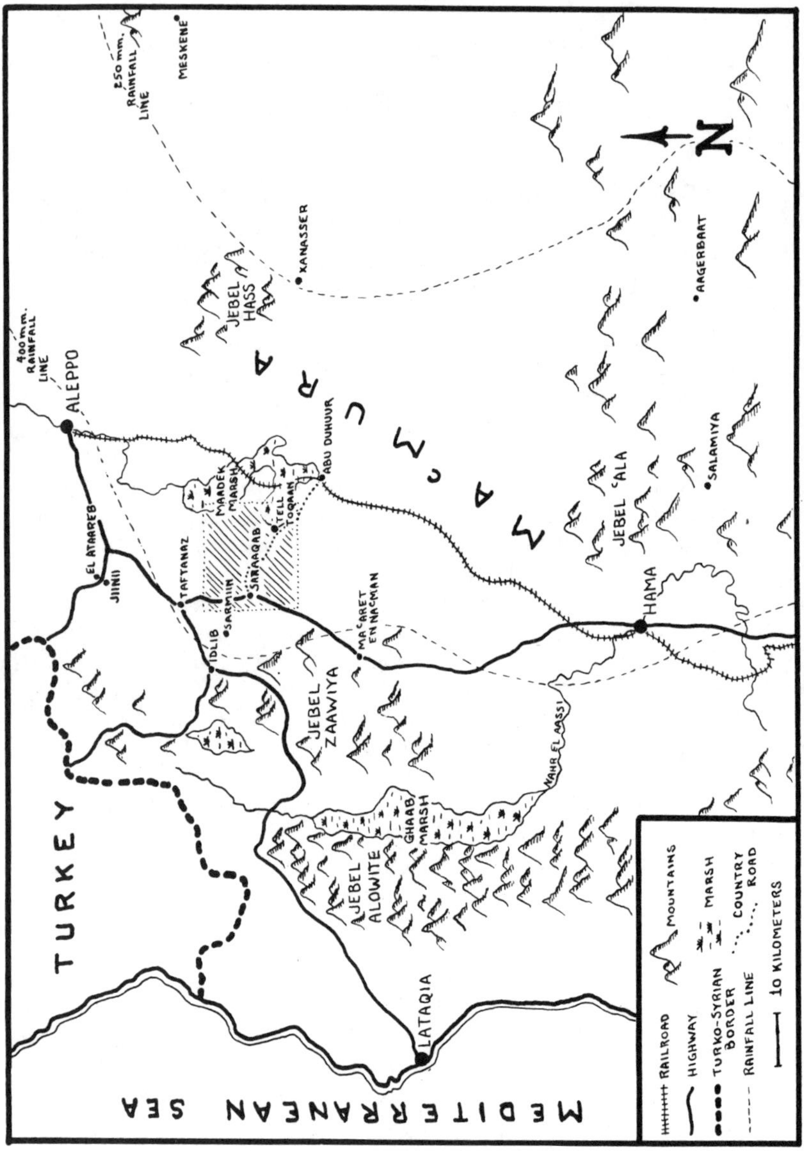

Fig. 1. Northwest Syria.

The area east of the coastal range, sighted from the village, is a part of northwest Syria called the interior plain and dry-farming area. Here in the north the narrow band of arable rain-fed lands between the coastal ranges and the dry eastern steppe widens out to some 150 kilometers in breadth. It is a region that has passed back and forth many times, between agricultural and pastoral exploitation and control, over the millenia of culture history in the Near East.

Topography and Drainage

The earthen houses and compounds of Tell Ṭoqaan spread out over an uneven area above a small spring which, in 1954, sent only a small trickle of water down a reedy bed to the marsh east of the village. This prong of the big marsh is called Es Siiha and its surface lies at about 245 meters altitude. Tell Ṭoqaan is situated on a level about 10 meters higher. In the immediate vicinity of Tell Ṭoqaan contour lines on the 1:50,000 scale map (French Levant Series, Saraaqab Grid, 1943) show a gradual and undulating rise of the terrain north, west, and south. About 2 kilometers from the village the first of a series of ridges of weathered limestone outcrops just reaches 300 meters altitude and closes the villagers' horizon as it curves from southwest of Tell Ṭoqaan around to the northwest. Called Es Skayk, this low ridge marks the southwest boundary of the village lands with those of the neighboring settlement of Shuuḥa.

In 1943, date of the scale map, the Siiha marsh edge lay about one and a half kilometers from the village on the northeast side, but in the spring of 1954 the water stood much higher. It lapped within 10 meters of the tell and inundated good wheat and cotton land north of it. One of the peasants told me that the water level of the marsh usually rose and fell over a four- to eight-year natural cycle, and the present height was owed to the government, which had recently allowed or caused more water to enter the big marsh from the Quwayk River.

The most prominent topographical feature of Tell Ṭoqaan and its land is not, however, a geological formation but a cultural one. Across the road on the north side of the village and approximately 300 meters from it, rises a great city tell or mound, probably of Seleucid times. It is roughly oval in shape and approximately 700 meters long and 500 meters wide. Three levels are pronounced and its highest point, at the end nearest to the village, is 30 to 40 meters above the level ground at its foot.

No prominent wadis or seasonal stream beds cross Tell Ṭoqaan lands. The Wadi Hassaniyyaate bed twists down the Skayk ridge from Shuuha, 3 kilometers southwest of Tell Ṭoqaan, but it peters out in a gravelly patch of earth just before it reaches the village. I never saw it filled with water during the winter nor heard that it ever was. Six kilometers west of the village and close to the boundary between Tell Ṭoqaan and Islamiin lands, the Wadi Rmass, or Luuf (as it was always called locally) has cut a wide bed with steep banks in places and its course is directed in a generally southwest to northeast direction. The Wadi Luuf runs well to the north of Tell Ṭoqaan, beyond the Skayk ridge and the villages of Zahabiyye, Ajlaas, Osmanniyye, and Jazraaya. Ultimately, it empties into the marsh in the area of Zammaar, 8 kilometers north of Tell Ṭoqaan; in late winter of 1953-54 it flooded several times and temporarily cut off travel north and westward.

Because of its proximity to the Siiha prong of the Maadek marsh and the descending contours of the terrain from the north, west, and south, Tell Ṭoqaan has an unusually shallow water table compared to that of other villages nearby. Water begins to fill a well excavation at 10 to 20 feet in the higher places in the village and at only 3 to 6 feet in the lower places and in the low land around the tell. But ease of reaching a water-bearing level is not an indication of inexhaustible abundance. Wells that fill several feet deep when they are first opened may be used up in a few days of mud-brick making and time must be allowed for them to fill again. There are a number of reservoir pits for irrigation which have gone permanently dry or which have only a little water standing in them, insufficient for further use. The year the spring was cleared (1953) the flow was so abundant as to give rise to disputes over the distribution, but the following year there was only a trickle which went untapped, and the pool of the spring stood only a few inches deep.

In the interior plains area of northwest Syria ground waters are fed by infiltration from the surface during the winter rains and are conserved at the impermeable level of subsurface rock strata (Dubertret and Weulersse, 1940: 42; Weulersse, 1946: 39). Undoubtedly, the basin of the marsh close to Tell Ṭoqaan collects most of the seepage from a wide area of diffuse subsurface movement. The village wells and reservoirs make only slight interruptions and small collecting pools which are quickly used up; rarely do they tap any considerable sources from this general infiltration and flow toward the lower level of the marsh basin.

Soil Types and Distribution

Tell Ṭoqaan stands at a boundary of soil types. As viewed from the tell, its lands to the north, west, and southwest are the dull red of the terra rossa, which continues and becomes deeper in color to the west and north wherever it is not interrupted by rocky outcrops and ridges. A characteristic soil of the Mediterranean climate area, terra rossa is widely distributed in the Near East and particularly in the northwest sector of Syria around Idlib, a town about 30 kilometers northwest of Tell Ṭoqaan. The soil in the Idlib area is considered one of the most fertile in Syria. Terra rossa erodes easily, but cereals and cotton do well on it and, if it is deep, fruit trees also. (Blanchard 1929: 209; Fisher 1950: 64; Weulersse 1946: 47). Terra rossa has resulted from the solution and erosion of the products of the disintegration of limestone, the parent material (Reifenberg, 1938: 39-40). With the exception of imported stone, limestone appears to be the only native rock and stone to be found in the immediate vicinity of Tell Ṭoqaan.

Eastward from Tell Ṭoqaan the color of the earth grays and whitens and thus marks the beginning of steppe soils. The midden soil of Tell Ṭoqaan, the low and wet ground along the thin stream bed from the spring, and the higher land northeast of the village and along the marsh are black or gray earth. The black soil of the midden is distinct in origin from that of the last two sites, since it is the product of village debris; the gray of the other two, closely associated with the marsh, is alluvial soil.

Local farmers distinguish and classify these soils by color, if not by constitution, and accord to each type certain qualities and uses. The villagers pointed out that the red earth ended at Tell Ṭoqaan and the west edge of the marsh. They added that the gray or white steppe soil which stretched eastward from the village was frequently interrupted by stony land over which the soil cover was so thin that it could not be cultivated and supported only grazing grasses.

Climate and Seasons

Since Tell Ṭoqaan lies well behind the costal ranges of the Levant, it is in the area subject to the "interior regime of temperature." Isohyet maps indicate that in this region, 45 kilometers south southwest of Aleppo, the median temperatures of January and July are a few degrees less extreme than those encountered in the immediate vicinity of Aleppo, where the medians are 42° F. in January and 88° F. in July (Dubertret and Weulersse, 1940: 32, 33; Fisher, 1950: 390). It was, in fact, perceptibly (if only slightly) warmer in Tell Ṭoqaan in December and January than in Aleppo. Growth of crops and the first harvests also preceded the Aleppo area by a week or so.

This inland plains region is part of the climatic zone of the "Mediterranean steppe" (Dubertret and Weulersse, 1940: 37) a zone characterized by dominance of summer and winter seasons and little marked by the short transitions of spring and autumn. The cold winters, when temperatures frequently drop below freezing and snowfalls may last several days, and the long, rainless summers result in two "interruptions," or dormant periods, of plant and animal life that are characteristic of Irano-Turanian zoogeographic regions (Bodenheimer, 1935: 20). Rainfall in this climate is confined to winter; summer is long, hot, and dry—five months of almost cloudless, rainless sky.

During the 101 days I resided in Tell Ṭoqaan from January 4 to May 20, 30 days with rain were recorded. These 30 days of rain were distributed as follows: January, 10; February, 8; March, 6; April, 5; and May, 1. The last rainy day for March and those of April were only passing thundershowers. The last occurrence of rain, during the night of May 3, was unusual and scarcely more than a heavy dew, and a rainless month had preceded it. From then on no more could be expected until late September when the first autumn showers would come.

In the Mediterranean steppe zone the winter rains occur in two periods, October-November and late December-March, with the maximum in January (Fisher, 1950: 48). Formerly, eastward movement to the steppe grazing began with the first winter rains, but in recent years, as in 1954, the shepherds have not left until February.

Tell Ṭoqaan is located in the 500-250 millimeters annual rainfall zone (Dubertret and Weulersse, 1940: 31). The 250-millimeter line lies 70 or 80 kilometers east of Tell Ṭoqaan and marks the environmental limit for dry agriculture. Local concern about rainfall focuses upon the time of its occurrence, in conjunction with the growth stage of the crops, as well as upon its abundance.

The people of Tell Ṭoqaan recognize all four seasons, but spring, however brief, is distinguished from the others by the pleasantest aspects of nature: abundant grazing and beautiful flowers, birth of young animals, greening of fields, and pleasant weather. Spring is the time for visiting and relief from heavy work between the winter plowing and planting and the summer reaping and threshing. It is the time when the heavy winter diet is lightened with fresh milk products, green vegetables, and the first fruits.

Vegetation

The geographical location of Tell Ṭoqaan places it within the vegetation zone or botanical province variously termed the

"Irano-Turanian (Fisher, 1950: 70, map), the "cultivated steppe zone" (Dubertret and Weulersse, 1940: 87), and "the domain of cultivated steppe and Mediterranean oasis" (Weulersse, 1946: 50). The last of these descriptive terms emphasizes the dominance of the vegetation developed by man. Notable features of the vegetation are the absence of trees and shrubs, unless introduced by man; the presence of steppe grasses; the adaptation of plants to the climatic conditions of seasonal dichotomy; and the long summer period of dessication from drought and high temperatures.

The few trees in or near Tell Ṭoqaan and the more extensive orchards said to have been present in the past, were all planted by man. A few pine, mulberry, fig, apricot, and apple were the only trees that I observed; a few rose bushes and one grapevine were set out in compounds while I was in the village. With a more abundant water supply, closer to the surface than in nearby villages, Tell Ṭoqaan is potentially a "Mediterranean oasis" in its capacity to support trees or orchards. The orchards existent before the Mawali-Hadiidiin war were located in the low land along the stream, and here young fruit trees had recently been planted again.

With the exception of the spring and streamside, however, the vegetation of the surrounding lands of Tell Ṭoqaan conform to the characteristics of the "cultivated steppe zone." In this zone natural vegetation adapts to the marked seasonal dichotomy in two ways. The cereals and grasses complete their growth during the winter rainy season and survive the dry summer as seed. Other plants adapt structurally and are helped to survive the arid period by extended root systems, bulbs and tubers in which nutrients are stored, reduction of leaf surface, and other mechanisms. Late winter and early spring, after the midwinter pause, are blooming periods for both categories of plants. Wherever vegetation was found on the village lands, March and April were the green and flowering months. But during the first weeks of May this vegetation began to wither in the increasing heat and soon only the edges of the stream and the irrigated gardens remained green.

Few parts of Tell Ṭoqaan land support wild vegetation, but there appear to be more than is available around villages to the west and north because there are more stony outcrops of limestone which cannot be profitably cultivated. Grasses and many plants flowering from bulbs or tubers and the "camel thorn" flourish in season on the Skayk ridge, on the slopes of the great tell, and along field and path edges where plowing has not disturbed them. Marsh reeds and grasses are thick along the stream and at the edge of the marsh. Water plants grow abundantly in the shallow spring and stream, among them the familiar, peppery water cress.

One of the characteristics which makes Tell Ṭoqaan a crossroads village, I was told, is its location in relation to vegetation. It was said that the shiiH, the best grazing grass, begins on the south and east side of Tell Ṭoqaan and that from there onward there is much good grazing; and, further, that none of the land north and west is good for grazing since it does not have the steppe grazing grasses. The local movement of flocks in February from the northern villages down to Ras l Ain, the first village southeast of Tell Ṭoqaan, seems to confirm this.

A number of spring plants, including a mint, are gathered from the wastelands for salad greens and spices. The inner stalk of the cotton thistle (salbiin) is collected in quantities and eaten raw or cooked. Several herbs have medicinal usage, and these include camomile (babuunij), which is brewed as a tea.

Fauna

Owing not so much, perhaps, to the paucity of wild fauna in the Tell Ṭoqaan area, but rather to the season of my residence in the village and the habits of wildlife, little was seen of the wild animals or came up for discussion. The Skayk ridge, the slopes of the tell, and the marsh appear to provide an ample nearby habitat for wild fauna. Dubertret and Weulersse pointed out that Syria is a meeting place of many regional faunal types; although, according to Bodenheimer, Irano-Turanian types dominate in the steppe area, particularly burrowing rodents.

Actually noted among wild mammals were bats, hedgehogs, rabbits, a jackal, and mice. Rodents of many species are considered the most abundant group of animals (Bodenheimer 1935: 95, 104), but they are largely nocturnal in habit. Accounts of wolves as threats to sheep and the hyena as a threat to man were given me. For two days early in March the villagers were excited by the report of a hyena in the neighborhood and a hunt was organized which was unsuccessful. A few gazelle skins and a skull seen in the village were said to be trophies from hunts in the Beriyya (grazing steppe) to the east.

At all times, however, birdlife was abundant. Wild geese and ducks wintered in the marsh. Other large water birds like herons were also found there. A solitary stork appeared briefly on migration; the Arabs call him Hajj Luugluug and say he makes the pilgrimage to Mecca. Sparrows, swallows, hawks, and ground owls are in the neighborhood all year. Early in March a great many, brightly colored, small, field and song birds and larger species arrived, among them the hoopoe, horned larks, and especially the warwar, (the bee eater *Merops piaster*). This bird, with its brilliant blue and orange, black and white plumage, arrives about bee-swarming time and is regarded as the chief threat to the villagers' hives. When the day is cold, I was told, the bees cluster together and the warwar will swoop down to eat them; then people go out and beat pans to frighten the bird away.

In the spring and stream and in the reservoir pools frogs and water insects abound; many small fish live in the spring at Tell Ṭoqaan and in the one at Ras l Ain. But the marsh was said to be too brackish to support such life.

During the late winter and early spring snakes were not in evidence, nor were insects with the exception of a small house-dwelling gnat or fly (barghash) and a large moth (bsharra). The larvae of the gnat live in the mat or thatch ceiling of some room types. The moth is believed to be an omen of good news to come. Toward the end of March mosquitoes and houseflies began to appear. Mosquitoes breed prolifically in the marsh; some of the villagers, as well as sources in Aleppo and Beirut, said that they carried the malaria parasite. Horseflies and other insects become annoying pests for the horses and mules in spring; and the villagers are forced to protect the nostrils of their working animals with burlap sacks.

Local people said that in the hot summer both scorpions and snakes are plentiful; both are greatly feared, but especially the scorpion which frequents the dwellings. In spite of dire predictions by urban dwellers, I did not encounter or hear of lice or fleas infesting the human population. Perhaps, the availability of water and evidence of regular bathing and laundering, as well as the season, contributed to keeping these pests down.

Settlements and Communications

Tell Ṭoqaan lies in an area well populated with villages, each surrounded by its own agricultural and grazing lands. Distances between villages are short and vary from 2 to 6 kilometers; the five nearest villages to Jazraaya are visible from the village or tell.

East of Tell Ṭoqaan and close to the marsh is the large compound of Bayt Sharqii ("East House") inhabited by the members of a single family, all of whom work for the Aleppo landlords who own border and marshland there. It is the only occurrence in this area (that I am aware of) of a homestead type of dwelling and land-unit relation, and as such is in contrast to the nucleated village settlement pattern general in the Near East. Tell Ṭoqaan people work for Bayt Sharqii and the family there is closely associated with the life of the village.

There are no uninhabited or unutilized stretches of land and, to my knowledge, all of the local terrain is allocated to some village or the landlords thereof. Even the shallows of the Siiha marsh have been surveyed and belong to Tell Ṭoqaan and Bayt Sharqii landholders. The pastoral grazing zones, tribally allocated by the government, begin now about 70 kilometers to the east.

A comprehensive network of roads and paths connects all the villages with each other and with the more important country roads. None is surfaced or tended, but they are traversible in dry weather by automobile. A main route of country travel joins Tell Ṭoqaan with Saraaqab, a large market village, 14 kilometers northwest and located on the major north-south highway of Syria which links Aleppo and Damascus. Another country route begins at Tell Ṭoqaan and runs northward through villages situated along or close to the west shore of the Maadek marsh and arrives at Aleppo after about 65 kilometers. The route to Aleppo by way of Saraaqab and the highway is about 85 kilometers and, south to Damascus, approximately 285 kilometers. When the shepherds move eastward down the major and minor country roads for the spring grazing, many flocks, family groups, and attendant caravans of merchants and Qirbaat ("Gypsies") converge and pass by Tell Ṭoqaan on the road which continues southeast 14 kilometers to Abu Duhuur and beyond.

Abu Duhuur is a market village and station stop on the railroad line which runs from Aleppo south to Hama and Homs. The railroad crosses the west side of the marsh and the trains are visible from Tell Ṭoqaan. In winter when deep mud made automobile travel west to the highway impossible Shayx Nuuri and members of his family drove east along the limestone ridges to Abu Duhuur and took the train from there to Aleppo.

During the dry season buses on two lines operate two or three times daily. One line runs southeast and northwest between Abu Duhuur and Idlib. Idlib is the government administration center which has jurisdiction over the caza (kaẓa, administrative district) that includes Tell Ṭoqaan; it is situated on the Aleppo-Latakia highway about 30 kilometers northwest of the village. The second bus line runs from Abu Duhuur around the south end of the marsh, past Tell Ṭoqaan, and north to Aleppo by way of the villages along the marsh. Travel is especially heavy on days when markets are held in Idlib, Saraaqab, and Abu Duhuur. At this season Tell Ṭoqaan is a bus stop and in 1954 one of the men of Tell Ṭoqaan secured a ticket concession and planned to construct a coffee shop for waiting passengers.

From Saraaqab to Abu Duhuur, beside the main country road which passes Tell Ṭoqaan, there runs a government telephone line which is primarily for the use of the gendarmarie. The nearest telephone is at the gendarme post at Tell Suultaan, 6 kilometers southeast of Tell Ṭoqaan; the next are at Saraaqab and Abu Duhuur. With fair regularity planes of the various air lines which service the Near East are seen to pass high over Tell Ṭoqaan.

The people of Tell Ṭoqaan are in frequent contact with a considerable number of other villages and the market towns and cities through marriage and kinship ties and commercial and legal dealings. Aleppo and Idlib are regularly visited or visitors are received from them. Other communities of contact are as far away as Marayya, some 90 kilometers north, Alowite villages 100 kilometers to the west, Salamiya 60 kilometers south, and the Circassian village of Khan Aasser, 50 kilometers or more to the east. But most of the regular week-in, week-out contact is bounded by Aleppo (north), Maar Shuuriin (about 26 kilometers southwest), Idlib, and the Beriyya (grazing area) to the east; it focuses largely on the villages of the Bu Layl tribe and the town nearest to Tell Ṭoqaan.

In the wet winter season when country roads are deep in red mud, only foot travelers, riders of animal transport, and tractors can pass from village to village, but even so people come and go continuously by these means. Villages of the interior plain, particularly those which, like Tell Ṭoqaan, stand next to a well-traveled road, are in no way isolated by season or terrain.

Ethnogeography

Tell Ṭoqaan is in the northwest corner of the Ma^{c}mura ("populated" or "inhabited" area), the intermediate and "recently" sedentarized zone which lies between the "old" peasant agricultural region west of the Aleppo-Damascus highway and the eastern limit of agriculture and beginning of the pastoral zone. The line that separates the first two runs from Meskene on the Euphrates in the north southward in an irregular fashion east of the Jebel Hass and east of the villages of Agerbat and Forgloss, which are situated east of Hama and Homs, respectively. The western boundary of the Ma^{c}mura is fairly accurately marked by the Aleppo-Damascus highway. The nomadic zone termed the Menaader bounds the Ma^{c}mura on the south (Weulersse, 1946: 64, 303-04, Fig. 49; De Boucheman, 1934: map, 12; Mouterde and Poidebard, 1943: map, 14).

The Ma^{c}mura, long contested by the two major shepherd pastoral tribes, the Mawali and the Hadidiin, and their respective allies, is now populated by agricultural villages of various tribal affiliations or of peasant origin from the west (De Boucheman, 1934: 12, 14, 17).

Immediately surrounding Tell Ṭoqaan, the villages may be classified, as the people themselves do, into three types: (1) Nontribal peasant (fallaaHiin) villages; (2) tribal villages, whose residents regularly belong to one section of a tribe; and (3) mixed villages (shuurba, "soup" villages) whose populations are of diverse tribal and peasant origin and whose landownership was mixed. For twenty-eight of thirty-seven villages in an area roughly 20 by 20 kilometers, which includes Tell Ṭoqaan, the distribution by type is as follows: Tell Ṭoqaan and Tell Suultaan are the only small mixed villages; Saraaqab and Afess are large, ancient, mixed villages close to town category in size and are situated on the highway. Kafer Aamiin is the only nontribal village. The remaining twenty-two are tribal villages and represent sections of the Aghaydaat-Bu Layl, Na^{c}im, Bu Shab^{c}an, Mawali, and Hadiidiin tribes.

Since 1928, the time when property and territorial disputes were settled between the two major tribes of the area (Mawali, Hadiidiin) by the establishment of a boundary (Von Oppenheim, 1939, I: 299), the villages of the Hadiidiin and their satellites have been located north of Tell Ṭoqaan and east of the railroad; those of the Mawali and their allies south and west of this line. Long before 1928 Jazraaya had been, and Tell Ṭoqaan now is, the headquarters of the paramount shayx of the Bu Layl, a splinter tribe of Aghaydaat origin. How the five or six Bu Layl villages are strung from Ras l Ain northward along the western shore of the marsh to Zammaar and Tell Aalluush are shown in Figure 2. West of them are located other tribal villages, mostly Na^{c}im in affiliation in the central part and Bu Shab^{c}an toward the north.

The Tell Ṭoqaaniis believe that their village stands at a crossroad of ethnic distribution as well as at one of communication routes, soil types and vegetation, and agricultural-pastoral economy. All the territory to the north and east, they said, is under the Hadiidiin or Hadiidiin power; all that to the southwest and south is Mawali or under Mawali power; while in and around Tell Ṭoqaan, between these two, are the villages of the small tribe of the Bu Layl. Distribution of the tribal villages in this small area does not appear to bear out this generalization precisely. Such information as is available suggests that in fact this northwest corner of the Ma^{c}mura is mixed and shows a transition in territorial dominance. To the north of the narrow strip between the highway and the railroad and marsh are some villages of a long sedentarized tribe, the Bu Shab^{c}an, satellites of the Hadiidiin (De Boucheman, 1934: 38); many more are found northward to and around Aleppo (Von Oppenheim, 1939, I: 294). Among them, and increasing in number in the Tell Ṭoqaan area,

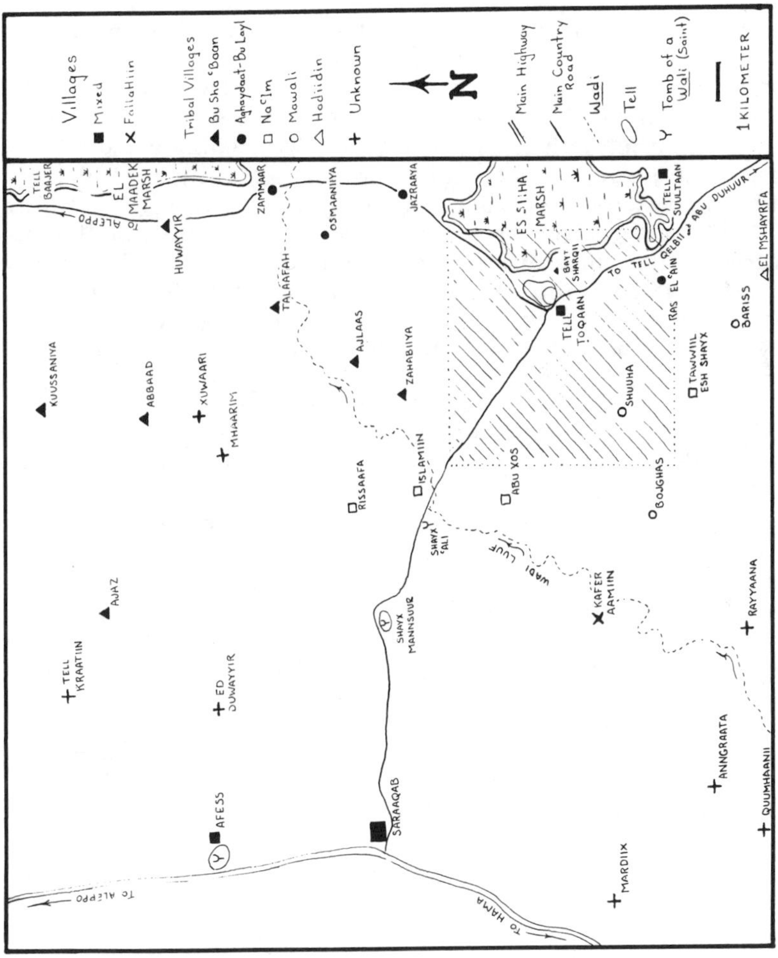

Fig. 2. The Tell Toqaan Area.

are villages of the Na^{c}im, a tribe associated with the Mawali. About the latitude of Tell Ṭoqaan villages of the Mawali and their allies begin to predominate and they increase in number southward. But at the foot of the marsh appear a few Hadiidiin villages—only Masaade and Tell Qelbi are in the Tell Ṭoqaan area. Abu Duhuur, southeast and on the railroad, is locally counted as Hadiidiin.

The "Tell Ṭoqaan area" appears to be very small and arbitrarily drawn on the map, but as outlined here it has several interesting ethnogeographic characteristics in relation to neighboring areas and the Ma^{c}mura zone as a whole: The area (1) includes a group of villages of a single tribe, small but distinct, the Aghaydaat-Bu Layl, members of which are allied to the Mawali but who also have connections by marriage with the Hadiidiin and Bu Sha^{c}baan; (2) represents from north to south a shift from predominantly Hadiidiin-allied tribal villages to predominantly Mawali-allied tribal villages; and (3) has predominately tribal villages to the east and in the area in general; fallaHiin or mixed villages appear increasingly to the west. Nevertheless, from the point of view of the villagers, Tell Ṭoqaan is the center of a small universe to which the surrounding area is satellite or upon which it converges. But it is probably the presence in the village of the tribal headquarters of the Bu Layl which gives the greatest weight to this concept.

Besides the tribal and peasant Arabs two other ethnic groups in the Ma^{c}mura should be mentioned: the Circassians, whose northern villages of Membedj and Khan Aasser are located in the northeast corner (Proux, 1938: table opposite 54), and the small continually wandering bands of Qirbaat or Gypsies. The gypsies stop two or three days at this village or that, go on, and return a month or so later, as though each band followed its own restricted circuit. There are several such groups in the Tell Ṭoqaan area, and each provides the villagers with customary services or products.

The mixed character of the Ma^{c}mura zone may be judged by other cultural criteria which are important to the population. Particularly in the Hama and Homs area there are a number of villages of the Metwaalii, Alowite, and Isma?iilii sects of Islam (Lewis, 1955: 54-7; Weulersse, 1946: 302-3; De Boucheman, 1934: 17, Note 2). Most of the Ma^{c}mura is Sunni Muslim, however, and to the best of my knowledge all of the villages in the Tell Ṭoqaan area are likewise.

Throughout and characteristic of the Ma^{c}mura, as an intermediate zone between the peasant and agricultural west and the tribal and nomadic pastoral east, are people of nomadic background now sedentarized and agricultural as well as groups of people who remain nomadic pastoralists; there are also peasant people wholly of agriculturalist tradition. All of these socioeconomic categories are found in the Tell Ṭoqaan area. The Bu Shab^{c}an villages are made up of long sedentarized pastoral peoples; the Na^{c}im villages are more recently settled from pastoralism, one as recently as 5 years prior to the field session. Sections of the Bu Layl and of the Harraamshii who summer at the Bu Layl villages, especially Ras l Ain and Tell Ṭoqaan, are still nomadic shepherd pastoralists.

III

PEOPLE OF TELL ṬOQAAN

Population and Vital Statistics

THE YEAR-ROUND RESIDENTS in Tell Ṭoqaan in the early part of 1954 were computed from the family charts to be 319. If one adds to this figure the seven members of the family at Bayt Sharqii (see p. 70) 326 persons lived permanently in or very near and were part of the life of the village. During the four and one-half months of my stay there were five births, one death, and one marriage. Two persons moved into Tell Ṭoqaan, a Negress and her child, and the nine persons of three family units moved out.

This population census does not include the eight "tents" (families) of nomadic shepherds who were camped on the south side of the village when I arrived. Members of these families set out on their annual grazing round early in February and were not expected to return until after harvest in June. They numbered 25 or 30 persons and moved with other shepherd families who camped annually at Ras l Ain. In Shayx MaHmuud's history they are described as Bu Layl and Harraamshii "followers" of Shayx Nuuri Shwatiyya, paramount shayx of the Bu Layl and a resident of Tell Ṭoqaan.

Physical Appearance

If the expected impression of Arabs of the interior plain is one of a gracile, slight, brunet, white-skinned type, then the expectation is only partly fulfilled. The people of Tell Ṭoqaan are, in general, sturdy and even stocky in build, but with great variation in stature; there are many tall individuals, both male and female. This agrees with what Shanklin (1936: 227) found concerning the Mawali and Aghaydaat between Hama and Aleppo, that they were taller than the Rwala Bedouin. For the most part, the Tell Ṭoqaaniis are a brunet, wavy or curly haired, white-skinned people—the "Mediterranean" type. Faces and hands are tanned deep brown by the sun. Exceptions were, of course, more noticeable. The Circassians present in the village were markedly more blond than the majority in skin and hair, with lighter eyes. Some members of the Mabruuk family were distinguished by prognathism and kinky hair. They belong to the Hanaadii tribe which came into Syria from Egypt during the last half of the Nineteenth Century.

Pathological Condition

The people of Tell Ṭoqaan present the appearance of a hardy population, once childhood is survived. And at least three men, it was said, were over 70 years of age. There were noticeable some congenital and functional disabilities however. Several members of one family showed marked dwarfism or spinal curvature. One boy in another family suffered from a deformed hip, so that at the age of six or seven he was only able to hobble with a stick; most of the time he crawled or was carried about the village by his older cousins or by playmates. Another boy was hunchbacked. There was one small child who perhaps suffered a central nervous system deficiency, for at an age when other children were learning to walk and talk he was unable to sit up and was quite unresponsive.

One woman in the village, described as majnuunii, "possessed," was irrational. Her condition was said to have developed after she saw her son hanged in Aleppo by the French. She wandered about in colorless rags, was given food scraps, tolerated amicably, and slept wherever she found shelter. She was unable to speak coherently, but begged or scavenged enough to keep herself alive. No family claimed her, so far as I could discover.

Malaria was said to be endemic in the village; respiratory illnesses seemed chronic but mild during the winter; there were many complaints of eye, headache, and gastrointestinal illnesses. One child had lost an eye by surgery in Aleppo. Only one individual, however, was chronically ill and unable to work at any time. Another, an elderly man, became very ill and it was expected he would die. However, he recovered a few days after he had been taken to a doctor in Idlib.

Infected wounds and sores were most feared and much talked about. "Spiritu" (alcohol) was liberally applied to all cuts and abrasions to prevent infection and blood poisoning. Medical treatments and beliefs are more fully discussed in Chapter XIV.

Census Categories

The following censuses of family and personal or individual origin and affiliation illustrate the basis for the Tell Ṭoqaaniis' description of their village as "mixed" in comparison to most other villages in the area; they also provide information relevant to description and explanation of the social organization of the village.

Not all the members of the population of Tell Ṭoqaan also belonged to one of the 56 families in the village; there were a number of men who had no family status. The local definition or understanding, of a single-family unit is taken here to distinguish 55 families (as such) from individuals who were residents only by virtue of economic or other personal status. "Family" in the following censuses, therefore, signifies a group of two or more members (related by kin or marriage) who have their own dwelling. This excludes single men without dwellings, widowers without co-resident kin. It includes widows or widowers with children and siblings with a brother, married or single, who acts as head of the household.

This definition of family corresponds to one of two important sociological applications of the term bayt in Tell Ṭoqaan. The two uses of bayt distinguish two orders or levels of social organization. When bayt is used with the name of the living individual recognized as head of the kin inhabiting the dwelling, it corresponds to the term "family" as defined above, and represents the smallest unit of social organization on kinship lines recognized. For example, Bayt AHmad Ibraahiim was composed of the members by kin and marriage of AHmad Ibraahiim's household, his wife, daughters, and sons. When bayt, however, is used with the name of the progenitor of a lineage, the place of origin of a lineage, or the tribal affiliation of a lineage, it signifies a "group of families" or biyuut ("houses") that are lineally related. Thus, Bayt Tell Haanii included the families of Bayt AHmad Ibraahiim, Bayt Xaliil Hassuun, Bayt Husayn Xaliil, Bayt MHammad Jumca, Bayt Ibraahiim Naayif, and Bayt Hammuud Hassuun. The kind of proper name connected with the term bayt distinguishes the level of organization.

I have used the smaller unit of family organization in the censuses, because difficult questions are raised when one applies such terms as "extended family", "patrilocal" and "neolocal residence" to conditions in Tell Ṭoqaan (see Chap. XIII). The primary unit is the more consistent and simple to deal with in a census. Such units were recognized in Tell Ṭoqaan as distinguishing groups from individuals who were not members of families and who stood alone or were identified only by economic relations with a "house" (bayt).

With the exception of Shayx Nuuri Shwatiyya, chief of the Bu Layl tribe, whose wives and children lived in Tell Ṭoqaan and who himself spends much time in the village, the other landlords and their families are not included in the censuses. They were not considered to be local residents by the villagers, who categorized them in a group as the effendiin (plural form of effendi; Tell Ṭoqaan pronunciation is ?affandii, ?affandiin), educated city men; they maintain their regular residences and families in Aleppo. This group includes the two landlords who are cousins and grandsons of the founder of the village. A third cousin in this family is a peasant farmer and lives in Tell Ṭoqaan.

In my classification of the villages of the area into (1) nontribal peasant or fallaaHiin villages, (2) tribal or ᶜashiirii villages, and (3) mixed villages, the primary ethnic distinctions between local people were made on their own terms. The peasants (singular, fallaaH; plural, fallaaHiin) are village-dwelling agriculturalists who have no other ethnic affiliation; they may be further identified by Muslim or Christian sect, but not by ethnic distinction. They are, and their progenitors have always been, peasants and Arabic-speaking, in contrast to tribal pastoralists, to urban people, and to the ethnic groups.

Among the peoples of tribal or ᶜashiirii affiliation, however, a number of distinctions are made, but the major category is that of ᶜarab ("Arabs"). In Tell Ṭoqaan these are the people and families of shepherd pastoral tradition who formerly lived in tents and nomadized with their flocks. With them is to be associated the pastoralist dialect, many specific traits of culture and behavior, and a tribal affiliation. In the Tell Ṭoqaan area peoples of the agricultural tribal villages, of pastoral background but long sedentarized, are more often designated by tribal name than as ᶜarab.

The other ethnic groups in the village are locally classed as ᶜashiirii category. These are the Circassians, Turks, and Kurds. The possible subdivision of these peoples into tribes is not taken note of in Tell Ṭoqaan, since only single individuals or families are present.

The peasants in a village form social units of one or more patrilineally related families, each of which is designated as a bayt ("house"), but the tribesmen belong to the larger social unit of a tribe, ᶜashiirii, which may include many villages and nomadic units as well. Owing to the broken and mixed composition of Tell Ṭoqaan my informants found it difficult to clarify for me, or for themselves, their usage of the two key terms, bayt ("house") and ᶜashiirii, ("tribe"). On the one hand, it was said that Tell Ṭoqaan is made up of many "houses" (biyuut) and that Mawali and Kurd ᶜashiiraat ("tribes") are now equivalent to the "houses" of peasant families like Bayt Tell Haanii. On the other hand, it was pointed out that Bayt Tell Haanii, a peasant lineage, and Bayt Darwiish, a Kurdish lineage, are the same as ᶜashiirit-Bu

Layl, "the tribe of the Bu Layl." Distinctiveness and separateness of these as descent determined units, regardless of relative size or status, seemed to be the chief concern.

In the censuses that follow the composition of the small population of Tell Ṭoqaan has been divided according to the locally recognized categories which distinguish urban versus rural origin, socioethnic type, and tribal representation. A census of individuals is also included, because of the number of solitary men and because wives always retain the affiliation determined by their own patrilineal descent.

Urban or Rural Origin

Urban or large town origin was attributed to six of the 55 families in Tell Ṭoqaan. Damascus is represented by two brothers whose father had settled in Tell Ṭoqaan. Aleppo is represented by three families: two of brothers who had moved to the village 13 years before to work as gardeners and one established by the grandfather of the present head of the family. This last family and the two descended from the Damascene are ranked as old families in the village society and belong to the "peasant core." The origin of the Aleppo family is commemorated in its local title, Bayt Halabii, "the house of the Aleppene," but because the lineage comprised of the other two families is considered to be of Kurdish origin it is named after its local progenitor, Bayt Darwiish al Kuurdii, "the house of Darwiish the Kurd." The administrative town center of Idlib is represented by one family which was established by the father of the present head.

The remaining 49 Tell Ṭoqaan families are rural in origin. In most cases, the place of origin of peasant and a few tribal families was said to be villages near Tell Ṭoqaan. More remote places, such as the Hauran (south of Damascus) area, the Latakia, and the Euphrates (near Deir ez Zor) and the Circassian villages and other settlements in the eastern grazing area, were mentioned as the original residence of immigrants to Tell Ṭoqaan. This variety of geographical origin in families illustrates the contrast between such "mixed" villages as Tell Ṭoqaan and either the traditional peasant or the tribal type. The last two types seem generally to show much greater social continuity and unity. Peasant villages frequently form as a result of the migration into new territories from crowded villages of a few related families. The subsequent increase and expansion of the daughter village continues to draw from the village of origin. Tribal villages often represent the settlement of tribal sections united by kinship ties.

All but three individuals of the present Tell Ṭoqaan population are themselves of rural origin by birth; these were one woman from Aleppo, the wife of the Circassian carpenter, and the two brothers from Aleppo. None of the people of urban origin, as families or as individuals, displayed in their habits or materials of living any indication of urban traits.

Over 62 per cent of the families and over 57 per cent of the total population of Tell Ṭoqaan belonged to the tribal Arab category by patrilineal descent. In the small "Non-Arab Ethnic Group" category are two Kurdish families.

Socioethnic Type

	Families	Persons
Nontribal Arab Peasant	13	67
Tribal Arab	35	187
Non-Arab Ethnic Group	7	37
Unknown	1	23

Tribal Representation

Fourteen Arab tribes are represented in Tell Ṭoqaan. To these tribesmen the village is a Bu Layl village, a tribal village, but to the peasants it is a mixed village. If it were not for the presence of the peasant core families and their historical priority in the village, and perhaps for the fact that two-thirds of the lands are held by urban men, certainly the strength of local sentiment and Bu Layl political power would favor classification of Tell Ṭoqaan as a tribal village. Peasants, Circassians, Kurds, and Turks aside, the relationships of some of the tribesmen or families in the village to the Bu Layl may reflect alliances established by the shayxly family of the Bu Layl with their tribes. These alliances would affect the Mawali, Na^{c}im, and Bu Shab^{c}an. But there are also in the village Hadiidiin, traditional enemies, as well as others not of allied tribes. Probably past and present intertribal alliances count for less than economic opportunity, for most of the tribesmen in Tell Ṭoqaan are poor men and are employed as members of a class of casual agricultural labor. The economic and social links involved are more fully discussed in the chapters on the division of labor and social organization. The data below serve merely to point out the problem in its demographic aspect.

Tribe	Family	Persons
Buchamal	1	4
Dlim	1	4
Sa^{c}ab	1	5
Bu Sarawwii	3	14
Bu Layl	5	39
Mawali	5	28
Hadiidiin	3	24
Bu Shab^{c}an	1 (Bayt Sharqii)	9
Bu Shayx	3	16
Na^{c}im	-	2
Hanaadii	5	21
Baggara	2	6
Bu Harb	2	8
Harraamshii	2	7

IV

LANGUAGE IN TELL ṬOQAAN

DIFFERENT KINDS OF ARABIC are spoken in Tell Ṭoqaan and the interest of the villagers in them deserves mention and illustration to whatever extent is possible. Some of the differences between Beirut Arabic and Syrian village and shepherd pastoralist Arabic are readily apparent and discussed briefly below.

Local Knowledge of Language

The Tell Ṭoqaaniis distinguished not only the dialects and local mannerisms of speaking Arabic, but many had heard and had picked up a few words of Turkish, French, Italian, and English. They recognized that the Qirbaat (Gypsies) spoke a distinct language and could imitate its intonations and sound patterns cleverly, though none of them claimed to be able to speak it. The three Circassian men in the village also spoke their own language, only one of the three had grown children, but these spoke only Arabic. Among the landlords French was spoken by both the men and the younger women. Shayx Nuuri's eldest son, Husayn, who attended a school in Aleppo, was learning English. A number of visitors from other villages were also able to speak a little English.

It was common knowledge in Tell Ṭoqaan that every city and village, every region from the mountains to the desert, and every tribe had its own "tongue" (lugha). According to my host, Damascus Arabic is soft and slurred as compared to the hard and forceful speech of Aleppo. He imitated these for my benefit, and to the amusement and agreement of the villagers with us, and also the speech mannerisms of Abu Xoss, a village to the west of Tell Ṭoqaan. His wife explained some of the differences between the speech of Saraaqab (her village) and local Arabic. Two Mawali tribesmen and an elderly Hadiidiin shepherd provided examples of the speech of tribal shepherd pastoralists. To cite an instance, for the phrase "What do you (f.) want?" they say in Saraaqab, "?ashuu baddik?"; in Tell Ṭoqaan, "?ish baddik?"; but a Mawali tribesman says, "shuu triidii?."

The Tell Ṭoqaaniis agreed that village speech and pastoralists speech were not the same kind of Arabic. Furthermore, the villagers said, the Arabic of the Anaza, camel-herding Bedouin, who live far to the east and no longer come into the Tell Ṭoqaan area, is unlike either and resembles ancient Arabic, that of the Koran and considered the best. City Arabic, village Arabic, and pastoralist Arabic were the three main dialects which they distinguished. But in Tell Ṭoqaan, it was said, these forms were "maxluuṭiin," "all mixed together," everyone knew them all.

Of the differences in intonation, vocabulary, and phonology, those of the first two were of greatest interest to the villagers; that of the last was noticed but least commented upon. The differences between city, village, Mawali, and Hadiidiin kinship terms were considerably discussed, and a few are incorporated in the section on kinship terminology.

Features of Arabic Spoken in Tell Ṭoqaan

In the main, there were only two kinds of Arabic, "village" and "pastoralist" spoken;their usage corresponds to some extent with the nontribal peasants and the tribal Arabs, respectively. In the course of my stay I learned to follow conversations in village form of Arabic with some understanding of its general intent. But the pastoralist form, unless spoken very slowly for my benefit, and with many yacnii's, "it means," was often incomprehensible, even though it concerned some object before my eyes. The pastoralist Arabic of one young Hadiidiin woman from Tell Qelbii, in particular, was difficult for me, beyond the understanding that she regarded me as her sister (saying, "ya?uxtii"). I finally perceived that she also spoke with a pronounced lisp which was not part of Tell Qelbii Arabic.

Three phonological differences are listed in Table I. They are those of which I was most aware and which I noted as regularly distinguishing the speech of villagers of peasant background and villagers of pastoralist background. It was also noted, however, that individuals might use both, depending on to whom they were speaking.

The speech of all villagers, of Tell Ṭoqaan and other villages in the area alike, can be distinguished from that of city

TABLE I

PHONOLOGICAL DIFFERENCES IN TELL ṬOQAAN ARABIC

Arabic Letter	Transcrip-tion	Village Arabic	Pastoralist Arabic	Meaning
ث	θ	tlaatii	θalaaθa	three
ق	q, g	qubqaab	gubgaab	wooden clogs
		waraqaat	waragaat	papers
		qassal	gassal	wheat straw
ك	k, ch	kalb	chalb	dog
		?akal	?achal	food
		diik	diich	cock

people of Beirut and Aleppo by its retention of the qaaf (transcribed as "q") sound, where it has been replaced in city Arabic by the hamza or glottal stop (transcribed as "?"). As an example of the variation to be found in this sound alone the name of the village of Saraaqab was heard as: saraa?ab (city speech), saraaqab, saraajab, and saraagab (among villagers).

Finally, the speech of Syrians of Aleppo and of villages of the Tell Ṭoqaan area alike was distinguished from the Beirut form by the use of "j" instead of "zh" for the zhiim. Examples:

Syrian	Beirut	Meaning
ṭanjara	ṭanzhara	kettle
jamal	zhamal	camel
darj	darzh	drawer

The feminine suffix which is regularly pronounced "ii" in both city and village speech, is pronounced "a" in pastoralist speech and serves further to distinguish the two forms of Arabic in Tell Ṭoqaan. Examples:

Village	Pastoralist	Meaning
najii	naja	old ewe
farwii	farwa	sheepskin coat

City and village Arabic both employ the "b" prefix tense in present tense constructions, but it is characteristically absent in pastoralist Arabic. I was regularly scolded by my Hadiidiin "teacher" for using it in his presence. Examples:

Village, City	Pastoralist	Meaning
bishrab	?ishrab	I will smoke, drink
briid xubz	?ariid xubz	I want some bread

Vocabulary differences also distinguished village and pastoralist speech. Besides those given in the ethnographic account and to be found in the list of kinship terms, the following will serve as examples here:

Village	Pastoralist	Meaning
laban	xaaθir	laban (cultured milk)
kuzluuq	naḍaraat	eyeglasses
kumbaz	zubuun	man's gown
kwayyis	zayn	nice, pleasant

I was not able to form any definite opinion whether village or pastoralist Arabic held more prestige among the Tell Ṭoqaaniis, or whether one form was superseding the other. They were distinct, however, and like culture traits, helped to identify that which was pastoralist from that which was agricultural peasant. It was my impression that some of the tribal Arabs, particularly those of long sedentarized tribes (Bu Shayx, Bu Shab^{c}an, Baggara) spoke the village form, but that the Mawali, Hadiidiin, Bu Harb, Bu Sarrawii, and other tribal Arabs closely connected with pastoralist background, spoke the pastoralist form. The prestige of the Bu Layl shayxly family in the area certainly may be considered a factor in maintaining the pastoralist dialect.

V

HISTORY OF TELL ṬOQAAN

The Villagers' Historical Concepts

LIKE MOST VILLAGES of the Levant States, Tell Ṭoqaan is surrounded by the ruins and remains of past cultures. Ancient stone foundations underlie the midden or are incorporated in the structure of stable compounds. The tell is quarried for building stone. Artifacts, from scarabs and seals to heavy plumb weights and column capitals, are found on or beneath its surface; roughly finished limestone troughs on the slopes of the Skayk ridge. Here and there and on the slopes of the tell are scattered potsherds that represent millenia of history.

On the fine days of spring the villagers climb to the top of the tell. At its summit they point out the place where Shayx Abdullah Ṭoqaan, for whom the village is named, pitched his tent and hung the three golden apples which figure in the legend of his settlement there. Here also the Osmanlii Agha built his stone house when he founded the present village of Tell Ṭoqaan four generations ago. The tell itself was once an ancient city that was walled and had gates of stone on the east, north, and west. The villagers point out where their grubbing for camel thorn roots on the slope has revealed the traces of ancient mud-brick walls. It is recognized that the city flourished in antiquity before the Muslim Arabs came, in a period ascribed to the Ruumii ("Greeks" of Byzantium). If it were to be properly excavated, as they have seen or heard done to other tells, they say treasures would be found--for the real name of the great mound is Tell ađ Đahab, the Golden Tell.

On cold winter nights my host told stories that recalled medieval Islamic times and invoked the name of the Abbaasid caliph, Haruun ar Rashiid (786-809 A.D.), and those of rival kings of Aleppo, Hama, and Damascus. Occasionally, Shayx MaHmuud or on one of the young men read classical Arab poetry. This too was qadiim, "ancient."

Among the older and illiterate residents of the village the remote historical past is divided into two periods. The first is that of the pre-Arab period. Its content and extent are unknown to them except for such evidence as the tells of ancient cities provide. The second period begins with the Arab Conquest (622-642 A.D.). Its Arab history remains to them largely in picaresque tales and legends which depict a feudal or tribal way of life, and in retention of the names of a few rulers, but within no chronological framework.

Events closer to the present are more realistically conceived. For example, the presence of the Hanaadii in the village was referred to the time, "over a hundred years" before, when these tribesmen followed Ibraahiim Pasha from Egypt on his conquest and brief rule in Syria (1831-40). Recent history which falls within the life spans of the older residents is well known, not only within the village dimension, but also in terms of the tribes and area between Aleppo and Damascus and east of the coastal ranges. It is divided into the period of the "rule of the Osmanlii" or Ottoman Empire, the period of Franji (French) rule, and the present Hkuumii, "government," of independent Syria. The three periods were more than once discussed and compared before me or with me in terms of changes in the conditions of life for villagers.

Under the Osmanlii, they said, life was doubly insecure for villages in the Tell Ṭoqaan area. Both the Osmanlii army and the Mawali tribes harassed and oppressed them. But under French rule, this jeopardy ceased, and under the present Syrian government life is yet more secure. Today, when a known thief is sought in his village, the police take only that malefactor and his property. The rest of the men in the village are safe from seizure. No longer do they have to flee as they did under the Osmanlii.

Recent decades and the French rule are said to have brought many changes for the better in technology and economics. The Ottoman period is, in part, looked upon as a period of ignorance. Now, in every village, they say, there are people who read and write; there are new foods, crops, and tools. Everyone knows more. Little by little the tribes are disappearing, and after a while they will all be gone.

But along with the changes which are looked on with favor there have been losses: the traditional pageantry that accompanied bringing home a bride is gone; the cattle herd and the rich grazing are gone; men no longer know purebred mares; the excitement of the departure of the village camel caravan for Aleppo is gone. Those days, said my host are dead—"maat, mitl maat jamal, maat faras" ('dead, as the camel is dead, as the purebred mare is dead'). Now is the time of cotton, the tractor, and the truck.

In local history years are named by an outstanding event. There was, for example, the "year of the forty days of snow" in the Tell Ṭoqaan area; my host and several others were born in that year. There was also sinit-Harayyib, "the year of the fighting," when the Mawali and Hadiidiin tribes fought between Ras l Ain and Tell Ṭoqaan for five months, when the orchards were cut down and the people fled, and the French bombed the villages from the air and shelled them from the train. I was also told that 1954 was already spoken of in the village as sinit-Louise! There was not any evidence, however, that each year was given a name and a sequence so remembered or recorded. Use of the Muslim chronology was cited only once, and that by a literate person. Such absolute dating systems are less important in village life than is the sequence of months and seasons and days of the year. Past events are set in a pattern of relative and vague antiquity; depending on the context, qadiim may thus mean "last year" or "antiquity," before the Muslim Arabs conquered this land. Historical priority is remembered in connection with the first men to come to Tell Ṭoqaan, or the first buildings erected. Some sections of land are supposed to be named after the men who first plowed them.

Explanations of events in recent local history are psychologically realistic and eminently practical: the progenitor of one family in Tell Ṭoqaan came to the village to escape service in the Ottoman army. But, as incidents told in Shayx MaHmuud's history (see below) show, the explanations for wars, raids, and migrations of the past follow the romantic pattern found in ancient Arabian poetry: most frequent precipitants of war between tribes are insults to the honor of a shayx or to the sister of a tribesman.

Besides the teacher, Shayx MaHmuud AHmad, and his students, three or four of the young men in the village were able to read and write; they had learned these skills in some other village, usually Saraaqab. Occasionally, they referred in conversation to historical events or recounted the rise of the Arabs in conventional historical fashion within a political framework. Shayx MaHmuud, who had been educated in Aleppo, and who claimed to know "all the histories of all the peoples of the world," demonstrated his knowledge one evening by giving a brief but reasonably accurate account of America from the time of George Washington, who was the father of "my" country as Shukri al Quwatli was the first president and father of independent Syria.

As will be more apparent in the following section on the history of Tell Ṭoqaan, as recorded by Shayx MaHmuud, the histories of men, families, and tribes form an important body of the historical knowledge present in the community. History as a sequence of unique events of specific changes through time is a distinct part of the ideology in Tell Ṭoqaan; however, the closer the events are to their own experience and way of life, the more precisely they are placed in relation to each other.

Shayx MaHmuud and His History

In 1954 Shayx MaHmuud AHmad Cholak had lived in Tell Ṭoqaan only three years and he left the village the following one. During his stay he lived most of the time in my host's household and conducted a school in the room set aside for him in our compound. He served also as reader and scribe for the villagers, performed religious services, and occasionally, but not regularly, conducted Friday prayers in the mosque. Although he was not in very good standing with either the urban landlords or Shayx Nuuri, they tolerated his presence.

Shayx MaHmuud was a Na^{c}im tribesman from Tar Rifaat, north of Aleppo, the same village from which the progenitor of one of the local families derived. He had been educated in an Islamic school in Aleppo, and was locally considered to be qualified as a religious shayx; that is, he could teach the Koran and Hadiith. My host met him in Idlib and brought him to Tell Ṭoqaan in order to give his sons a traditional Muslim education in the Koran and teach them the rudiments of reading and writing and arithmetic.

In the course of my stay I was able to employ the Shayx to write a history of Tell Ṭoqaan. Since he was not a native of the vicinity he sought out the oldest men in the Area and took down their accounts and versions of local events. From time to time these elders were guests of my host and I could observe his procedure. While they talked, he wrote, and from time to time asked a question. When a group was present, a general discussion and argument often arose over the course of events and identities of participants. Generally he ended the disputes himself by selecting the version that seemed most plausible to him and writing it down with a decisive flourish of fountain pen and paper.

The manuscript is not chronologically arranged and comprises a jumble of tales, poems of praise, narratives of personal experience, and genealogies of families traced down from the man who first settled in Tell Ṭoqaan. The completeness of the genealogies and inclusion of female members, even those who were unmarried or still children, may have been a result of the questions I asked in securing family charts. There is also a considerable amount of material on Arab-French relations and the political leaders of Syria. Interestingly enough, the name of General Adiib Shishekly, President of Syria at the time the first part of the history was written, is not mentioned. Occasionally, there are passages which suggest that the Shayx felt ready to attempt a whole history of the Arabs and the rise of Islam from the time of the Prophet. Since he used a few government texts in his school, it is possible that he has drawn on some of these, in part, but the bulk of the material was taken down from the tales of his informants. From time to time he gives the name and position of one as qualified by age, experience, and integrity to speak.

In spite of the disorder in his manuscript, Shayx MaHmuud clearly had in mind a number of topics or historical problems relevant to a history of Tell Ṭoqaan and its area, for he returns to them time and again. His major aims were to account for the arrival of the Mawali tribes in the area; to account for the name of the village; to account for the presence and importance of the Bu Layl tribe in the area and in Tell Ṭoqaan; to narrate the founding of the village; to account for and name the families and their members resident in the village; and to narrate the events of the Hadiidiin-Mawali wars, particularly as the fighting affected the local scene. It is the last topic that frequently takes him far afield.

History of Tell Ṭoqaan

From Shayx MaHmuud's manuscript I have extracted and summarized the following history of Tell Ṭoqaan. Some corrections and confirmations are available from other sources on the area. The emphasis of the Sahyx's account is political; some other historical material has been incorporated in the ethnographic chapters and derives from other informants.

Arrival of the Mawali tribes; the Ṭoqaan —Shayx MaHmuud selected the arrival of the Mawali tribes as the beginning of events relevant to the history of Tell Ṭoqaan. They were said to have come into the area under the leadership of Hamd al Abbas, a former emir of the Mawali, who lived in the Jezira and ruled from Deir ez Zor to Hasakah. In a series of raids and battles "more than three hundred years ago" the tribes of Tai, Bani Xaalid, and Al Abiid were defeated and driven out, and the Mawali under Hamd al Abbas occupied the area between Homs, Hama, and Ma^{c}aarat an Na^{c}man. Hamd al Abbas was succeeded by Emir MuHammad al Xarfan.[1] During Xarfan's emirate the long history of war and raiding between the Mawali and Hadiidiin tribes began, and the Mawali were divided into the northern and the southern Mawali, and subsections appeared.

The name of the village.—Among the subsections of the Mawali were the Ṭoqaan, whose shayx established himself and his people in the neighborhood of Tell ađ Đahab, the "Golden Tell." The fame of this shayx was such that it resulted in a change of name for the tell and locality to Tell Ṭoqaan. Shayx MaHmuud records several tales current among the villagers of the area which illustrate the generosity, wealth, and noble character of Shayx Abdullah Ṭoqaan. Ultimately, however, his independence and reputation brought about his downfall and death at the hands of the Mawali emir. After this defeat the locality is said to have become, as it was before Abdullah Ṭoqaan's local rule, a pasturing and watering place for all the shepherd Arabs, and to have been a headquarters for thieves and robbers until an Ottoman military post was established at Tell Ṭoqaan and the area "pacified."

Establishment of the Bu Layl tribe.—After the dispersal of the Ṭoqaan, the Bu Layl tribe was among the Arabs who moved into the vicinity from the area of Homs. The Bu Layl were said by the Shayx to have formerly been called Shammar, but both the villagers and Von Oppenheim commonly refer to them as Aghaydaat from the tribe located in the region around Deir ez Zor on the Euphrates. Furthermore, although the Shayx's history would establish them in the Tell Ṭoqaan area long before this, Von Oppenheim (1939 I: 322) says that they first immigrated about 1860 from the Euphrates.

From the time of their arrival in the Homs area and their later move northward the Bu Layl have been allies of the Mawali. They lived as shepherds and tent dwellers in the Tell Ṭoqaan area under an Ottoman sultan whose name is given as Arslan. Under this sultan, the history says they were forced to take up cultivation—that, according to the Shayx, was two hundred years

1. Von Oppenheim (1939 I: 313) places this emir in the latter part of the 18th century.

ago. They settled in the present Bu Layl villages of Jazraaya, Osmaniyya, Tell ᶜaaluush, Zammaar, and Ras l Ain. It is more probable that this sedentarization took place in the third quarter of the 19th century during the reign of the Ottoman Sultan Abdul Aziiz (1861-1876).

About seventy years ago Hajj Mustafa al Shwaṭiyya, shayx of Jazraaya, established himself by force as shayx of all the Bu Layl. He was supported by the Ottoman government and dissenters from his rule were driven out. It seems clear that Hajj Mustafa owed his security as leader of the Bu Layl to the Ottoman army officer in command of the post at Tell Ṭoqaan, four kilometers from Jazraaya. And, according to the Shayx's history, because of the good relations this officer maintained with all the leading tribal shayxs and the services he performed for them, his sons were able to retain their landholdings in Tell Ṭoqaan after the fall of the Ottoman rule, even though they were Turks.

Founding of Tell Ṭoqaan.--The present village of Tell Ṭoqaan first appears as a military post of the Ottoman Army under the command of a Turk from Salonika, "Baynii Basha," YaHya Agha Ṣalaa H ad Diin.

One of several treatments of the subject which occur in Shayx MaHmuud's history reads as follows:

> And among the great people which we shall record in this history are the people of the village of Tell Ṭoqaan. And among them are people like YaHya Agha, who was the first one to build the first farm in the village after it had been all leveled. And he started agriculture in it and he started the sowing of wheat after it had been left for hundreds of years. And the beginning of this building started in the year 1831 *[sic]*. And YaHya Agha ṢalaaH ad Diin, from the city of Salonika, came to the village of Tell Ṭoqaan when it was nothing but a desert which used to be the point where Arabs would come from four countries to pasture their cattle because it had great and fertile fields and a lot of good water and it was the crossroads of Arabs of the desert.

Elsewhere in the History it says the military post was established in the reign of the Sultan Abdul Aziiz (1861-1876) and the area pacified at that time by the garrison. The post was moved to another place, but when the Turkish officer YaHya Agha retired, he returned to Tell Ṭoqaan with a number of his former soldiers. To some of them he gave land; others were employed as farmhands. Three grandsons still hold among them a major portion of the land, and several of the present families in the village are descended from his followers. Families of other original settlers have emigrated or become extinct for lack of male descendants.

Shayx MaHmuud also explains that the village is now "disunited," because its present population derives from the mixed contingent of soldiers and refugees who settled there under the Ottoman commander; they were Turks, Arabs, Kurds, and not all of one tribe. The Bu Layl apparently began to move into Tell Ṭoqaan at the end of World War I as the Turkish rule was ended and as Hajj Mustafa, then, paramount shayx of the Bu Layl, began to acquire land from men in Tell Ṭoqaan.

Hadiidiin-Mawali Wars.—Most of the local historical events which followed the imposition of French control after World War I and the short reign of Feisal (1920) are concerned with the fighting between the Hadiidiin and Mawali tribes. This flared up again about 1920 and continued through the 1930's. Shayx MaHmuud is of the opinion that the continuous fighting was stimulated by the French as a policy to prevent Arab unity. He says, "This misfortune increased day by day. More troubles took place, and the foreigner played his part in arousing the hatred. This foreigner is France. At first France began to strengthen Shayx Nawwaaf al Salah [Hadiidiin], and at the same time she strengthened the Emirs [Mawali]."

Some of the accounts given the Shayx by men who participated in or witnessed the fighting indicate that in the 1920's Tell Ṭoqaan and the Bu Layl villages were at least partly deserted. French Levant army units, planes, and artillery mounted on railroad cars, bombarded and devastated the area. Throughout this period the Mawali remained stubbornly anti-French. The Bu Layl, as Mawali allies, were implicated with the rebels (as the French called them). At one time Hajj Mustafa and the lesser Bu Layl shayxs were imprisoned for real or supposed collaboration with and aid given to the Mawali.

> Three attacks were made on the Al Bu Layl Arabs by the French who arrested Shayx Dalbash al Xarfan, Shayx of Al Bohalahal, and took him in chains. In this battle the Al Bu Layl Arabs, who were left without leaders—for their leaders were arrested and imprisoned—could not stand the airplanes from above and the guns and tanks which were firing at them. So they ran away with the French planes bombing them until they came to Al Amk. All the people of the Al Bu Layl villages and Tell Ṭoqaan ran away from the ever increasing ferocity of the enemy, who had no mercy nor conscience. You could see Tell Ṭoqaan at that time, as dark as clouds, and the men running away for their lives; they were like sheep and the French like wolves. (I: 123-24)

Again, when the fighting was proceeding on three fronts, one of these was located between Ras l Ain and Tell Ṭoqaan. The

French and Hadiidiin took positions at the former village and the Mawali at the latter. And in the year 1925, a year marked by general revolt in Syria, particularly in the Druze area south of Damascus, the Mawali were among the most active "rebels." At this time Jazraaya and Tell Ṭoqaan were shelled from the railroad, and the people fled to the Skayk ridge where they took shelter in the caves there.

Incident follows incident in the Shayx's history, and no chronological sequence is clear. When compared to De Boucheman's brief history (1934), there seem to be a number of overlapping accounts. Even though these may be the same incidents repeated in different versions by different informants, it is apparent that the Tell Ṭoqaan area was one of the centers of disturbance for a number of years.

The Shayx's history stops abruptly (and unfinished) with one of many incidents in the attempt of the French to capture Emir Abdul Razzak of the Mawali, the chief hero of Arab resistance. A final historical note may be added here from the events of the early part of 1954. On February 25, 1954, the government of General Adiib Shishekly fell and he was forced to flee the country. In Tell Ṭoqaan I learned of the event immediately from the villagers who heard the radio announcement. The next day the chief government official at Idlib came and ordered all radio aerials to be pulled down. Although there was considerable discussion of the course of events in the village, there was no disruption of daily activities. News continued to come over radios in automobiles owned by Shayx Nuuri or members of his family who lived in Jazraaya. The deposition of Shishekly was justified for me in simple terms: he had thrown good men into prison without reason. Shishekly was removed from office by a rebellion of the army, and it is interesting that, while Shayx MaHmuud does not mention Shishekly by name, he frequently pays tribute to the Syrian army.

General Historical Setting[2]

Since the rise of civilization in the northwest quarter of Syria, where Tell Ṭoqaan is located, the culture history of the area has been dominated by a group of urban centers. These

2. See Hitti (1951b) for the history of Syria from ancient times to the Ottoman conquest. The sketch here is concerned with the Tell Ṭoqaan area from about 1517 to the present.

lie east of the inner mountain range and are aligned from north to south in well-watered and fertile sites. They came into prominence in antiquity, flourished through many peoples and dynasties, and most of them continue to thrive at the present. Of chief interest here is the northernmost city, Aleppo, which has rivaled Damascus in size and power throughout most of its history. Qinnasrin, now an Arab village, located at the head of the Maadek Marsh, 18 kilometers north of Tell Ṭoqaan, was an important urban center from Seleucid to medieval Arab times. Ma^{c}arrat an Na^{c}man, home of the medieval Arab poet Al Ma^{c}arri, lies on the Aleppo-Damascus highway about 20 kilometers south of Saraaqab. Today it is a large market town and the location of a Bedouin control post. Southernmost of this group of urban centers is Hama, one of the four major cities of interior Syria. It has been in continuous occupation since the Neolithic and today is a Muslim religious center and a focus of commercial enterprise.

The Spanish Arab traveler Ibn Jubayer, noted in 1184, in the course of his journey from Aleppo to Damascus, that these towns were surrounded by populous agricultural villages attached to them. Of the lands around Ma^{c}arrat on Na^{c}man he wrote: "They are all dark with olive, fig, and pistachio trees, and all kinds of fruits; and their luxuriant gardens and well-ordered villages stretch for a distance of two day's journeying. It is one of the most fertile and productive of Islamic lands." (Ibn Jubayer, 1952: 264). But by the time of the Ottoman conquest the Mongol invasions of the 13th and 14th centuries and especially the decimations of the great plagues of the 14th and 15th centuries had broken up the panorama of flourishing medieval prosperity in this area. It is estimated that plagues alone, in the last two centuries mentioned, reduced the population of Syria and Egypt to one-third its former size (Hitti, 1951*b*: 631-38).

In 1516, following the defeat of the Ēgyptian Mamluke army north of Aleppo, Syria "passed quietly into Ottoman hands" (Hitti, 1951*b*: 658), and the four centuries of Ottoman imperial control began.

Ottoman administration of the Arab provinces left the Egyptian Mamluke divisions intact, and the area of Tell Ṭoqaan probably remained within the pashalik of Aleppo throughout the period. Interested primarily in taxation, the rulers continued the already ancient practice of farming out tax collection to the highest bidder (Hitti, 1951*b*: 664). Pashas sent out from Constantinople to the urban centers had a free hand in governing their districts during their tenures and were supported by Janissary contingents. Ottoman control was imposed over the local pattern of feudalism; local chieftains retained considerable power so long as tax levies were passed on by them to the pashas (Hourani, 1954: 24).

During the first three centuires of Ottoman rule both population and economic conditions steadily declined. In the late 18th century only 400 taxable villages were left in the Aleppo area of the 3200 counted at the beginning of Ottoman rule (Hitti, 1951*b*: 674). During this period nomadic shepherd peoples and camel Bedouin began to move into northern Syria. At the beginning of the 19th century the countryside around Aleppo was dominated by nomad tribes, probably the Mawali, who were paid tribute by Aleppo and who controlled both security and trade movement (Olivier, 1807 IV: 169-70). But throughout the 18th and 19th centuries nomad pastoralists began to drift into the area from the vicinity of Euphrates, and many settled down to village and agricultural life (Von Oppenheim, 1939 I: 292). Among those who came, about 1860, were the Aghaydaat-Bu Layl, now established in the Tell Ṭoqaan area (Von Oppenheim, 1939 I: 322).

Under the last century of Ottoman rule the structure of political control changed and the prevalence of local despotism gave way slowly to more centralized administration. Land registration was begun with the intent of eradicating the system of village collective land tenure. Codification of the Ottoman land law came in 1858. A number of attempts were made to abolish in practice, as well as by edict, the tax-farming system and to substitute direct tax collection by the state (Bonné, 1955: 39-78). Among the many evidences of the influence of Western culture now penetrating the area was the completion of the Hedjaz railway in 1908.

During the last half of the 19th century re-expansion of agriculture into the east began. Circassian refugees were settled along the border from North Syria to as far south as Amman, the present capital of Jordan (Lewis, 1955: 48-60). Exemption from military conscription was offered in exchange for reopening cultivation in the deserted zone, a zone largely controlled by shepherd pastoralists, particularly in the Sultan's domains. The founding of Tell Ṭoqaan by a retired Ottoman army officer appears to be one such event in the revival of agriculture during this period. This expansion was accompanied by efforts to compel the border shepherd tribes to settle in permanent villages. The history and present situation of the Bu Layl indicates participation in this program

During the 19th century the population of the area began to increase and the rate was accelerated by the beginning of the 20th century. Communication lines were extended and between 1902 and 1911 a hard road from Aleppo to Homs and Tripoli was completed (Baurain, 1930: 110-14). Between 1880 and 1914, the Hadiidiin tribe gained in importance and the size of the grazing area under its control southeast of Aleppo nearly doubled (Von Oppenheim, 1939 I: 298).

In 1914 Turkey entered the First World War on the side of the Central Powers. The British conducted negotiations during the war, which at first appeared to consider as well as encourage the ambitions of Arab nationalists for independence. But these finally resulted in the mandate arrangements which set arbitrary boundaries and divided the control of the Levant between Britain and France. After a brief five months of self-declared independence as a kingdom under Faisal (May-July, 1920), Syria capitulated to the French forces and remained under French control as a mandated territory until 1941.

During the Mandate Period a number of national institutions were introduced, largely of French design, which served to incorporate the old Ottoman provinces into the present political units of the Syrian and Lebanese republics. These were extensions of a road system, the beginning of a national secular school system, the organization of a parliamentary form of government with the Syrian capital at Damascus, and the levying of a military force from the general population. French policy, however, secured its position by keeping the area divided into separate and more or less autonomous states. The army was organized by ethnic units, and these were used in disturbed areas in such a fashion as to maintain or increase tensions between such groups.

Meanwhile steady Arab pressure for independence continued. The Druze revolt of 1925-26 spread through southern Syria, and in the 1930's there were "local and ephemeral" disturbances farther north (Hourani, 1954: 188-96). Two kinds of pressure for freedom from French control seem evident. Agitating from urban centers and from cities as far outside as Iraq and Europe, "nationalists", who seem to represent the landowning class, sought to organize political party pressure after European fashion. Within Syria the Druze in the Jebel Hauran and the Mawali confederation of shepherd tribes in the north sought to maintain local independence and to continue their own autonomous political organizations.

Brief accounts of the feud between the Mawali and Hadiidiin shepherd tribes are to be found in De Boucheman (1934) and Von Oppenheim (1939, I: 298, 309). From the 16th century on the Mawali, a large confederation of nomadic shepherd tribes led by the Emirs, often dominated the borderland from Hama to the Khabur river. During the Mandate Period they consistently opposed and resisted French control, while the French supported and protected the Hadiidiin against the Mawali. The fighting between the two tribes and the French took place, as Shayx MaHmuud's history shows, in the Ma^{c}mura zone and much of it close to Tell Ṭoqaan.

Following years of tribal feuding, the Mawali in 1921 cut the railroad tracks near El Hamra. This was interpreted as active hostility and rebellion against the Mandate government, and from then on the French took military action against the tribes. In 1925 members of the confederation with other supporters attacked Hama, Ma^{c}arrat an Na^{c}man, and Abu Duhuur. They were soon put to flight and spent the winter in Iraq. On their return in 1926 to their customary summer grazing grounds they were bombed from the air by the French and suffered considerable loss of flocks and men. In 1928, the boundary between Hadiidiin and Mawali was drawn and marked by the railroad line from Aleppo to Hama. In 1930, Emir Abdur Razzak, hero of the Mawali, was assassinated by a Hadiidiin tribesman, but the French ruled against the Mawali claim for blood revenge. The years of 1932-33 were famine years in this area, and in 1933 a new incident provoked hostilities. The accounts of De Boucheman and Von Oppenheim end at this point, but a third source mentions a new outbreak in 1942, which involved not only the two shepherd tribes but two camel Bedouin tribes of the Anaza, the Sbaa and the Fedaan (Delegation Générale de la France Combattant au Levant, 1943: 141-43). It is in this source that the only historical record of Tell Ṭoqaan occurs of which I am aware. The anonymous author, in an account of the origin of the Hadiidiin, says that conflicts in 1850 between the two groups included an incident in which Mawalis drove back Hadiidiin "as far as Tell Ṭoqaan" (Delegation Générale...1943: 153).

When the Second World War broke out in Europe in 1939 measures were immediately taken by the French to secure their position in Syria and Lebanon. Their occupation troops were reinforced, leaders of questionable political groups were imprisoned, and the Lebanese Chamber was dissolved. After the capitulation of France (1940), the interference of Axis powers in the Levant increased and Britain extended her blockade to Syria and Lebanon.

The French withdrew from the League of Nations in April, 1941, and Syrian and Lebanese political leaders considered that the legal basis of the mandate was thus ended and the general strike which had begun in February continued. In June of that year mixed forces of British Imperial, Free French and other Allied troops crossed Syrian frontiers from the south and from the northeast. The campaign of the Allied troops against the Vichy French occupation army from June 8 until July 12 does not appear to have touched the Tell Ṭoqaan area, although the Allies probably used the Aleppo-Damascus road 14 kilometers to the west. From this time the Free French under DeGaulle were in territorial command of Syria and Lebanon, but the area was garrisoned by British troops. "Economically and financially it has become a part of the bloc of British-controlled Middle Eastern territories" (Hourani, 1954: 244).

In September, 1941, General Catroux proclaimed the independence of Syria, and in November of that year a similar proclamation was made for Lebanon. In March, 1943, steps toward restoring constitutional government began in both Syria and Lebanon as provisional governments were set up and plans were made for general elections. The Syrian elections were held in July, and in August the new Chamber of Deputies met and elected Shukri al Quwatli as president of the Republic of Syria.

France relinquished her hold on Syria and Lebanon slowly, but by the end of 1944 most of the government administration had been transferred to Syrian or Lebanese control, except for the army. These troops comprised the Syrian and Lebanese levies and formed part of the French Army of the Levant. Because of the general social situation in Syria and Lebanon, the faction that controlled the army controlled the governments. This was especially true in the case of Syria "where semifeudal tenures were still to be found, localism was so strong a force, and there existed large Bedouin tribes traditionally recalcitrant to civil government" (Hourani, 1954: 292).

Syrian independence was fully achieved in 1945. In April 1949, parliamentary government was overthrown by military coup d'etat and Husni Zayim established a brief military dictatorship. In 1951 Adiib Shishekly, chief of staff of the army, succeeded to head of the government by a similar move; his regime continued until February, 1954.

Throughout the recent years of increasing political activity in Syria, the towns and cities have been the centers of such work. The rural countryside, particularly the peasants of the plains, has not engaged in significant political action. The resistance of the Mawali tribes during the mandate appears to have been the only such nonurban activity to take place in the area that includes Tell Ṭoqaan. However, there is brief mention of "Socialist" agitation west of this area, in the rural districts around Homs, Hama, and Aleppo (Tadmor, 1952: 109).

VI

LAND SYSTEM OF THE TELL ṬOQAAN

Settlement and Lands

TELL ṬOQAAN is a small settlement of buildings and compounds surrounded by its lands. These form a unit which has endured beyond changes in landholders, changes in the demographic features of the population, and, up to the present time, changes in technological and sociopolitical features. The location of Tell Ṭoqaan is advantageous for water supply and convenient access to the irrigated gardening area, but as its history indicates, it has no apparent natural defense.

Distribution of the dwellings and compounds of the village is not as compact as that in such older and more populous places in the area as Saraaqab and Afess. There are many instances of open spaces between blocks of several compounds whose walls are shared; a number of compounds and dwelling units stand free. At Zammaar and Ras l Ain, both tribal villages of the Bu Layl, the houses and compounds are detached and do not share walls with neighbors.

The lands of Tell Ṭoqaan may be divided into those which are public to any villager's use and those which are privately controlled by holders' rights and partners' contracts. All cultivated lands are thus closed to public use; but waste or non-cultivated land is open to any villager of Tell Ṭoqaan, with the exception of that next to the boundaries of fields. The common land of one village is not generally used by residents of other villages. In Tell Ṭoqaan the tell slopes, shallows of the marsh, stream and path borders, and the stony ridge of the Skayk are public land.

Except along the boundary set by the marsh, the lands of Tell Ṭoqaan extend outward until they meet the boundaries of the lands of the surrounding villages (see Fig. 3). Although its lands appear to have been surveyed, judging from a map of the marsh shallows which I saw at Bayt Sharqii, I was unable to secure a map of the property boundaries of the village. The local view is that Tell Ṭoqaan possesses more arable and waste land than other villages around it. Unlike Jazraaya and Afess, its lands

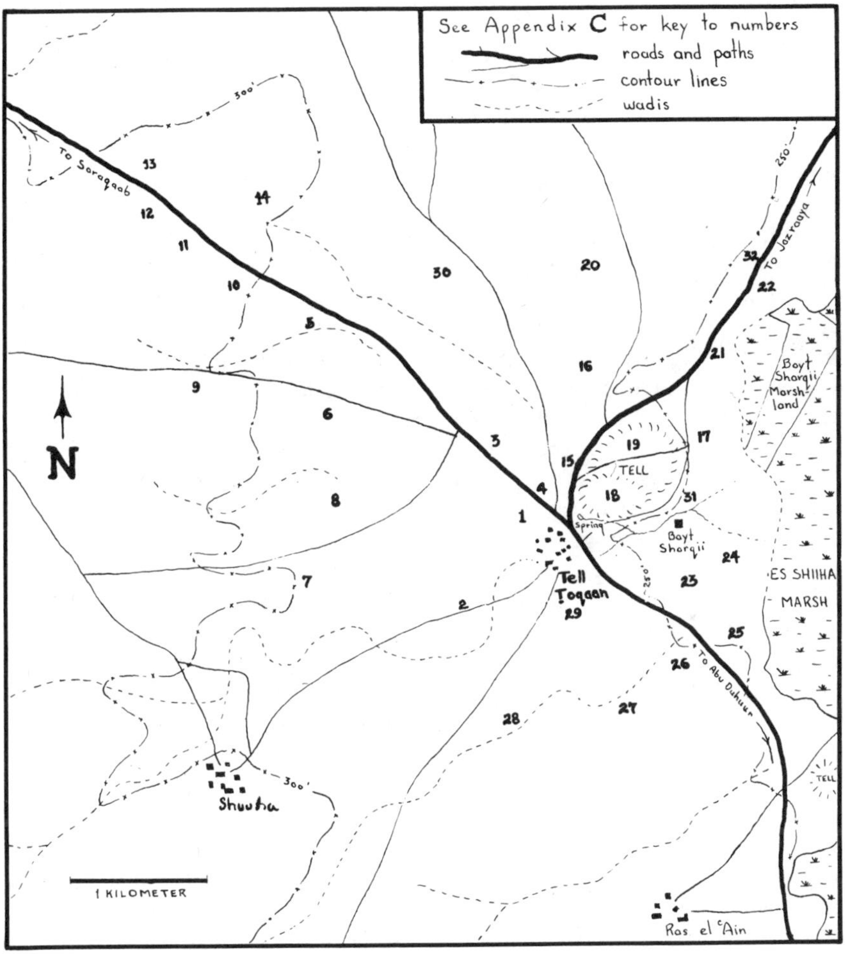

Fig. 3. Land divisions of Tell Ṭoqaan.

have not yet been measured in hectares and the extent is described in faddaan (see p. 58). In midspring, when the field crops are well up and brilliant green, it is possible to see at a glance from the summit of the tell where the lands of Tell Ṭoqaan end. The two-field system of cultivation and fallow is followed in the area, and in 1954 all the villages in the part east of the Aleppo-Damascus highway left the south and east sides fallow and planted the north and west sides. As a result the fallow of one village abutted on the cultivated of the next and so on. The color contrast of bare red earth next to green wheat and barley was striking. There is considerable variety in economic exploitation of their lands by the Tell Ṭoqaaniis. Besides cultivation and grazing, the village territory is hunted over, gathered from, and mined.

The cultivated lands which lie around the village are divided into irrigated gardening and dry farming lands. On the south and west sides the dry farmed fields begin at the edge of the settlement and extend outward to the boundaries of the lands of the next villages. On the northeast side, however, across the road which borders the village, the garden area extends around the west and east sides of the tell, for it is possible to take advantage there, with irrigating apparatus, of the shallow water table. Beyond the gardens, as the terrain rises to east, west, and north, are more fields. On the northeast, however, the Siiha marsh and the land of Bayt Sharqii bound Tell Ṭoqaan lands. The tell is cultivated only on the first two lower levels; the topmost is too small and stony.

Two kinds of grazing land can be distinguished by the herd or flocks pastured on them. The village herd of cattle, horses, mules, and donkeys usually grazes on the tell slope and along the marsh and stream borders. In spring, when the barley is up and there are foals to feed, small barley fields around the foot of the tell may be set aside for horses and mules by their owners. The flocks of sheep and goats graze on the fallow fields and, when the spring grasses are up, on the stony ridge of the Skayk. The few camels are fed barley straw or graze in fallow fields where passing rains of late spring bring up plants for which they seem to have specialized tastes but which grow more randomly than other pasturage. They may also be seen feeding around the foot of the tell and around the spring.

Bird hunting and trapping exploit such opportunity as time and place provide; geese and ducks are found in the marsh; small birds are trapped in the fields by the plowmen; hawks are occasionally lured and snared out on the Skayk ridge.

In "gathering" activities materials are sought along pathsides, on the Skayk, and along the spring and marsh borders. In these places wild plants grow which provide salad greens. Rushes and reeds used in roofs, mats, and tent screens are found in the marsh and along the spring; stalks of asphodel for fuel or roofing material are collected and dried in bundles on the Skayk; camel thorn, which provides a gnarled root used for fuel, is searched for in fields and on the tell slopes.

The earth of the village lands is in itself a major natural resource; large stones or chunks of limestone are excavated from the tell or found in the course of spading up soil for mud bricks; gravel is brought from the bed of the Wadi Luuf. Finer soil is needed for various purposes and is dug within the precincts of the village. It may be the finely sifted red earth used for powdering babies or the black soil of the midden used as compost in the gardens.

It may appear from this sketch of Tell Ṭoqaan lands that many needs, in terms of the basic subsistence and maintenance pattern are well met by local resources. The village has water supply, arable land, grazing land, building and fuel materials, and various supplementary items that are gathered or hunted all within its boundaries and control. But the more one examines technology and economics of life in Tell Ṭoqaan, the more it is seen that much must come from outside and that village life here is not self-sufficient.

Settlement Pattern

At first view the settlement of Tell Ṭoqaan appears open and to have grown up by random accretions wherever there was space to build. Paths do not run a straight-lined grid throughout but twist around corners of large blocks of compounds and divide and veer off at angles. Except on the northeast side, bounded by the road, the village is surrounded by a wide uncultivated flat; another broad area divides the settlement unevenly into a north and a south sector. Within the built-up area the terrain is uneven, pitted with shallow excavations or rising in small hillocks. In retrospect, one might suppose that, over a long period of time, a natural shallow depression had become partly and irregularly filled by the debris of past constructions, each built over the preceding one. When the level of the surrounding land that sloped gradually inward was reached, some of the building then began to spread out over it. Excavations for building earth in the midden have turned up ample evidence in the shape of finished blocks of limestone or basalt, of such previous occupation. The excavators interpret these to be from the ruins of an ancient khan.

The layout of the settlement was on one occasion casually sketched for me by Shayx MaHmuud. As he set it down the arrangement of the village showed a definite pattern of three major clusters of buildings which was not at first apparent to me but which proved to be clearly so conceived and respected by the villagers. On the south there is the Nuuri side and the intervening Nuuri threshing ground; along the west side are the compounds or dwellings of the Aleppo landholders and of a peasant who is related to them, and their threshing grounds; and, finally, there is the village proper. My further acquaintance led me to add the camping ground for tent dwellers and the cemetery, both on the east side of the village, and the jurin ("basin"), a depression at the north end used as garden or grazing land. The midden is rough and irregular and separates the "village proper" into north and south portions. Across the country road separating the settlement and the tell, lies a triangular plot of land at the foot of the Tell called the zawra. It is owned by Shayx Nuuri and in 1954 was planted to barley for pasturage for his animals. The Nuuri side of the village spreads out between the Nuuri threshing ground (baydar) and the border of fields at the south end of the settlement. The buildings there are well separated from each other and are scattered over the whole space available without encroaching either on fields or threshing ground. Shayx Nuuri's stone house at the southwest corner commences the series; behind and beyond it is the Nuuri compound which contains stables, sheepfolds, grain storage, and quarters for hired men and foreman. East of these are the compounds or dwellings of six families and the small house of one widower. Two of the six families are tent dwellers, the only ones who remain all year round in the village. Near them the Bu Layl shepherds who spend summer, autumn, and early winter at Tell Ṭoqaan also locate their tents; during most of my residence in the village they were away on their nomadic grazing round in the east. (See Figure 4.)

The Nuuri threshing ground lies between the Nuuri side of the settlement and the rest of Tell Ṭoqaan. On fine days in winter the young men of the village play ball on it. Toward its east end the itinerant Qirbaat ("Gypsies") pitch their small tents when they visit the village. When the pastoralists begin to move east for the spring grazing Shayx Nuuri has a black tent

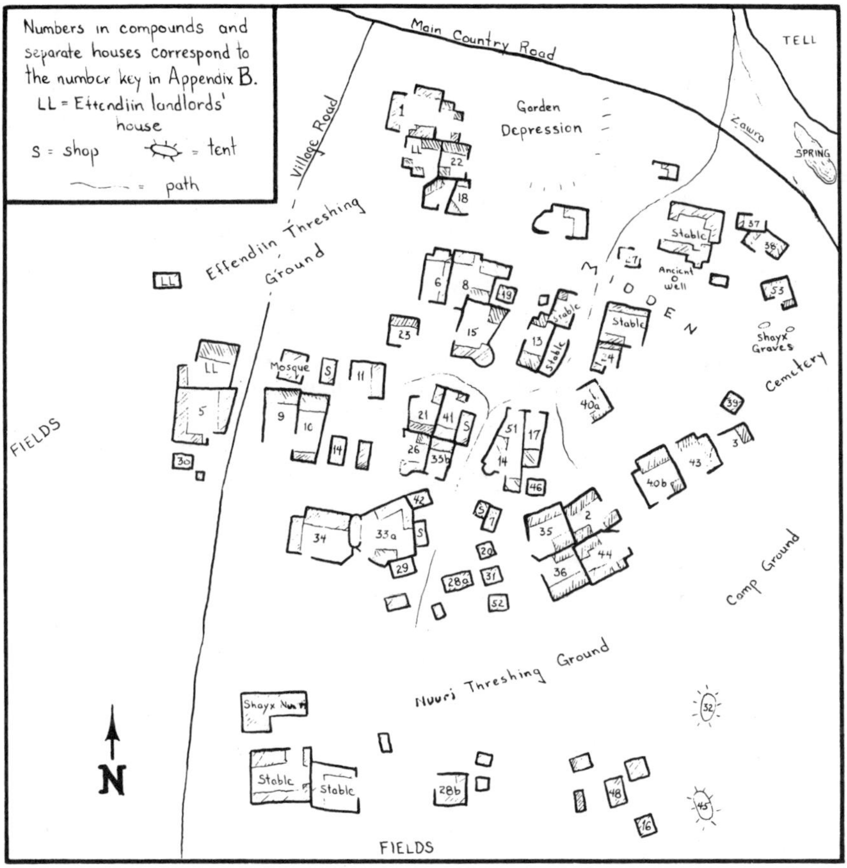

Fig. 4. Settlement pattern of village. Sketch made by Shayx MaHmuud.

raised near the center to be used as a sheepfold by those who stop overnight in Tell Ṭoqaan. In 1954, in the spring, following the wedding of a young couple in the village, a lantern was hung on a long iron stake set in the middle of the threshing ground and for three nights the villagers circled it in the dabkii dance, while others stood about watching the celebration. And during the summer the Nuuri grain is piled here for threshing—wheat, barley, lentils and jilbaan (a vetch), each kind in its customary place.

The dwellings of the urban landholders and their peasant cousin are distributed along the western edge of the settlement and the threshing grounds which they use lie between their buildings and the fields. These threshing grounds are also used for games, by casual social circles gathered to enjoy the spring sunshine, and for a little grazing. During my stay no tents were pitched on them and it was not clear whether they ever served as a camping ground.

The only path or road which was pointed out as the official village road passes along the west side of the settlement, close to the buildings, between the muxtaar's compound and the buildings east of it, and across the Nuuri threshing ground. From the southwest corner of the village it runs through the fields and over the stony ridge to the village of Shuuha. Other thoroughfares in the village are mere paths or ḍarb baqar ("cow path"). There are several of these which can be traced on the sketch map of the village.

The "village proper" is regarded as a separate unit of the settlement from the bordering establishments of the landlords. This view was reflected in the scolding my host's son received from his mother, after he and several other boys got into a scrape in the village one evening. Our compound belonged to the Aleppo landlords' group on the west side. She instructed him: "ma btruuH bi Tell Ṭoqaan ?abadan ba^{c}d mughrib" ("Don't you ever go into Tell Ṭoqaan again after sunset!") Also, the Nuuris' foreman was once heard to remark to a friend that he "never went into the village."

Buildings of the "village proper" stretch from the public road on the north side south to the edge of the Nuuri threshing ground, and the most compactly built area is between the midden and the Nuuri threshing ground. The compounds along the road and the east border, all fairly recent in construction, are inhabited either by newcomers to Tell Ṭoqaan or by old inhabitants who have built new dwellings. No clear or predominant pattern in the arrangement of dwellings, in relation to each other within the "village proper," emerges. There are in all 58 separate dwellings or compounds of families. Six belong to three men who have two wives apiece; in each case the compounds of the man's wives are in different parts of the village. Thirty families and households have no immediate patrilineal kin in the village, and their houses are found scattered throughout the settlement. Twenty-three families are grouped in eight kin groups of two to six families each, but in only one instance, that of the six families of one lineage, can it be said that their dwellings are all in the same part of the village; and even the compounds of this lineage do not comprise a solid block. Both in Saraaqab and in Afess I visited families where the several houses of one lineage were built next to each other and were separated as a unit from the village path or street by a wall and gate.

In Tell Ṭoqaan there are examples of compounds of brothers built next to each other (four), and compounds of brothers that are widely separated from each other (three). With one exception, no compounds of cousins are contiguous. Of seven instances of family heads who have married sons with families, five of the sons maintained their dwellings within their fathers' compounds, and two lived in separate houses. The father of one of the two that lived apart had moved to the Nuuri side and left his old compound to his son. Thus residential unity of kin groups is not a Tell Ṭoqaan practice except in the cases of men whose fathers were still living. The general feeling was that a man could build a house anywhere he chose within the village precincts. It is tempting to think that this independence of family units reflects tribal pastoralist custom rather than that of agricultural peasants in whose villages there tend to develop virtually exclusive quarters occupied by a large group of patrilineally related kinsmen.

There is a dual arrangement in the whole settlement pattern from the Nuuri side on the south to the country road on the north. Tribal affiliation seems to influence the location of families somewhat on the Nuuri side of the village. Several families dwelling there are Bu Layl, as is Shayx Nuuri, but other Bu Layl live in the village. When the nomadic shepherds pitch their tents on the east side of the village, however, the Bu Layl tents are raised at the Nuuri end on the south, and the Harraamshii tents at the northern end, beside the "village proper." Within the village itself the houses of tribal, ethnic, and peasant families intermingle.

So far economic affiliation does not seem to have affected location of dwellings in the "village proper." Houses of employees of all the landlord employers, including Shayx Nuuri are scattered at random throughout it. But there appears to be a definite trend for Nuuri workers to build on his side. None of the dwellings on that side was said to be more than 10 years old and most of the families there were employees of Shayx Nuuri.

Duality of settlement pattern is described by the people in Tell Ṭoqaan as characteristic of large villages nearby, such as Saraaqab and Afess. They said that these villages are not only divided into West Side and East Side, but that each side often has its own muxtaar (village chief), mosque, ?imaam (leader in prayer), shops, and wells. According to informants, the people of one side live only on that side and work only for employers associated with that side, and moreover, this affiliation is or should be maintained from father to son. In Tell Ṭoqaan, however, people change employers from Nuuri to urban landholders each year, depending on the money offered. There is only one muxtaar, one mosque, and every house can have its own well. In the opinion of some villagers, there are two sides—the Nuuri side and the effendiin (urban landholders). Others say they are all one and not divided. But the expression of unity came, in fact, from men who spoke also in terms of national unity.

On the east, between the village and the fields, lies a wide level area used by the nomadic pastoralists as a camp ground when they are at the village. Otherwise, except for occasional grazing of the flocks of sheep and goats during the spring it is idle. Close to the northeast corner of the village is the cemetery. The graves, all oriented east and west, are low hillocks. A few are covered with small stones or marked at head and foot by plain slabs.

Toward the north end of the village the midden interrupts the continuity of settlement. A much traveled path runs across the middle and the midden rises up on each side of it steeply and roughly. Here refuse is dumped and quickly disintegrates; old excavations provide the only latrines in the village aside from those in the landlords' dwellings. At the east edge deep excavations have been made and straw is buried there until it is called for by the owner. Some parts are used by the women to make fuel molded of manure and straw. The midden is mined for compost, or "black earth," to be used in the irrigated gardens, and for earth to mold mud bricks for building.

Besides the major parts of the village that constitute its settlement pattern, there are particular places of use and interest in the village. Tell Ṭoqaan has five shops, but scattered rather than located in one area. Three of them may be called actively flourishing, and all three serve as occasional social gathering places for the men. Next to one shop in the path is set a large block of black stone hollowed in the top. It is used by any woman who needs a mortar for pounding up wheat, pomegranate peel, and the like.

The spring and its shallow pool lie across the main road near the northeast corner of the village. Families which do not have wells or access to a neighbor's well, or those whose well has temporarily gone dry, fetch their water from the spring. Travelers stop there to water their animals and to drink. Occasionally, a woman will bring her laundry or raw wool to the pool to wash. It is not a social gathering place for the women, because, as the Tell Ṭoqaaniis point out, almost every house in the village has its own well and people do not have to use the spring.

At the north end of the village, next to the road, are the graves of two shayxs, MHammad-l-?aajamii and his younger brother. There was once a dome over the elder shayx's grave, but none over that of the younger. Now, that dome has fallen, but each grave is protected by a low wall and the tombs appear to be kept up to some extent with a new layer of plaster-mud each year. The two shayxs are long dead and are regarded as having been honorable and good men, but neither tomb appears to be a place of pilgrimage.

Tell Ṭoqaan has a mosque, but the exterior does not distinguish it from an ordinary double-domed house except for a few points. Windows are left blocked-up all year. The apse projection of the prayer niche on the south wall has not been pierced with vents, as are niches for fireplaces or baths in the dwellings. And unlike most of the dwellings, its door faces north rather than south or east. Neither mosque nor the graves of the shayxs figure largely in the daily life of the village. Friday prayers were not held regularly in the mosque, but each evening the muezzin's call was given at sunset from the slight rise of ground in front of the mosque.

Legal Category of Lands

The Tell Ṭoqaan land belongs to either of two legal categories: jifitlik ("estate of the Sultan let out to tenants") or ?amlaak dawlii ("freehold or private property of the state"). Neither category corresponds precisely to miirii, a term applied to the state-owned land that was the source of fiefs during the feudal period of the Ottoman rule. Rather, they trace back one, the jifitlik, to the private estates of the Sultan and the other, the ?amlaak, to lands controlled by tax farmers. Weulersse (1946: 94) mentions that two large sectors of the private domain of the state were amassed under Sultan Abdul Ḥamid (1876-1909), one southeast of Aleppo and the other in the vicinity of Salamiya, and these were exploited in the manner of the great estates held by landholders in the miirii areas. At the fall of the Ottoman Empire (1918) they became the property of the state of Syria and at the disposition of the French as the mandate power. The French administration attempted to put into operation a new agrarian policy (particularly comassation of fragmented holdings) in these areas following the cadastral survey. At both Afess and Jazraaya this comassation had been completed, but not that I heard of elsewhere in the Tell Ṭoqaan area. All the land from Saraaqab and Afess to the east was said to be "jifitlik," while the Saraaqab land and all that to the west was called "miirii." But they both are now state-owned land and to be contrasted to mulk, private property, or waqf, religious or charitable endowment properties. There are no waqf properties in Tell Ṭoqaan.

The land on which the buildings of the village settlement stand is likewise state land, but constructions are private property and are bought and sold by, or rented to, individuals. That is, the landholders of Tell Ṭoqaan do not own their land but only the right to work it. This usufruct is heritable and can be bought and sold. Landholders pay a tax, locally called mtaa, equal to 10 per cent of the harvest. The amount of the levy was formerly collected in kind at Ras l Ain, but is now paid in money after estimation by a government appraiser. In cases of share cropping, the tax is taken from the gross harvest and the partners divide the remainder according to the partnership contract.

The land attached to the homestead of Bayt Sharqii is marshland (mawat) and is not included in the land attached to Tell Ṭoqaan. It is held by an Aleppo man, whose name suggests kinship with a family which once held land in Tell Ṭoqaan.

In amount the land attached to Tell Ṭoqaan was stated to be 16 faddaan; but if individual holdings are totaled it amounts to at least 36. The term faddaan here refers to the amount of land one plow team and plowman can take care of in one year of agricultural labor. The exact size of this measure of land in the Near East, therefore, varies with the region and quality of soil, and with the ease or difficulty of working (cf. Grannot, 1952: 183-84; Latron, 1936: 11-12, 14-17; Weulersse, 1946: 122). Estimates only are available, and the closest comparable area is the Homs-Hama region, for which Weulersse gives the approximate equivalent of 30 hectares to one faddaan. Using this, 16 faddaan would amount to 480 hectares, or 1186.08 acres; 36 faddaan, to 1080 hectares, or 2668.68 acres. The larger figures seems the more probable for Tell Ṭoqaan but they must only be taken as a tentative estimate of the amount of land which supports the Tell Ṭoqaan population and landlords.

For comparison, a visitor from Afess, one of the two large villages on the highway, said that his village had a population of 950. The two largest landholders held 2400 hectares between them and there were many more small holders whose lands amounted from 10 to 40 hectares each. Jazraaya, the first village to the north of Tell Ṭoqaan, was said to have 1500 hectares.

Landholders in Tell Ṭoqaan

Most of the cultivated lands of Tell Ṭoqaan are held and controlled by four men of the landlord class. Three of these are city men, the effendiin, and one is the tribal shayx. Of course none of these cultivate their lands themselves, but delegate management and labor to others through customary procedures described in the section below, Subtenures and Contracts (pp. 65-66).

The urban landholders live regularly in Aleppo and visit the village only occasionally. They are YaHya Agha Ṣalaah ad Diin and his cousin, Shanaasii Agha, both descendants of the founder of the village, and Mazhar Effendi. Among these three, as Table II shows, 22 faddaan or about two-thirds of the land are held. Shayx Nuuri, the second largest landholder (10 faddaan) and paramount shayx of the Bu Layl tribe, maintains two large households. One, where his three wives and smaller children reside along with other kin, is in Tell Ṭoqaan; the second, for his mother, is in Aleppo. He himself divides his time between Tell Ṭoqaan and local interests in the Bu Layl villages and residence in Aleppo, but is regarded as a resident by the Tell Ṭoqaaniis.

The remaining 4 faddaan of land are held by peasants. One, YaHya ^{c}aarif, is a grandson of the founder of the village, like the two effendiin cousins, but the smallness of his holding and his personal history and mode of life have cast him with the peasants of the village. A second peasant landholder, MHammad Daduu^{c}, lives in Saraaqab, and even though he has a son living in Tell Ṭoqaan, his land (one faddaan) was worked on a partnership basis by the farmhands of Shanaasii Agha. Apparently the son had nothing to do with his father's property, for he worked as a day laborer in the village. The last holding of one faddaan was

TABLE II

LANDHOLDERS, LANDHOLDINGS, AND MANNER OF SUPERVISION IN TELL ṬOQAAN

Landholder	Number of Faddaan	Manner of Supervision
YaHya Agha Ṣalaa H ad Diin	12	4 faddaan - Partners 3 - Jum^c a Sarawwii 1 - Hammuud Hassuun 8 faddaan - laborers Foreman - ^c aali Sariyya
Shayx Nuuri Shwatiyya	10	All worked by farmhands Foreman - Husayn the Circassian
Shanaasii Agha Salaa H ad Diin	7	2 faddaan - Partner, Xaliil Hassuun 5 faddaan - Laborers Foreman - AHmad Bagg
Mazhar ?ibn ^c aali Effendii	3	Partner - AHmad Ibraahiim (muxtaar)
YaHya ^c aarif	2	Self and sons
Ta^c lib Halabii	1	Self and brother
MHammad Daduu^c	1	By Shanassii laborers

that of a young peasant, Ta^c lib Halabii, who inherited it from his father. He worked it with his brother's help, but since his brother was unmarried and lived with Ta^c lib, the holding was undivided and generally ascribed to Ta^c lib as the head of the family.

The details of the holdings, the sectioning of the land into 32 divisions, and the cultivation and crop system present such an intricate meshing of egalitarian and hierarchical principles that they are hereafter broken down in analysis into three topics, Divisions of Land and Field System, Subtenures and Contracts and, in Chapter VII, Agriculture and Gardening. It is clear, however, that the hierarchical system of landholding, through the landlord-tenant contracts, is in control of the whole cultivating system and surplus production of the village lands. But it has not wholly replaced or obliterated the egalitairan field system. This latter system represents a close adjustment of land use by a small peasant community to the local variation of soils and their productivity in a precarious climate for agriculture. Like most agricultural villages of the Levant States, however, Tell Ṭoqaan can and does usually produce a marketable surplus beyond the peasant's subsistence needs and it is this surplus which supports the major landholders.

Divisions of Land and the Field System

All the cultivated land of Tell Ṭoqaan is portioned into thirty-two divisions (quṣm, "division"; pl. quṣuum). These divisions represent an egalitarian apportionment of the land in terms of soil type and quality so that each landholder will have a share of each kind of land and none will have all his holdings in the best or poorest only. A landholder's property in land thus comprises scattered plots which are located one in each of the thirty-two divisions. The size of any man's plot in a division is supposed to be in proportion to that of the other landholders. Thus, a peasant who holds one of the thirty-six faddaan of Tell Ṭoqaan lands, will have a plot in each division which is believed to be one thirty-sixth of that division.

The thirty-two divisions are, furthermore, grouped into four sectors that are designated directionally, as the north, east, south, and west sides. In conformance with the two-field system, alternate cultivation and fallow, the north and west sides go together and the south and east sides. Since no survey map of the properties was available, I can only refer the reader to the sketch map (Fig. 4, p. 53) for the relative locations of the 32 divisions.

The divisions have certain attributes in common. First, there are no fences dividing any one from the next or any of the individual holdings from each other. In both cases, a boundary (taxm) is established by a double furrow; one furrow each is plowed by the adjacent landholders with a narrow space left between the two. The low ridge of earth thus formed is used as a path by residents of the village and by people and animals coming and going from the village. Second, each division has a name. Most of the names are descriptive and relate to shape, location, or some unique feature. A few names derive from past landholders who were reputed to be the first men to cultivate them (see Appendix C, List of Land Divisions).

And last, in cutting up of each division into individual holdings, usually the same order of landholders is followed. Division is made across one end, or raas l ?ard ("head of the land"), so the holdings lie in parallel lines and run the full length of the division. The method of measuring out for the individual holdings and the order in which they lie was as follows: The unit of measure is the maras ("rope"). No source or standard for this measure was described or referred to in the village; it was simply the "rope." It appeared, however, to be equivalent to about 40 feet. If it is necessary to remeasure the amount of land which a man holds in each division, because the boundary furrows are somehow obliterated, a group of men who represent the landholders, their partners, or their foremen, go out together. At the end of the amount of land each man holds, as measured by the "rope," there is placed a stone or clod of earth; space is left for the boundary furrows. Then stones are set down the length of the strip to the ends of fields. When it is seen that they line up properly, each man plows a furrow marking the boundary.

The order of plots or fields within each division has been stabilized in Tell Ṭoqaan and is followed each year. Originally, it was decided by the procedure of casting lots (niirmii qawra, "we cast lots"), which was thus described: If the order in which two men shall hold their strips is disputed, or they dispute which shall have the best of two adjacent strips, a third party takes the qawra which consists of two talleys, one for each man, holds them behind him so he cannot see which he has, and drops one in each plot. The disputing parties must accept the plots they get, for Allah decides who shall have the best. In relation to each other, each of the plots has a name: fay for the one to the north or west of the other, and shamis for the one to east or south of the fay plot. This manner of settling disputes and the procedure of casting lots itself are said to have survived from the days when the egalitarian collective tenure system prevailed, and each year village lands were divided and redistributed among the peasants.

In the standard division of land the present order of plots and proportions in terms of the "rope" measure is given below. A typical section is considered to be 30 rope measures wide (marasaat, pl. of maras). Divisions are apportioned and ordered from east to west, or from south to north.

Order of Plot	Holder	Proportion (in marasaat)
1	Shayx Nuuri	8
2	Mazhar Effendii	3
3	Ta^{c}lib Halabii	1
4	Shanaasii Agha	5
5	YaHya Agha	11
6	YaHya ^{c}aarif	1
7	MHammad Daduu^{c}	1

The thirty-two divisions are not uniform in size, shape, or in the direction in which the parallel plots of the individual holdings lie. Only two examples of the variations from the general rules of division and arrangement are given here, but they will illustrate the abundance of difference in details that exist.

A section devoted to growing watermelon (quṣm jabas, "watermelon division") was pointed out as departing from the general system in many respects. It is only 27 1/2 rope units (marasaat) wide, and is designated in nine groups. The holding and working is shown in Table III.

TABLE III

LANDHOLDING, LANDHOLDERS IN QUṢM JABAS DIVISICN OF LAND

Order of Plots	Number of Units (Marasaat)	Landholder	Supervision or Subtenure
1	2	MaHya Shwatiyya	Partner
2	5-3/4	Shayx Nuuri Shwatiyya	Foreman
3	1	Ta^{c}lib Halabii	Self and brother
4	2	Shanaasii Agha* YaHya Agha*	Foreman Foreman
5	2-3/4	Mazhar Effendii	Partner
6	4	Shanaasii Agha	1 unit - Partner 3 units - Foreman
7	8	YaHya Agha	2 units - Partner 1 unit - Partner 5 units - Foreman
8	1	YaHya ^{c}aarif	Self and sons
9	1	MHammad Daduu^{c}	Shanaasii Foreman

*1 unit each.

A section of land called shaqaf ma^{c}aysra lies northwest of the village along the stony rise of land which is physiographically an extension of the Skayk ridge. When referred to, it is designated by the term shaqaf rather than quṣm ("division") because it is not divided as one. Each person's holding in it is called a shuqfii ("potsherd," "piece"; pl. shuqaf), because the plots are laid out wherever the land is cultivable, for in general the soil cover is very shallow and stony. It was said to have been named ?arḍ mushaa^{c} formerly, that is, land subject to the regime of periodic redistribution among the cultivators by casting lots. The plots of each holder are designated here not by an area measure but by seeding capacity.

Number of "pieces"	Holder	Capacity (in shimbal)[1]
1	YaHya ^{c}aarif	11
2	YaHya Agha	20
1	Shanaasii Agha	10
1	Shayx Nuuri	10
1	Mazhar Effendii	5
1	Ta^{c}lib Halabii	7

Wherever a section borders on an uncultivated area, as do the two preceding, the landholder of the adjacent cultivated plot has authority over that abutting his. But he may then give permission to a man working for him to till any portion of the border which he does not himself use. In 1954 one landholder had allowed a farmhand to cultivate a small piece of land near the stream which bordered on his holding in the division south of the tell. Unwisely, perhaps, this landlord's foreman had allowed the man to use his employer's tractor to plow the small tract and it became mired in the soft earth near the stream. The incident gave rise to interesting repercussions, because the foreman's wife was a sister of the farmhand and the interference of kinship relations with economic relations was a topic of local gossip.

1. Latron (1936: 10, 12-13, 25) has pointed out that the quantity indicated by the shimbal varies from locality to locality in Syria and according to the context of usage. It is a "plains area" measure. It may mean a half or a full camel-load (100-150 kilograms or 200-260 kilograms), or it may refer to a quantity similar to a bushel. There was no certain way of knowing the equivalent in Tell Ṭoqaan. On one occasion when a grain sack was filled with what was called "one shimbal of barley," it appeared to mean half a camel-load. This was the only time when a scale was present, however rough, to provide an idea of what was meant.

Subtenures and Contracts

Most of the land of Tell Toqaan is farmed or gardened by the peasant holders or by hired farmhands working under supervision of foremen. Only 9 of the 36 faddaan were definitely stated to be worked on the tenant or partnership basis. Four men of the village were designated as the partners (shuraka) cultivating these 9 (see Table II, p. 60). A fifth man farms at least a part of one division as a partner of Shayx Nuuri's brother, MaHya Shwatiyya (Table III).

The lands fall into two categories and different contracts apply to each. Grain or cotton lands are subject to the partner contracts or to foreman-hired-hand contracts. Garden and melon lands, ?arḍ maqaatii (a term more or less equivalent to our "truck garden"), are subject to the tilit ("one-third") and foreman-hired-hand contracts. Most of the land of Tell Ṭoqaan is cereal and cotton land; not more than four or five divisions are garden land.

The partnership contract is made anew each year with the landholder on yawm l baydar, "threshing ground day," the day or time when all harvesting operations are finished at the end of summer. There is no guarantee that it will be renewed from year to year, and the trend in Tell Ṭoqaan seems to be, from the landlords' point of view, to reduce this type of contract in favor of foreman-hired-hand contracts. On the other hand, I was told that it was the aim of every farmhand to become a partner.

Under the partnership contract the landholder provides land and seed and the partner provides labor and plowing team (dawwab); the crop is divided equally between landholder and partner after the tax deduction. The partner takes full responsibility for farming the land under his contract and is not subject to the foreman (wakiil) who may be supervising farmhand labor on the same landlord's neighboring plots.

A second type of contract, not in use in Tell Ṭoqaan at the time of my stay but which had been, is the murabbi^{c} contract. In this type the landholder provides seed, land, animals, and the dayn, money for clothes and house. Terms are agreed on at the beginning of the contract year. At the end of the year the crop is divided: three-fourths to the landholder and one-fourth to the murabbi^{c} contract holder. As it affects the village, this is the intermediate step between farmhand status and that of partner. Two peasants in Tell Ṭoqaan were cited as examples of men who had worked up from farmhand, through murabbi^{c}, to partnership status.

The "one-third" (tilit) contract for garden work, like the partnership one, is on a yearly basis, but in this case the gardener provides only labor; the landholder furnishes land and seed, and does the plowing. The crop is divided two-thirds to the landholder and one-third to the gardener after the tax portion is taken.

In addition to those described, there was in Tell Ṭoqaan a type of very small partnership, shikara or flaH shikarjii, in which the partner provided, according to contract, seed only or also team of plow animals and work, for an agreed portion of the crop yield. The partner's share was for his own domestic use and needs and not for sale. A peasant farmer cited two sections in his holding in one division as examples of this type of contract. In one section he shared the yield half and half with a local man whose property was in sheep. The peasant farmer provided land and seed, and the partner provided labor, team, and plow. In the other, one of the wives of Shayx Nuuri provided jilbaan (vetch) seed, and the farmer provided land and labor. The division again was half and half.

Such are only the general rules of contract arrangements as I learned them. There was indication from brief conversations with landlords, and from various accounts in the literature, that landlords, tax collectors, and peasants all have their customary ways and practices of trying to extort a little more than the contract allows to each.

VII

AGRICULTURE AND GARDENING

Agriculture

ALL AGRICULTURAL tools and equipment, or their constituent materials or parts, must be purchased outside the village. Tell Ṭoqaan has neither the timber for the wooden parts of tools nor the raw material or complex metallurgical techniques for making metal parts. The sources of supply are the markets of neighboring villages, of the town of Idlib, or of the city of Aleppo. Even the fabric materials of such accessory items as baskets and grain sacks come from outside, and almost wholly in ready-made form. Only the broad sieves used in winnowing and cleaning grain are purchased from a different source, the itinerant Qirbaat (Gypsies).

Tools and equipment.—The agricultural equipment may be divided into two classes: traditional peasant tools and industrial equipment. Both are shown in Table IV, with the farming operation in which each is used and kind of labor involved.

The peasant group of agricultural tools and equipment found in Tell Ṭoqaan are described in the order in which they are used during the agricultural year. Faddaan, a term which has many meanings, in this connection refers to the plowing unit comprised of plow (^{c}uud), team of two animals (dawwab), yoke (niir), and reins and collars of the harness. It also includes the plowman and the plowman's combined whip and plow-cleaning tool (masaas). To the plow may be attached the seed tubes (zummir or kshaaf ad diik) and the drag (kaluul).

The plow (^{c}uud) is a composite instrument. The seven wooden parts are assembled from pieces which are straight or appropriately curved in growth and which need only adzing down to be fitted to each other. Heavy nails and iron bands hold the parts together. The metal bands are tightened by hammering small wedges of wood under their edges. Hard daily usage loosens the joints, and every day throughout the plowing and planting season the carpenter is busy tightening parts or replacing sections of wood that have split. In this area the plow is a single-handled tool. Near the end of the beam are seven notches (nukuur) on the upper side; these were said to control the depth

TABLE IV

COMPARISON OF PEASANT AND INDUSTRIAL EQUIPMENT AND LABOR IN AGRICULTURAL OPERATIONS IN TELL ṬOQAAN

Operation	EQUIPMENT		Labor	
	Peasant	Industrial	Peasant	Industrial
Plowing	Team and harness; plow with 2 shares, masaas	Tractor; disc plow cultivator plow	4 plowings for cotton; 1-5 plow units; 6-8 hours per day	2 plowings for cotton; 1 tractor, 1 or 2 drivers; 12-24 hours per day
Planting	Plow unit with 1 seed tube attached	Tractor with 3 seed tubes attached to cultivator plow	Broadcast (winter crop), 1 sower per plow; summer crop, 1 sower per plow	Broadcast (winter crop), 3 sowers per tractor; (summer crop), 3 sowers ride tractor
Harvesting		Combine		
Reaping	Sickles; fingerguards; 2 types of pitchforks		About 4 weeks; gangs of fieldworkers 6-12 per field	Not observed
Transporting to threshing grounds	Camel; team and wagon; pitchforks		1 week	
Threshing and winnowing*	Threshing machine (haylaan); winnowing forks (?); sieves		2 months	

*This operation includes the grading of straw which is not a part of the industrial operation of harvesting. One peasant said that industrial machines cut and threshed in such a way that there was no straw which could be used for customary village purposes. Peasant-threshed straw is hard and solid, not beaten to a pulp as when grain is threshed by combine.

of plowing. But from the loose manner in which the beam is chained to the yoke it does not seem likely that they are very effective in this respect.

There are two types of plowshare: one a broad blade for use in soft soil; the other sharply pointed and suited to stony soil. Both blades make a furrow which pushes the earth to both sides; the depth varies only a few inches and in the softest soil does not seem to be more than 8. Depth of furrow attained seems to be chiefly a function of the angle at which the plowman controls the plow. Grains which are sowed by broadcasting may be plowed under with either share

Seed tubes are locally made and fastened to the plow for planting sesame, cotton, and corn. The zummir is made in several fashions depending on available materials. One type is of four pieces of wood nailed together so that the tube tapers slightly and it is fastened by ropes to the plow so that the seed will fall between the "ear" of the plowshare and the sayf (the beam over which the share is fitted). Another type of zummir, attached in the same position, is made of metal from the standard tiniki (a rectangular, 5-gallon gasoline tin) bent into a tube about 4 inches in diameter and soldered at the seam. Stovepipe sections were also used. In either case a funnel is placed in the upper end of the zummir and into this the seed is dropped.

The kshaaf ad diik is used for the same purpose as the zummir. It is made of a gasoline tin from which top and bottom have been removed; a wooden frame covered with burlap is mounted above it to gain the height needed for hand sowing through it. It is mounted over the diik of the plow. The kshaaf ad diik is only employed on heavy soil, whereas the zummir is used on all soils where cotton, corn, or sesame are grown.

A drag (kaluul) is fastened to the handle of the plow. It is a device, used in conjunction with the seed tubes, to cover the seed and make it unnecessary to do so by replowing the field. The drag is a short log tied to the ends of two sticks and the whole suspended loosely from the plow handle.

A combined whip and share-cleaning tool (masaas) is carried by the plowman. The masaas is a stick of wood, about 3 1/2 feet long, over one end of which is fitted a short spatulate iron blade, and to the other end of which is fastened a length of rope. Frequently at the end of a furrow the plowman will stop to clean off the plowshare with the blade.

A team of two animals (dawwab) drag the plow. In the Tell Ṭoqaan area they are either of mules or horses or one of each. Mules are, however, preferred because of their greater endurance on less food. Until four or five years ago cattle were the draft animals, and cattle still predominate west of the highway. Neither camels nor donkeys are ever made to pull the plow. Multiple teams are not necessary in Tell Ṭoqaan soils.

The yoke (niir) by which the team is harnessed to the plow is shorter and smaller than that used for oxen to the west but similar in pattern. It is a straight, unshaped bar of wood. Two wooden pegs at each end are spaced so they will fit over the neck of each draft animal. A pair of pegs in the middle of the yoke takes the end of the plow beam between them. The beam is held in place by a well-wrapped chain of 1-inch iron links. Padded collars fit over the necks of the mules or horses, and, under the tension of pulling, the pegs of the yoke press against them. But the collars give a minimum of protection, for they are scarcely more than a roll of canvas or burlap packed with straw, the ends of which are pulled together and tied with a rope under the neck of the animal. An additional scrap of sacking fits under the yoke and collar to help prevent chafing. The weight and pressure do not fall on the animal's shoulders or chest, but on the neck and throat. Each animal wears a very light halter of leather straps and rope; on the outside of each animal's halter one end of the rein rope (mruud) is attached. The loop thus formed is carried back over the yoke of each animal and comes between the animals to the plowman's hand. Six baa? (one baa? is the distance between the closed fists of the outstretched arms) of rope are needed for one rein rope. The rope, like that used elsewhere in the village, is market bought, twisted of three or four strands of some brown vegetable fiber such as hemp, and no larger than the standard clothesline familiar to Americans.

The plowman may be any male from a boy of thirteen or fourteen to an elderly man; women never plow. He guides the plow with one hand on the single handle. In this hand is also held part of the rein rope, the other hand carries the masaas and controls the rest of the rein. Since the plowshare neither has a moldboard nor turns a furrow to one side, furrows can be plowed in both directions and up and back the length of the field. The team is guided or urged on chiefly by shouts. An inexperienced animal or a young one is harnessed with an experienced animal to learn, at first only an hour or so at a time.

The reaping tools for the field crops are the mughmaara, pitchfork, and sickle. Jilbaan (vetch) is pulled by hand; barley may be also, or it may be cut with sickles if the grain is thick. Sickles are always used with wheat. In pulling grain the reaper moves along from a squatting position and the instruction is always to grasp the plant min taHt (from below) near to the ground. In cutting wheat with the short-handled iron sickle, the reaper moves along stooping from the hips and cutting as close as possible, because both barley and wheat straw are, as a peasant pointed out, "money" and are important ingredients and resources in the village economy.

In many parts of the Near East sheaths or fingerstalls (sharaaṭaat) are used to protect the fingers from chafing, thorns, or the sickle blade (Du Buisson, 1932: 110; Crist, 1953: 410). These are an ancient Near Eastern trait and are made of wood, copper, tin, or tubes of reed. Although none was observed in Tell Ṭoqaan, the reapers regularly wrapped small rags around their fingers as bandages.

Grain is collected into piles with pitchfork and mughmaara. The pitchfork is a four-tined, long-handled fork similar to the tool common to Western farming; none of the locally made wooden type was observed in Tell Ṭoqaan. The mughmaara is a short-handled, one-pronged rake made of two curved sticks. The end of the smaller stick fits through a slot in the end of the larger, and the brace which crosses the acute inner angle is an iron nail. Du Buisson (1932) pictured a mughmaara from the Hama area, which had the two parts lashed together with leather thongs. Those I saw in Tell Ṭoqaan were said to be Hama work and lighter in weight than Idlib work. There are two sizes: the smaller, about 2 1/2 feet long, is used in the field during reaping; the larger is to load grain onto the wagons; it is about 3 1/2 feet long. As much grain as possible is packed into the angle between the two sticks, held in place with one hand, and the whole is lifted above one shoulder and carried to the stack.

Transportation of grain from field to threshing grounds is in a four-wheeled wagon or on camel back. During the rest of the year the sides of the wagon are of solid planks painted blue on the exterior. For this work these are removed and a special frame of wood placed on the wagon bed.

Grains are threshed with the haylaan ("village" term) or jarjar (pastoralist), an implement also called in the literature by its Latin name, plostellum (Weulersse, 1946: 147). The tribulum, or threshing sled, is not used. This machine consists of a wooden frame mounted on two axles. The wheels on the axles are four-toothed iron discs, each made of half circles of metal set in slots in the axle; a single rivet holds the two parts of the toothed wheels where the edges of the metal semicircles are overlapped. The whole axle turns on pegs driven through the heavy side planks of the frame; there are no nails or bolts in its construction. The haylaan is purchased dismounted in town or city bazaar and assembled in the village. One from Aleppo costs sixty Syrian pounds.

The haylaan serves to chop the grain straw as well as thresh the grain from the heads. It is dragged by a single animal around the stack of grain until the whole stack has been worked down. One person, often a child, rides the threshing machine.

Winnowing is performed with a large-sized sieve (gurbiil) purchased from the Qirbaat (Gypsies). The mesh of the best kind is said to be made of mare's-hide thongs. Since I did not observe this operation in Tell Ṭoqaan, I do not know whether winnowing forks are also used. None was seen. The chopped straw and grain is tossed and poured from the sieve from a standing position, so that the breeze will blow away the chaff and straw and the grain falls in a heap at the winnower's feet. Practiced and skillful handling of the sieve (tossing, tapping, and rotating it steadily) seems to be the primary technique for successful winnowing and cleaning of grain with this instrument as well as dependence on the wind.

The industrial equipment in the spring of 1954 consisted of two tractors with plow and disc attachments. They had been purchased in Aleppo and were the property of Shayx Nuuri and an urban landlord. Although harvesting and threshing machinery are known, all the vetch (jilbaan) and barley harvesting in 1954 was done by hand in the traditional peasant manner. After I left the village in May, I learned that an American-made combine was rented for the wheat harvest on one urban landholder's fields and that another urban landholder had purchased a tractor.

While it is difficult to estimate how much of Tell Ṭoqaan land is plowed by tractor and how much with animals, the former amount may be set roughly at a little less than half. Peasant partners and the peasant small holders all use the animal-drawn plow. Some of the sections of the large holders' lands that were worked by farmhands under a foreman were likewise plowed with peasant equipment. Both landlords who own tractors also engage in contract plowing at other villages. They may find this more lucrative, if there is a choice between plowing more of their own land or undertaking to plow another farmer's land for payment. As a peasant farmer remarked, it was cheaper to hire tractor plowing than to invest in a new team of mules or horses. A team eats up in a year the amount in barley that tractor plowing costs.

The two tractors in the village are used wherever draft animals are to plow or pull wagons. One is a heavy caterpillar type said to be suitable for heavy soils; the other is a lighter Fordson tractor. With both tractors plowing can be done with both discs and "plows." The plow is a multiple cultivator-type blade which does not turn a furrow to one side. It is used in planting cotton, sesame, and corn with a seed tube of the same type used on the peasant's plow, mounted behind each of three blades. Three sowers sit on straw-filled sacks and feed the seed down the tubes as the tractor moves down the field. I did not see this practiced anywhere else; perhaps it can be counted as a local adaptation. Both tractors are mounted with strong headlights, and during good weather in plowing season it is not uncommon for them to be operated night and day. At such times two drivers are used; one works all day and the other all night.

Crops.—Wheat, barley, and cotton are the major field crops. Besides these and smaller amounts of other field crops, the irrigated gardens make possible the cultivation of a considerable number of vegetables. The crop list is described in terms of winter and summer crops; both groups include field and garden varieties. The winter crops are planted during late autumn and early winter and are harvested by June; the summer ones are planted in spring, and the last of the harvests, that of cotton, is finished in early autumn.

The winter field crops (musim shitta) are wheat, barley, vetch, and lentils. Wheat and lentils are for human consumption, and the former is the major cash crop. Wheat and barley straw, as will be seen, have various uses. Barley and vetch are fodder crops. Beans, onions, and garlic are winter garden crops and are planted in late winter in fields near the village. All seven are considered to be "old" crops, in that the peasants have "always" planted them.

Although several varieties of wheat, barley, vetch, and lentils are known, only one of each is cited as the best. Except for new varieities sometimes tried by the big landholders, the local (bilaadii) one prevails. For most plants seed is saved from year to year, but is also occasionally purchased from an itinerant merchant. The kind recognized as "best" is usually named after its provenience; that is the best beans come from Damascus, the preferred onion sets from the Hama district.

The field crops of the summer list (musim ṣayf) are cotton, corn (maize), popcorn, sesame, and watermelon. Cotton as an important cash crop was said to be about 20 years old in Tell Ṭoqaan and to have been introduced by the French. Before that time only a little cotton (?utn bilaadii or jawz) was grown for local use. Jabas, recognized as an American variety of watermelon, has been planted in the village in the last 4 years only. "French" cotton and "American" watermelon are considered crops "new" to the peasants; corn, popcorn, and sesame seed, "old." Corn is frequently mixed with wheat in certain dishes; popcorn and toasted watermelon seeds are a popular snack, as in the city.

Included among the summer crops are the majority of garden vegetables, of which the Tell Ṭoqaaniis boast a long list: chick peas, eggplant, cucumber, melon, summer squash, and red peppers are "old" crops; tomatoes and potatoes the people were less certain about in this respect; carrots, cauliflower, turnips, and radishes were known but not frequently grown. Different varieties were not recognized among these plants; each year's crop was grown from seed saved from the previous year. Tomatoes, cucumbers, squash, and red peppers appeared to be the most popular.

As a general rule the size of a crop yield is not predicted in Tell Ṭoqaan. The yield is from Allah and the peasant never knows what it will be. The fertility of each land division is different, and there are good years and bad years. However, one peasant pointed out that in a good year he gets 15 shimbal of wheat or barley from one shimbal of seed, and from the best land, near the marsh, the yield may be 40 to one. It is preferred to distinguish among fields by the amount of seed required to plant them. One peasant said that he needed 15 shimbal of seed to sow half a faddaan, and 25 to 30 for a full faddaan.

Soils, fields, and rotation.—Tell Ṭoqaan lands have many kinds of soil suitable for different crops. The black soil along the marsh is good for cotton. The red earth to the north and west of the tell is good for all the grain crops and especially for cotton. The stony land near the ridge (the shuqaf macaysara division) is good only for such field crops as wheat and barley. And the gray earth to the south and away from the marsh on the east is good for the winter field crops but not for cotton. Sessame, too, is planted on the gray soil. The soil on the top of the tell (comprising two divisions) is good only for barley.

The 32 sections into which the Tell Ṭoqaan lands are divided are further separated into east and west sides: numbers 1 to 15 are the West Side and 16 to 32 are the East Side (see Appendix C). Cultivation of one side in the winter crops, while the other side lies fallow, is alternated year by year. The winter of 1953-54 was sinii Hunṭa (wheat of grain year) for the West Side and sinii ma flaH (no cultivation year) for the East Side. Crop as well as land rotation is also practiced. A peasant pointed out that it is necessary to rotate crops or the wheat will be poorer each year. The best wheat, he said, follows vetch or lentils; wheat comes poorly after watermelon, sesame, and cotton, and poorest of all after popcorn.

Two kinds of crop rotation can, therefore, be distinguished, that by which winter and summer crops are alternated within the two-field system, and that by which species of the same seasonal group are rotated with each other in cultivation years.

The sequence for the winter-summer crop rotation of the divisions of one side is as follows: on sinii Huṇṭa the fields are in wheat (or other winter crop) all winter and spring; following harvest they lie fallow and open to grazing during the summer. The following autumn and winter they are in sinii ma flaH, and are prepared for cotton. Cotton is planted in spring and harvested in early fall. The fields then enter the cultivation cycle again and are immediately plowed and sown to the winter crops. During this sequence divisions of the other side are in the opposite position.

Just as Huṇṭa (wheat) stands as a general term for all winter field crops, so ?uṭn (cotton) appears to signify all summer crops. Hence, although the sequence noted above seems to make wheat follow immediately upon cotton, which is undesirable, the particular crop may be some other member of the same seasonal group. Thus, in the rotation of species within a seasonal group, jilbaan or lentils are often planted in the fields where wheat or barley was sown in the previous cultivation year. Moreover, not all divisions are good cotton land, especially those of the eastern peripheral divisions. These in a no cultivation year remain fallow throughout the winter and summer. They are, however, plowed at regular intervals.

Tree fruits, grapes, artichokes, oranges, and lemons are well known in the village, but have to be purchased. Before the tribal wars, apple, plum, and apricot trees grew in the orchard located near the stream. At the present time there are two or three mulberry trees in villagers' compounds and a few young apricot trees have recently been set out on the old orchard site.

Control of planting has been said to be invested in the village council of elders, particularly in collective, mushaa^{c}, villages (Latron, 1936: 226-28); each farmer must plant the crops his neighbor does, each division of land must be uniform. From my observation this does not appear to be so in Tell Ṭoqaan. Also, I was told that the only crop in Tell Ṭoqaan on which the farmers have to come to an agreement with each other is popcorn, and that because the birds eat it and guards are needed. There is never any question which winter crop a man might plant in his various holdings on the winter-crop side. Only on the fallow side is there question and then only whether all of the holdings in one division are to be planted to popcorn—Hakii, "talk," decides it. The other summer crops, cotton, sesame, or watermelon, may be planted as the individual farmer decides.

Operations and techniques: plowing.—For 8 months of the year the peasants are plowing. From October through December the fields of the winter-crop divisions are plowed and planted with the winter field crops, wheat, barley, vetch, and lentils. Weather conditions may push the schedule a few days into January. For winter crops, two good days in a row are needed for each field: the first day the field is plowed; the second day the seed is sown and then plowed under.

After the winter crops are in, around the first of January, the plowman moves to land in sinii ma flaH ("no cultivation year") and begins the series of preparatory plowings for the summer crops, especially cotton. Fields to be planted with summer crops are plowed four times between January and April, approximately once a month. A fifth plowing goes along with cotton planting. If there is not time for four, three must serve. The peasants say that this succession of plowings is necessary to keep the surface of the soil broken and loose so the earth underneath will stay damp, hold water. For each field, 10, 15, or 20 days are needed between each plowing; some rain falls, a little grass grows, and then comes the next plowing. Moreover, the four plowings keep the soil clean (ndiif).

In the peasant's schedule the first plowing is called Hashka; as soon as the plowman has finished the first plowing of all his fields in the several divisions, he begins over again with the second plowing (tnayya) and so on through the third (tatliit), and the fourth (tarbi^{c}). Table V gives the schedule of plowings and other agricultural activities in Tell Ṭoqaan.

Sunrise begins the day's work throughout the village and throughout the year. The plowman starts work at sunrise. Throughout the winter, if the weather is good, he plows until early afternoon, but as the days lengthen and the heat increases, he returns to the village earlier in the day. By June the plowing hours run from about 4:30 A.M. until about noon. In winter, if rain sets in during the day, plowing may have to stop until the soil is easier to work. If a peasant has no watch and the day is cloudy, he figures he has done a full day's work if he has plowed 20 to 22 field-length furrows.

When a landholder has wide plots of land in his holdings, a number of farmhands working for him and the equipment for them to man, he may use echelon plowing to speed up the work. In this practice, two or more plow teams work one field at a time, each taking a furrow next to the other and starting a little behing the preceding. Sets of three and five teams were seen on the lands of the urban landholders.

If tractors are used only two plowings are needed to prepare the soil for summer crops. The first takes place in November, rather than January. It is reckoned that the second customary plowing is skipped, and that the one plowed in March is the "third."

A tractor can plow 100 dunum a day; the dunum equals 919.3 square meters (Latron, 1936: 20). On the one hand, it was explained to me that in Tell Ṭoqaan 10 dunums of land have a seeding capacity of 1 shimbal of wheat, and, on the other I was told that 1 dunum amounts to 800 square meters. This figure of 100 dunums for the amount of land a tractor plows in one day does not seem credible. It would amount to only about 1 hectare, or 2.47 acres.

Before tractors were acquired, a man from Idlib did tractor plowing at the rate of five Syrian pounds a "dunum." The prices charged by the local landlords (per dunum) were: YaHya Agha, 2 Syrian pounds for the discs and 2 1/2 pounds for the plows; Shayx Nuuri, three pounds for the discs and six for the plows. Nuuri's is the heavier tractor.

Planting.—Two techniques of sowing the field crops are practiced: the winter field crops (wheat, barley, vetch, lentils) are broadcast; the summer field crops (cotton, sesame, and corn) are planted with a seed tube attached to the plow. Only men broadcast the grains; but women sow with the seed tube. The only reason given for the prohibition against women was that they are too light, not strong enough to make an even cast. But the emphasis with which it was said that women *never* sow broadcast indicates a very strong prejudice; sowing broadcast was man's work.

On the one occasion that I watched wheat sown, the sower poured the seed needed into the skirt of his cloak. He paced off the width of the field and noted that it was 10 furrows wide. Starting at one corner, he walked up one side of the field casting seed over it, crossed the far end, and came back on the opposite side, casting from that direction also. His son then plowed the seed under. The son started at the same corner as his father, placed the plowblade between the previous furrows, and worked back and forth up the length of the field, plowing under furrow for furrow. It is customary for one man to plow and one man to sow. In tractor plowing, three sowers follow the tractor.

In sowing the summer crops with the seed tube, one man guides the plow and another, or a woman, walks alongside feeding the seed down the tube; the seed should fall at the bottom of the furrow. Cotton seed is prepared in advance. The morning before it is used the seeds are poured into a tinned copper household container and wetted down; they are covered with wet cardboard, cloth, or felt, weighted and left in the sun. The next morning ashes are rubbed through the seeds so they will not stick together. Sesame seed is mixed with finely sifted red earth before it is sown.

In the household in which I lived the growth of the crops was watched carefully and frequently discussed. Samples were brought in by any member of the family who happened to go out to the fields and the height, amount of blossom, or size of head were examined.

Stages of growth are named. Early in April barley was said to be in the hablaan stage, the head is still enclosed in the stalk, "as the young in the belly of a mare or ewe." The stages of wheat are Hashiish (grass), sab^c^al (swelling of heads), sha^c^ar (hair), Haliib (milk, in the kernels), fariik (green wheat from which the food dish fariikii is made), and Hunṭa (the wheat is nearly dry and ripe for harvest). Those of the vetch, are warid (flower), jilid (skin, i.e., the pod just formed), Habb zghiir (pod has small peas in it), and Habb kbiir (big peas in the pod). Vetch is harvested when the pod turns yellow.

From the many people who came to talk over the crops with my host, a peasant farmer, it was evident that he held in the village a particular role, as he was the man who gave the signal when the crops were ready and harvesting should begin, for his knowledge and judgment in regard to all cultivation was locally respected. On the 5th of May, he announced that the vetch harvest would begin the next day; the western or winter gate of his compound was thereupon blocked up with mud bricks and the northern or summer gate which had been closed was opened. On the 10th of May, he rode around all the wheat and barley fields estimating how soon they would be ready for cutting; barley he decided would be ready in a few days, wheat after 9 or 10. I did not observe any indication of formal decision, pronouncement, or ritual, other than the usual etiquette between visitor and host, when people came to discuss the crops, with him, and no special activities were connected with closing the winter gate and opening the summer one. Everyone helped casually. The summer gate opened toward the threshing ground and a bench of mud bricks was built against the compound wall near it. "Here," said my host, he would sit and watch the work.

Harvesting.—With the beginning of Hasaad (harvest) a marked change came over the economic activities and life of the village. Small groups of strangers appeared, people who had come from the west, often the Alowite Mountain area, to work in the fields. During the day the village was quiet; few people were around, most of them were reaping in gangs in various parts of the fields. Housebuilding and renovating, well digging and fuel making cease. The long social evenings of card playing and story telling stopped. People were up at dawn and worked until sunset under a broiling sun, and most of them retired soon after the evening meal.

The winter field crops are harvested in order: first vetch, then barley, then wheat. Each crop comes to ripeness in this order and there is just enough time to finish reaping one before the next is ready. The harvesting is divided into six operations; each step is completed before the next is begun. The first operation is reaping and stacking of the grain in the fields; the second, is bringing it to the threshing grounds; the third, is the threshing; the fourth, is the winnowing; and the fifth, is stacking the grain and straw. And, finally, on yawm l baydar (threshing ground day), the local harvesters are paid off, the government takes its share of the tax, and partners and landholders divide the remainder. Accounts carried over the past year are settled with merchants, clients, the carpenter, and others. All land and labor contracts end, and new ones are made for the following year. After this the grain and straw that have been sold are moved out of the village and the home supplies are stored.

During my stay in the village, I only saw the vetch and barley harvests. They are not considered as hard or as important as wheat harvesting, and younger boys and girls participated.

When a field of any grain is to be harvested, the laborers line up together at the head of field and each notes the furrows he will reap according to his agreement with the employer. Men reap two furrows at a time, women and boys one. Everyone starts at the same time. In reaping vetch and wheat the harvesters move at their own speeds and each places the handfuls of cut grain behind him. Barley is reaped by teams of three workers; the middle man is the leader and lays his barley directly behind him. His teammates lay their barley on this line of small piles. The grain is collected systematically into larger piles by other field workers.

TABLE V

AGRICULTURAL CALENDAR IN TELL ṬOQAAN*

Month	Weather and Season	Day-count Periods	Activities
August (?ab)	Summer Hot, little wind	The 40 days of murbaniyyit as sayf end August 10	Threshing Threshing Ground Day (yawm l baydar) about August 10
September (?ayluul)	Part summer, part autumn (autumn begins 25 days after end of murbaniyyit as sayf) Clouds and cold weather; rain		Cotton harvest Watermelon ripe
October (tishriin l ?awwal)	Autumn		Cotton and melon harvest Plow fields for wheat
November (tishriin ish shaanii)	Part autumn, part winter		Plow and plant winter crops First tractor plowing for summer crops
December (kanuun l ?awwal)	Winter	The 40 days of murbaniyyit ash shitta begin about December 13	Plow and plant winter crops Lambs should be born late in December
January (kanuun at taanii)	Winter Rain and hail	murbaniyyit ash shitta ends January 20 First period of sa^{c}ad dabaH, January 20-February 2 (12 1/2 days)	Plant winter garden crops First plowing for summer crops Lambs should be born by early in January Kids should be born in sa^{c}ad dabaH period

February (ʔishbaat)	Part winter, part spring (about February 12)	12 1/2 days of sa^{c}ad bala^{c} February 2-14 February 27-March 4, period of musta kurdat 12 1/2 days of sa^{c}ad s^{c}uud February 14-26	Second plowing for summer crops February 21-March 19, plant seedling beds February 3, shepherds leave Tell Ṭoqaan
March (ʔaadaar)	Spring Night alternating cold and warm (March 4-17)	12 1/2 days of sa^{c}ad Habayya February 26-March 10	Third plowing for summer crops, both tractor and peasant plow March 17—Former period of night herding of village herd March 10 to mid-April, plant all vegetables except tomatoes Plant trees
April (nisaan)	Spring		Fourth plowing and planting of summer crops
May (ʔayyaar)	Part spring, part summer		Harvest period begins Summer crops planted
June (Haziran)	Summer		Grain brought to threshing grounds Threshing Plant corn Shearing; end of shepherds' year
July (tammuuz)	Summer Much wind and heat	The 40 days of murbaniyyit as sayf begin about July 1	Threshing

*In Tell Ṭoqaan both Eastern (Julian) and Western (Gregorian) calendars are recognized. The Western calendar runs thirteen days ahead of the Eastern calendar. Villagers follow the dates of the Eastern calendar in economic activities; the state follows the Western calendar. Dates given in the text are according to the Western calendar. Dates cited in this table are those in the Eastern calendar.

When a peasant reaps his barley with a small gang of workers, the fields are divided into sets of three plots each. One of his two or three teams will reap the middle plot of a set first, then one side and then the other. As soon as one set of three is finished a team moves to the middle plow of the next set. When the fields of a large landholder are reaped, his larger gangs can reap the equivalent of a peasant's set of three in one trip down the field. But in both cases the teams of three and the orderly collection of grain, from the first piles left by the reapers, into the larger piles is the same. The result of this organization of reapers and stacking of grain are cleanly harvested fields as far as the grain is concerned. Care is taken to pull or cut only the vetch or barley and all other plants are left standing. The peasant foreman walks up and down among the reapers calling for clean work, "ndiif! ndiif!" Each reaping crew of the big landlords is directed by a crew foreman as well as the foreman of the landlord who oversees all the work. And two or three of the crew work as rakers.

Because the reapers stay all day in the fields, one laborer rides between the fields and the village two or three times during the day bringing water and lunch. At lunch the reapers sit in circles around the food, the women separate from the men. In the village, women are hired to work in the household of the foreman, peasant, or tenant landholder to prepare food for the noon and evening meals; both are part of the harvesters' pay. They are under the direction of the wife of the head of the household. The following example of an evening meal provided for a reaper is typical. After a day's work at reaping vetch for a peasant, his client came to the compound shortly after sunset. He received in an aluminum pail about a quart of beans cooked with olive oil and garlic and eight or ten pieces of bread. These he took back to his dwelling, where he lived alone.

Wages for harvesters are figured in terms of the number of furrows each person reaps and the type of crop. Wages in Tell Ṭoqaan are lower than in Saraaqab, but it was said that workers imported into the village were paid more than local residents. Imported harvest workers are paid and depart when the reaping is finished. For reaping one furrow of vetch the pay is half a Syrian pound a day, for two furrows 1 pound. This means that during the day, as each plot or field harvested, the reaper works on one or two furrows at a time, whatever the previous agreement. The pay for barley reaping is 1 1/2 Syrian pounds a day for one furrow, 3 pounds for two. The rate for reaping wheat is 2 pounds for one furrow and 4 pounds for two; in Saraaqab, by comparison, it is 7 pounds a day for two furrows.

Threshing.—Little can be said about the remaining farming operations, since they did not come under direct observation. From what was seen of threshing and winnowing in other villages in Lebanon and Syria, both are long and arduous procedures which take most of the summer. Discussions of the calendar of events in Tell Ṭoqaan indicated that normally these two operations took up the last of June, all of July, and part of August. Since combines were used in Tell Ṭoqaan in 1954 on some of the fields, on these this work must have been finished very quickly. Before I left it was noted that very few outside harvesters had been hired.

In the past, however, it was the custom on yawm l ?ijraad to bring the grain from the fields to the threshing grounds and to distribute it in orderly stacks for threshing. Under the direction of Shayx MaHmuud, I made a sketch of the order and number of stacks of grain that are customarily laid out on the Nuuri threshing ground. The number is not necessarily accurate, but the proportions between types of grain is probably a good indication of their relative importance in the local economy. Eighteen stacks are called for; of these ten are wheat, six are barley, and there is one each of lentils and vetch. Barley is threshed first. The vetch is tossed on to roofs to dry and is not threshed.

The preceding description has been concerned with the winter field crops only. Not only are these the oldest crops in the area, but their culture marks the major divisions of the economic year. The main events related to agriculture are concerned with their growth cycles and all techniques and operations are adapted to them. The summer crops ripen and are harvested after yawm l baydar, watermelon and cotton particularly in October.

Gardening

Gardening on a commercial scale, as well as for home use, is a feature of cultivation activities in Tell Ṭoqaan. The land around the tell and spring and near the marsh is of sufficient extent, and the water supply usually abundant enough, to produce more vegetables than are needed in the village alone. Most of the surplus goes to markets via the middlemen, but people come from the villages around about to exchange wheat for vegetables or to buy them with cash.

Vegetables of the winter-crop group (beans, onions, and garlic) are not irrigated. Those of the summer-crop group are, and the whole garden area close around the tell appears to be used every year rather than be subject to the two-field rotation.

While field crops were usually not irrigated, some cotton was expected to be in 1954, as well as the vegetable gardens.

Tools, materials, equipment.—As is true in the case of the tools and equipment connected with farming, all the implements concerned with gardening must come from outside. But there are not two groups of tools and operations to be distinguished in gardening as in farming. The only motor-driven machine is the pump used for raising irrigation water, and its use is restricted to that and is dependent on abundance of water. All other gardening tools are hand-operated.

The character of the irrigating machinery used in Tell Ṭoqaan has apparently undergone a change in the past 20 or 30 years. Before the orchards along the stream were cut down during the Mawali-Hadiidiin war, several norias, the vertical water wheels that are constructed entirely of wood, raised the flowing water to the plots to be irrigated. These have disappeared, except for excavations which indicate where they stood, and this streamside area has become marshy and too wet to till, because it is no longer adequately drained. Instead of norias, in the present gardens deep reservoirs are dug and over them are mounted all-metal wheels of small size, powered by animals, which turn an endless chain of buckets. Use of gasoline motor driven pumps by the major landlords began in 1954. The supply of water was found not to be sufficient in one landlord's pit to use the pump, and he replaced it with an animal-turned wheel. He took the pump, however, to the marsh and made plans to pump directly from the marsh for irrigation of cotton fields nearby. The reservoir diggers of the other landlord, fortunately struck a small subterranean stream, and that gasoline pump was successful there.

Initial plowing of the garden land is done by animal-drawn plow or by tractor. To enrich the soil black dirt or compost from the village midden is loaded into light four-wheeled wagons and drawn by tractor or team to the gardens. It may also be carried in burlap paniers on the back of a donkey.

Digging reservoir pits, wells, constructing gardens and seedling beds is accomplished by means of several tools. Of these, the hoe is a short-handled instrument with a broad triangular blade; this, and perhaps the "marr" type of shovel, are the two tools most closely connected with gardening. The hoe has few uses outside. The fas is a short-handled tool also, but with a narrow adzelike blade. Two types of long-handled shovels are employed: the krak and the marr. The krak may be a shovel that is similar to the Western type or one that has a much smaller, rounded blade with a broad flange along the top for pressure by the foot. The marr has a small sharp triangular blade and a stout wooden bar slipped down the length of the handle to a position a few inches above the blade. Both the marr and the krak with the small, flanged blade are more suitable for barefoot laborers than is the Western shovel. A short-handled pickaxe is also used.

In reservoir and well digging a tripod is set over the excavation, a pulley is attached, and the dirt is pulled up in baskets. The baskets are made of heavy inner-tube rubber cut in the same shape as is one of the several kinds of baskets and trays of traditional fiber. Hand-over-hand pulling may be used to raise the basketloads of dirt, but, preferably, the puller walks away from the excavation with rope over his shoulder or twisted around his hips. In reservoir digging a small ramp may be built so that he walks down an incline as the load is raised. This arrangement of pulley, rope, and inclined ramp is also commonly used for drawing water from deep wells in villages in the area and, on a much larger scale, in oases in Arabia as a means of raising irrigation or public drinking water (cf. Harrison 1924: 45-46).

The irrigation wheel (dulaab) is set vertically over the reservoir pit on a bolted frame of four heavy iron girders. The frame rests on large stones which are quarried from the tell. Cost of the wheel runs from 300 to 500 Syrian pounds, depending on whether it is bought new or secondhand. Six wheels were owned among the 4 major landlords; in 1954 a peasant purchased one, and he was the first peasant to do so. The chain of buckets can be made in the village with ropes, empty 5 gallon kerosene tins, and short bars of wood, but it is more often only repaired locally. The wheel is turned by a long pole fastened at one end to the set of gears connected with the axle of the wheel. A horse or mule is harnessed to the other end of the pole and paces slowly around a path around the reservoir. A clacking device is attached to the machinery so the boy or man, stationed to watch the wheel and water, knows when the animal stops moving and can urge him on. The whole assemblage is now made of iron, but like the rubber baskets is a replica in a new new material of a prototype in a less durable material, in this case wood (Thoumin, 1936: cf. Plate VII opp. p. 86).

The water spills out of the buckets into a trough and is led to the gardens in channels which are lined with cement. Three layers of cement form the channel lining. The first layer is mixed with fine pebble gravel, the second with sand, and the last with red earth. Each is smoothed with a trowel made by the carpenter of a flat, rectangular piece of metal with a wooden handle on one side. This same tool is usually used by the women in smoothing floor and wall plaster in the dwellings and, in fact, the cement work on the channels may also be done by women.

Garden crops.—The winter-crop vegetables, beans, onions, and garlic, are planted early in February. Green beans are ready to eat about May 1 and green onions are pulled beginning in late March. In 1954 the first seedling bed for tomatoes was made by my host, a peasant farmer, on February 21. From then until March 19 was the proper time to plant tomato seeds, and seedling beds appeared near many dwellings in the village shortly after my host's; if the plants fail, it was said, new seeds should be planted after the other vegetables. From March 23 to about April 23 was the right time to plant the other vegetables — two kinds of squash, eggplant, red pepper, cucumber, and potatoes. The irrigated seedling beds of the big landlords were made during this period. Transplanting the seedlings of tomato, red pepper, and eggplant begins about May 10.

Garden practices.—All of the gardening operations on the lands of the major landholders in Tell Ṭoqaan are carried out by contract gardeners with the exception of the preliminary plowing. This is done by one of the landholder's farmhands. When this is completed, the gardener takes over and directs or does the subsequent work himself. But like the farming partner, he is not under the supervision of the landlord's overseer or foreman.

Winter crops are planted without further treatment of the soil. When onion or garlic sets are to be planted a crew of workers is gathered. Each worker is assigned a furrow ridge and, with a supply of sets in the turned-up skirt of his gown, he moves along thrusting the sets into either side of the ridge. The soil is very soft and no tool is needed.

Of the summer-crop vegetables, tomatoes, eggplant, and red pepper require seedling beds, from which they are transplanted to the gardens. Nearly every household in the village makes such a bed near but outside the compound; these are not irrigated or watered. Seedling beds for the gardens of the landlords are laid out in the irrigation area and are spread with compost from the midden and regularly irrigated.

The villager's seedling bed is made with the adze; the earth of a rectangular plot (none was more than about 8 by 6 feet) is chopped up with the narrow blade, until it is finely pulverized; then the gardener makes a hatchwork of furrows with the end of the handle over the surface of the soil. The seeds are broadcast generously over the hatching. With palms and the long side of the adze handle they are covered lightly. Camel thorn is then spread thickly over the plot and tamped down to protect seeds and small plants. When the plants are 4 or 5 inches tall, the thorn is removed and stacked around the edge as a low fence.

The black dirt or compost of the village midden is taken to the plowed garden land and dumped in piles in convenient places. On a large melon or squash field, the black dirt is spread thinly along the irrigation furrows, but for the small plots of vegetables it is allowed to wash down the irrigation channel.

On the landlord's garden land the large seedling beds are so made that a group of three, about 40 feet of space in length, are leveled off, one a few inches below the next. Ridges of dirt control the water flow, and as the channel in one plot is filled, the gardener breaks down the wall of the ridge and allows the water to run into and spread out over the surface of the next lower plot. These beds are also covered with camel thorn, until the seedlings are well up.

The small irrigated gardens are made in sets of two to four plots surrounded by a well built-up ridge of soil. In a four-plot garden, there are four rectangular ridges surrounded by the trench for the water. Each plot is kept closed off from the others except when the water is let in. Tomato and other seeds are thrust into the sides of the ridges and it is not necessary to transplant seedlings from these gardens.

When the tomato seedlings are transplanted from the villagers' seedling beds to a garden plot, and when squash seeds are planted in a small plot, a qamuuc (lit., "cone-shaped column") is built of clods of earth piled on top of each other to a height of about 2 feet and set out at intervals. These are erected as scarecrows so the birds will not eat the small plants or seeds. As one rides along some roads in areas of rocky ridges where little pockets of soil are cultivated, a great many such columns of stone are seen, piled a foot high or more. When I saw the qamuuc made beside a small plot of squash I mentioned the similarity. The explanation was as above.

Labor organization in gardening.—Even though the operations connected with gardening are few, there are several features that suggest organization into working crews. A peasant may add to help from his family that of two or three men who have agreed to work for him year around; these are his "clients."

He may also employ a boy or youth by the job. One peasant specified particularly that he always paid in money and not in kind; he implied that payment in kind, like barter, was not infrequent. The three men who gardened on one-third contracts with major landholders called in members of their families to do the labor. Plowing, reservoir digging, and setting up the irrigating machinery came under the direction of the landlord's foreman and not the gardener. Day laborers were hired at 3 pounds a day, from among the Tell Ṭoqaan men and from nearby villagers for reservoir digging.

One peasant in Tell Ṭoqaan decided in 1954 to invest in an irrigation wheel to irrigate his plot of land in the qubblii tell division, a tract that lay on the southeast side of the tell and between it and the stream. The soil was a gray-black alluvial and the plot sloped gently from the foot of the tell down to the stream. Location of the wheel and reservoir, at an upper corner of the plot near the tell, was settled upon, because, he argued, he would find water there that derived from the rain which fell on the tell during the winter and seeped through the earth. Early in April, therefore, he made arrangements with his "friend" and money-lender, an effendi from Idlib, to purchase a dulaab. His patron agreed to put up the 500 Syrian pounds necessary for the equipment and to take in return one third of the vegetable and cotton profits. The peasant farmer, who would control two thirds of the crop, said he planned to hire a gardener with one third and that after a year or so, would be able to buy the irrigating equipment from his patron.

In due time the water wheel arrived; it had been purchased in Saraaqab, second-hand, for about 300 Syrian pounds. By the 13th of May the reservoir pit had been dug and adequate water found as predicted. The plot to be irrigated appeared to be about half an acre in extent. Most of it was planted to cotton, but the upper corner, near the tell and irrigating wheel, was made into a small kitchen garden and planted with squash. Tomato seedlings were transplanted from the seedling bed near the compound to two rows across the end of the plot nearest the stream.

VIII

ANIMAL HUSBANDRY

DOMESTIC ANIMALS are as important to the economy, and to the sentiments of the villagers as the agricultural activities. In a mixed village like Tell Ṭoqaan their value, both for work and products, seems higher than in such old peasant villages west of the highway as Jiinii. Sheep and goats are kept in proportionately larger numbers in Tell Ṭoqaan than in the villages whose economies are based primarily upon cultivation, and the pastoralist practices and lore are therefore relatively richer. In this respect the culture of Tell Ṭoqaan is clearly oriented toward the traditions of the shepherd tribes from which many of its residents derive.

The animals owned in 1954 comprised about 300 sheep (plus about 200 lambs born that season); 50 goats and 35 kids; 15 horses and mares and a few foals; 25 mules; of cattle, 12 cows and 3 calves, but no bulls or oxen; 3 camels; a dozen or more donkeys; and a considerable number of dogs and cats.

Two households kept hutches of domestic rabbits, but apparently for no other purpose than pets, since they were not eaten. Poultry owned included a great many chickens, a flock of geese, 40 in January which dwindled to three or four by May as they were consumed, and a few turkeys. Several houses kept beehives. Pigeons, which are believed to bless a household and which are much desired, had cotes provided for them. Nearby at Tell Sultaan there was a large rectangular building at the edge of the settlement built especially for them and owned by one man in that village. The nomadic shepherd families attached to Tell Ṭoqaan owned about 300 sheep and 20 camels.

Traditional Classes of Animals

In Tell Ṭoqaan two classes of animals may be distinguished by the tradition to which they belong: the peasant group and the pastoralist group. The difference of traditions is based on species (and sometimes breed), usage, and the consequent size of herd or flock kept by family units. Thus, the pastoralist economy depends upon sheep for subsistence and surplus, and traditionally upon camels for transport. The peasant economy depends upon working animals as the major nonhuman power resource for plowing, operating irrigation wheels, and transporting grain to market. Industrial equipment finds more traits of the peasant economy to displace than the shepherd tradition, but it has taken effect in both.

The peasant class of animals consists of cattle and oxen, the nondescript breed of village horse, the donkey, and the adjuncts of poultry and bees. In the west very small household flocks of either sheep or goats, or both, may be kept by peasant families, but they provide only enough milk for domestic use, and cow's milk may prevail in the area. Judging from information from the peasant village of Jiinii, such flocks may in even a fairly large village be the specialty of a few families which then provide the rest of the residents with their needs. Moreover, the proportion of goats to sheep seems much larger in the west than in Tell Ṭoqaan and its vicinity. In Aleppo, also, household flocks of goats are often seen, and sheep are rare. People in Tell Ṭoqaan clearly like sheep better than goats and display considerable pride and affection for their favorite ewes.

Mules appear to be very recent in Tell Ṭoqaan and to have been introduced from the north and east. I saw them at the tribal villages east of the highway which I visited, but did not see any west of the highway where peasant villages prevail. In the latter area oxen held their place as the draft animal. It is in the eastern area, where the pastoral tradition is strong, that mules have easily replaced oxen.

The pastoralist group of animals consists primarily of large flocks of sheep among which are mingled a few goats. Camels are still important to transport household equipment of the poorer nomadic families, but trucks are used extensively by the wealthier sheep raisers. And there is, in Tell Ṭoqaan, at least the nomad's memory of "purebred" Arab horses.

Other reminders of the importance of shepherd pastoralism in the area are the movement eastward of flocks of sheep to the spring grazing, the nomadic ranging of some small flocks and Bu Layl shepherds in the locality, and the extensive properties in sheep said to be owned by Shayx Nuuri which remained in the eastern grazing grounds all year.

The three camels which were kept all year in Tell Ṭoqaan by one family may be regarded as the surviving remnant of the former village herd used to carry grain to the Aleppo market.

Property in Animals

Whoever owns them, the domestic animals in Tell Ṭoqaan may be divided into two economic categories: work animals and product animals. Regarded as work animals are mules, horses, camels, donkeys, dogs, and even cats. The first four are draft and transport animals, dogs are kept as guards and scavengers, and cats are useful for catching mice. Since introduction of mules and tractors, cows are no longer worked and are kept wholly for their products. The expansion of cotton growing has cut down pasturage area and practices suitable to cattle grazing. As a result cattle are tending to decline in numbers. Horses, once used for riding and carefully bred as a prestige animal, have been replaced by the automobile. Those that remain are of bilaadii, or nondescript, breed and are primarily work animals. A few riding mares of "purebred" stock are owned by the wealthy landholders.

Only the major landholders, their partners, and the peasant farmers own mules and horses, for a team of mules or horses represents considerable investment and upkeep for a villager. A team costs 150 to 300 Syrian pounds and the pair will eat 18 shimbals of barley a year in fodder. There are a number of donkeys in the village, the usual transport animal of the poor man.

Only 3 camels are owned in Tell Ṭoqaan; those of the nomads numbered 20 but were not available all year around. The local camels belonged to one man and work regularly in the transport of straw between villages. Formerly, the village had a herd of 20 which carried grain to Aleppo all winter, but these disappeared long ago in favor of trucks.

The product animals are the sheep, goats, and cows. Eight or more families had cows, but no family more than two. Before the extension of cotton growing, there were many more, and one man was rated as having had a "large" herd, at least twelve. At the present time, the meager yield of cow's milk keeps these animals within the category of household or subsistence production. The local flocks of sheep and goats are of two types. One is the small flock whose yield in milk is for household use only and numbers no more than 4 or 5 females. The other is the large flock which produces a marketable surplus. Shayx Nuuris' household flock, however, as is commensurate with his position and obligations of hospitality, as well the feeding of a large household, is nearly as large as the largest flock belonging to a villager. Two of the large local flocks are held on a partnership-contract basis between two urban landlords and two villagers; both the village men are also the farming partners of their landlords. Eight other men owned flocks of from 6 to 60 animals, that produced enough surplus milk to sell. Male lambs or kids are also marketable items. As seen from this range, usage rather than size alone determines the kind of flock, but size indicates economic status, and flock sizes in Tell Ṭoqaan correspond to the economic differences which are characteristic of the society. A few men who hold no land or subtenure contracts own flocks large enough to produce a marketable surplus of milk, wool, and lambs.

Besides local flocks, Shayx Nuuri was said to own large flocks which stay in the eastern grazing area all year. One man in the village is a partner in sheep-raising with him, but the flock they own together remains in the village until February and is then taken eastward for the spring grazing. At this time many other flocks pass by Tell Ṭoqaan. Usually the property of men in such western villages as Saraaqab and Afess are under the care of hired hands who work under the shakkar contract and are paid 1 1/2 Syrian pounds for each ewe. No other type of contract in sheepraising was in force in Tell Ṭoqaan in 1954 except the one between partners. In this contract the pårtner, shariik, is responsible for the flock; he sells the products of wool, clarified butter, and milk, and pays the owner the amount agreed upon as the price of the sheep. At the end of the shepherd's year there is a division of the lambs; half the female and half the males go to the senior partner or owner.

Property Marks

Goats, sheep, and camels regularly carry the wasm ("branding," "marking") of the owner. Marking is done about the time the kids and lambs have begun to graze. Goats and sheep have their ears slit, cut, and notched in the owner's combination of two of the forms listed below.

riishii: diagonal slit cut upward in the fore edge of the ear

gubla: a triangular notch cut in the fore edge of the ear

jadda: tips of both ears cut off

shugga: a long slit, about 3 inches, cut upward from the tip of the ear

An animal which is not marked is called gaffal and is due for eating soon after it has been weaned.

Camels are branded with the tribal or sectional wasm xayyii ("branding of brothers"). The dagh is the brand of an individual owner, thus, while camels carry a lineage or tribal brand, sheep and goats do not. Other animals do not carry property marks.

Taxes

Only camels, sheep and goats are subject to a government tax. There is none on horses, mules, or cattle, which are shughl fallaah (a peasant's work animals). Formerly, camels were taxed up to 6 Syrian pounds a head, but now they are taxed like sheep and goats, at 2 pounds each because their use and number have declined. Each shepherd carries with him in a pouch slung around his neck an offical document giving the number and ownership of animals under his care. This paper is often wrapped in a page of the Koran for greater security.

Breeding

The gestation periods of the various domestic animals were stated to be as follows: cows, 9 months, mares, 1 year; sheep and goats, 5 months; donkeys, 1 year; camels, 10 to 11 months; dogs, 3 months; and cats, 40 days.

The Tell Ṭoqaaniis have definite ideas and practices as to times when animals should be bred, and the difference between the periods when the young of sheep and of goats are born indicates controlled breeding. Sheep and goats are in heat from June to September (Bodenheimer, 1935: 123). The villagers said that sheep should be bred at the first of the forty days of summer (murbaniyyit as sayf), that is, in July, and lambs should be born about the first of the forty days of winter (murbaniyyit ash shitta), or December. Lambing should be finished before the beginning of the fifty days of the four sa^{c}ad periods, about January 31. This schedule was successfully followed. Virtually all lambs were born before January 31 and were able to accompany the flocks as they moved east about the middle of February.

Goats should be bred after the forty days of summer are finished, that is, after about August 10. Kids should be born in sa^{c}ad dabah, the first period of the fifty sa^{c}ad days extending from January 31 to February 11. My observation records for the seven kids born in one peasant's compound show that this was the period during which they were born.

The generalization was made that all animals are bred so the offspring will be nursed and begin to graze during the spring abundance of grass. Besides sheep and goats, cows are bred in March. Mares should be bred in the cool of spring and not the heat of summer or the "offspring will not be strong or big." For mares there are two seven-day periods, each called musta kurḍat, when breeding should not take place. One must not plant trees during these periods, either; there also seem to be other prohibitions, particularly in regard to plowing. The musta kurḍat period extends from February 27 to March 4; both the Western and the Eastern calendar have a musta kurḍat including these days, and the prohibitions apply in full to both. Since the Western calendar runs thirteen days ahead of the Eastern calendar there is, however, an interim period of three days between the end of the Western musta kurḍat and the beginning of the Eastern when the prohibitions are not in force.

The musta kurḍat is a cursed period. The musta kurḍat, its name, and its prohibitions derive from the fate of one ?a^{c}ad ibn Mirwaan who declared himself to be Allah and was struck down. My informant declared that he did not know if the story were true, but he knew from experience that trees planted in these periods did not survive and mares bred did not produce young.

Local breeds appeared to predominate among the animals as among the varieties of crops, although other and superior breeds were known. Turkish sheep; the Shamwii, or Damascus, breed of cattle; and the baghl sultaanii, or best breed of mule from Mosul and Deir ez-Zor, were mentioned. While mules were bred from local animals, the Qurbaat mutarbii (Gypsies) were said to come around each year with the best breed of stallion donkeys from Damascus; they charged 3 pounds Syrian for stallion service. The Arab lore and sentiment concerning "purebred" horses, whose lineages are traced through the female lines, lingered among the older men, but the breeds are gone and only the kadiish biladii ("local nag") is found.

In sheep and goat flocks there are usually only one or two rams or bucks. Female offspring are always preferred, and the males are sold. The proportion of rams among sheep appears to be one to twenty or thirty ewes. When a man does not have a male in his flock he borrows, without charge, the services of a male animal from a neighbor.

When a ewe or female goat is ready to give birth she is closely tended, kept near the house, and helped during delivery. Men or boys care for the animals at this time and women withdraw from the scene.

If there is difficulty, an experienced shepherd is sent for. He may be paid a small fee or simply given tea and a package of cigarette tobacco.

The young is pulled gently but firmly as it begins to appear. As soon as it is free from the mother, it is squeeze-wiped dry and its nostrils blown into to clear them. It is then placed near the mother's head so she may lick it clean. Shortly afterward milk is forced into the young's mouth, its tail is flicked, and a teasing call given to coax it to nurse. The two are left for a short time, or until both animals come to their feet. Bread is immediately fed to the mother, and every morning for several days thereafter she is given a mixture of hot boiled wheat and lentils. When a female has had difficulty in delivery or is slow in lactating a hajab or charm (a verse of the Koran written on a scrap of paper and rolled in a bit of cloth) is hung around the animal's neck. If vaginal tissues have been torn, a protective apron is fastened over the rear of the animal. Placentas are thrown to the dogs.

All animals are individually referred to by descriptive names. The full "name" of an animal consists of several such terms, for example, saxla dariyya gharra hajla ("female kid with speckled ears and white on the lower forelegs"), but only the first and second terms, saxla dariyya, are used in casual reference.

The ewes and nanny goats are separated from their young most of the time, since the mothers are taken out to graze. When they are brought in at noon and evening they must be watched closely for the first few days and often coaxed to accept their young.

Newborn kids take milk from their mothers twice a day for 20 days; lambs and calves are fed thus for 30 days. After the first 15 days the goats and ewes are milked at noon and only a little is left for the kids and lambs which begin at this time to learn to graze. This milking is called Halbii wahdii (one milking). After 20 days or a month there are two milkings a day, the Haliibayn (dual form, "two milks") period, at noon and at sunset. The kids and lambs, which have been kept separate from the mothers at night, are now left with them in the folds until morning. After a month or so the young are grazed separately and kept separate at night for a few weeks, until offspring are no longer recognized and all can graze together. After weaning and for about a year goats are called jada and sheep are called garghuur; they are ready for breeding as two-year-olds. Very old ewes are called Hurmii, and occasionally kept somewhat as pets for as long as they live. Allowed to wander about as they please, they join any local flock as it passes, or even the village herd and their actions are a considerable source of amusement.

For 4 or 5 months the animals are fresh until lactating stops in summer at breeding time. Thus, there is not a year-round supply of fresh milk or laban for the average village diet, and spring brings with it a welcome change from boiled wheat, bread, and onions.

Care of Animals

Most of the food of domestic animals comes from natural grazing, but the different requirements of the animals are recognized, as well as their different tastes. The peasants work animals and cattle need grasses of higher quality and more green fodder than sheep, goats, and camels, and they do not graze on the stubble of the fallow fields. Sheep and goats graze the uncultivated and fallow lands selectively; they do not eat such plants as asphodel. Camels have even more discriminating tastes; during winter and spring their herdsmen follow the rains and let them feed in fallow and waste areas where plants to their liking are found. When there is no pasturage, they are given straw at the camp grounds.

Formerly, before the expansion of cotton farming, three divisions of land were set aside each year and barley planted in them for the working animals. In spring a system of co-operative night grazing was followed. At present, only a few plots of barley are set aside for pasturage, and the Hashiishaat glean the fields for green night fodder. The Hashiishaat are men and women, usually older and "unemployed" people, who earn a little money by this day labor. Jilbaan from a previous year's planting is gathered from plots of wheat and onion, or green barley is brought from the borders of outlying fields.

All animals are fed chopped straw when there is little or no grazing in summer and winter. Long wooden troughs are brought from the town markets and set up for the sheep; stables and courtyards are provided with mangers made of mud bricks. For the working animals and cattle, jilbaan is mixed with the straw. Throughout the winter and early spring chopped straw is transported east to the flocks of sheep kept there.

Large flocks or herds of animals are watered at the spring. A man who has only a few animals may provide water for them in pans or in a limestone trough. All the troughs were said to have come from the tell or Skayk ruins and are not locally made, and one stands by each well. Sheep and goats are not regularly watered until late spring, but the working animals are watered each day as soon as they return from the fields.

All animals are kept at night in stables, folds, or tents. Sheep and goats are always separated from the stable for working animals and cattle. The stable regularly has a manger of plastered mud brick built along one side, a small open wick kerosene lamp, and a few cleaning tools. The animals are not tethered to one spot in the stable, but each seems to take an accustomed place.

When the work animals return to the stable in late afternoon, they are immediately watered and fed. Straw is sieved of chaff, handfuls of jilbaan are mixed with it, and this is distributed in the manger. The fine chaff from the sifting is then thrown under the animals' feet. The following morning the stable is scraped down with a wooden shovel and the mixed dung and chaff carried out and dumped in a place reserved for it. Since this is an important fuel resource, it is not wasted and the stables are carefully cleaned each day. A man may clean the stable, but women carry out the dung in large, slightly concave, basketry trays. Sheep folds are not thus cleaned.

The nomadic pastoralists pitch black tents that are similar in general structure to the dwelling tents, for sheep folds. One end is banked off with feed troughs and brush into a smaller enclosure for lambs.

Camels are hobbled by tying one foreleg bent back at the knee joint and at night are also tethered by a light rope attached to the halter. The three camels which stayed all year in Tell Ṭoqaan were bedded down each night at one end of their owner's tent where the floor level had been lowered two feet or so by excavation to accommodate their height.

Among the itinerant specialists who visit Tell Ṭoqaan and other nearby villages is the horseshoer. Horses and mules are shoed with an ovoid metal plate which has a small round hole near one end. The shoer for Tell Ṭoqaan comes from Sarmiin, a village near Idlib. He charges three quarters of a pound for each animal for each servicing, and each family pays him for his year's services after harvest is over on yawn l baydar (threshing ground day).

Herding and Grazing

There is a definite caste or class flavor, projected from their rules for human society, in the villagers' statement that "Sheep and goats eat together; cattle, horses, mules, and donkeys eat together; but camels eat alone and go far off from the village." All the cattle, horses, mules, and donkeys of the village are grazed in one herd under the care of the village herdsman. He is responsible for their care during the day and is hired on a year's contract which begins and ends on yawm l baydar (threshing ground day), in August. His pay, expressed in terms of a quantity of wheat, is one-half kil (equal to one-fourth shimbal of wheat) for each animal, plus the zuwaadii (one kil of wheat "for bread" from each client). The first part of the fee may be paid in money; the second is regularly paid in wheat.

Each year the choice of a herdsman is a serious local concern; he is selected as the muxtaar is. Those men who have "many" animals in the herd make their decision after yawm l baydar as to whether the herdsman of the past year shall be kept for another year. Tell Ṭoqaan has had many herdsmen in the past 20 or 25 years. The list of names given included a number of the elder men in the village, some of whom had served as herdsmen for more than 3 or 4 years. Several times two men were partners in the herding.

The herdsman in 1953-54 was one of the two tent-dwellers in the village and a Mawali tribesman. While he took the responsibility and prestige of his position, the daily labor of minding the animals was performed by his two sons. However well known he may be to the villagers they address him as ya jawwaal ("Oh Herdsman—") rather than by his name.

Up until 10 or 12 years ago, there was a much larger village herd than the one at present, which numbers about sixty animals. There were, especially, many more cattle in it, and every man had six or more. All the land around the tell, now the garden area, was set aside as grazing land for the herd. Cattle were then used for plowing, and in spring they plowed from sunrise until noon; grazed from noon until sunset, when they were milked; grazed all night and were milked again in the morning. The Tell Ṭoqaniis got both milk and work from the cows. Spring grazing was important; the herdsman cared for the animals during the day, but at night, from the end of March to the beginning of harvest, the owners co-operated in night herding. Fifteen men took three watches through the night in groups of five and guarded the herd on horseback. The watches were called ?awwaliyyii ("first one") of 4 hours, nussaaniyyii ("middle one") of 3 hours, and ?axriyyii ("last one") lasting until sunrise. Then came the tractor and cotton, and now mules, and the night herding system has disappeared. In its place, green fodder is brought in by the Hashiishatt, or a man may take his own animals out by himself for the night and sleep during the day.

Sheep and goats are managed on a different system of which the basic component is the family flock. Every day families which are united by kinship or marriage customarily combine their animals into one large flock for the day's grazing. Unrelated families with small flocks may combine theirs, two families at a time arranging the co-operation through agreement between the heads of the households. In all cases the shepherd was a member of one of the families, an older boy or young man, but professional shepherds managed the flocks of ShayxNuuri and of the other landlords.

A professional shepherd's yearly contract ends, not on threshing ground day in August, but after the shearing is finished in June on the day called ᶜiid l ghanam (Feast of the Sheep). Lambs are butchered and the shepherds are paid four ewes and a set of clothing. They receive food throughout the year. A shepherd who is of tribal pastoralist background prefers his pay in sheep, but a man who is not prefers the money equivalent. The clothing consists of a short jacket, a sheepskin coat, a cloak to go over the sheepskin, two gowns, two pairs of the voluminous trousers called "Turkish," and two headcloths.

All the village animals except camels are grazed only on the village lands. From summer, after the reaping, until mid-February, the flocks of the nomadic pastoralists who camp at Tell Ṭoqaan are also present and graze the fallow fields or are fed barley straw. Everywhere in the area the black tents of the nomads can be seen pitched in well-spaced lines beside each village. Contracts hold between nomads and the villagers except in cases of mutual tribal affiliation. It is recognized that grazing on the fallow is beneficial for the fields because of the dung left by the animals but no contracts are in use in Tell Ṭoqaan for this.Contract arrangements for grazing were in use between landlords and shepherds to the west of the highway.

In spring shepherding families from the northern Bu Layl villages of Osmaniyya, Jazraaya, and Tell Aaluush move to the Ras l Ain and Tell Ṭoqaan area and to the east where there is a good deal of uncultivated land along the low limestone ridges around the southern boundary of the marsh. These people do not have many sheep, but enough to have to search for pasture and move from time to time. There is no payment involved between them and the villagers, since they are among fellow tribesmen.

Before the expansion of cotton farming in Tell Ṭoqaan, when there was much more rich pasturage between the tell and the marsh, flocks and cattle came in spring from many villages to the west such as Sarmiin, Taftanaaz, and Afess. Their owners paid the village a small amount per head for grazing.

On the morning of February 15, 1954, the tents of the nomadic shepherds on the south side of the village were gone. The day before, the sheep had started the trek eastward 60 or 70 kilometers to the spring grazing zone, and from then until the end of the month three or four flocks passed the village every day. Some were the property of landlords and city men, and were in the care of hired hands whose economic status was similar to that of the farmhands. Clothing of these men identified them as peasants and not pastoralists, for they wore black coats and black Turkish trousers and not long gowns. Other flocks were the property of nomadic shepherds, who like the nomadic shepherds attached to Tell Ṭoqaan, customarily camped at some cultivating village part of the year. But if they had no kinship or client ties like the Bu layl and Harramshii they did not "belong" to any village.

Each flock of 100 or so ewes and their lambs was led on foot and attended by three or four men and guarded by a few dogs. The personal goods of the men were loaded on donkeys, and often the shepherds carried lambs in their arms or put them in the saddle bags on the donkeys. Family groups of pastoralists followed their flocks, occasionally on a string of three or four camels. At night such small camel caravans could be recognized by soft clinking of the bells on the lead camel; they made no sound otherwise. But most often the pastoralist Arabs who were to work with the flocks in the east moved in trucks and automobiles.

Each spring the flocks are followed by donkey and camel caravans of merchants and artisans moving east to circulate among the shepherd camps with their goods and services. After a month or so these itinerants return to their town and city bases.

The flocks return from the east at two different times. Those which are the property of villagers or landlords of villages come back before the harvest period begins, so that the personnel in charge of them can participate in the harvest work. Those of the nomadic pastoralists stay in the east until threshing begins in June and return when the reaped fields can be grazed.

The pastoralists formerly started to move east at the beginning of the autumn rains and nomadized extensively. In recent years, however, expansion of cultivation has reduced the open pasturage and for that reason fewer pastoralists move east and they do not now go until the beginning of spring. In the cultivated west the increased planting of summer field crops has also reduced pasturage, and half the winter the sheep necessarily subsist largely on chopped straw.

Constant attention and control of the flocks characterizes the Arab shepherds' techniques, and their animals are noticably more tame and responsive to signals than sheep which are left to graze untended in fenced fields.

A shepherd's management of a flock of sheep and goats involves a number of techniques which indicate the constant control he maintains over the animals. The sheep dogs are a large and thick-furred breed, often black and white, and quite unlike the universally tawny village dogs. They are used only as guards against wolves and are not trained to drive or control animals. One shepherd and two dogs are needed for a large flock. The shepherd carries a light straight cane and a sling woven of white wool. These slings are made by the shepherds and are, like all hand-made wool work, considered a pastoralist handcraft. Touted as effective weapons against wolves, they are really used to cast stones beyond animals when they begin to stray from the flock and are most effective in turning them back.

A lead animal, whether a sheep or goat, is trained by the shepherd by petting, calling, and hand feeding of bits of bread. They are preferably selected as lambs or kids and are taken from the mother and fed separately. The lead animal, usually a female, wears a bell. When the lambing season begins, the lead ewes are often seen wearing, low on the left side, attached to their wool, a triangular decoration made of dyed wool with a circular mirror in the center and orange wool tassels hanging from the point of the triangle.[1] These female bell wethers are trained to follow close behind the shepherd when the flock is moving, and it is noticeable that, if the sheep are spread out, none of the animals moves ahead of the shepherd's position.

Each kind of animal is directed by a system of specific calls. There is even a separate set each for sheep and for goats although they are herded together. These are to keep the animals moving or turn them from wandering, to lead them to water, to bring lambs or kids to the mothers and encourage nursing, and to control or quiet the animals when they are being milked. The call for bringing the young to the mothers is used in social situations among people to tease or taunt, as in a game when one side taunts the other, or, with an appropriate gesture, as an insult comparable to nose-thumbing or biting one's thumb. As for sheep and goats, the other animals have their special calls to keep them moving, to hurry them, or slow them down. Several of those used with cattle are distinctive for nasalization.

Milk and Its Processing

In weaning the young of milk-producing animals, milking begins slowly and follows a schedule which leads to taking the total output human use.

1. The only name given me for this device was mrayya, "mirror." The only explanation was that it was for decoration, "to look nice." This is one of the instances of probable reticence in matters concerning folk superstition on the part of the speakers.

For the first 3 days after young are born cows, sheep, and goats give sumga; after this they give milk, Haliib. A little sumga is usually milked from each animal and cooked with sugar and a little saman (clarified butter) into a sweet custard-like dish, libbii, as a special treat. About 10 days after the young are born the tufii or small milking begins; each evening before the young are released to the mothers a little milk is taken from each animal for household use. After 15 days the Halbii waHdii begins, the single full milking a day, at noon. With the Haliibtayn (2 milkings), after 20 days or a month, the noon milking is sold to the cheesemaker, if there is a surplus, and the evening milk production is kept for household use.

From the end of March until May, when the weather becomes hot and the forage dry and the animals must come in for water at noon, the flocks stay out on the grazing areas all day. Shortly before noon and an hour before sunset each day the women and girls go out to the flocks with their wooden containers to do the milking. The shepherd ties the sheep and goats of his flock into the shbag, a soft braided wool rope, that is secured by a running loop to the first animal; as each animal is brought the rope is looped around its neck in such a way that when the whole flock is in position the animals stand in a double line, head between head. When the milking is finished they can be released by freeing the first animal and pulling the rope clear with a single jerk. Sixty or more animals can be lined up at one time and kept in place by one or two people while the women milk them. A woman squats behind each animal as she milks it from the rear and braces her head against its rump. With the first animal she often recites the universal charm, Bismillaah ar RaHmaan ar RaHiim (in the name of Allah the All-merciful).

When cows are milked from the side, the calf, if it is not yet weaned, must be held near the mother or the milk will not flow. If a family has cows, sheep, and goats the milk of all is usually combined, both when it is sold or when it is used in the household. Occasionally, the milk of a favorite ewe will be kept in a separate container.

Milking times each day are among the few occasions when a number of women of different families may be found together and temporary social groups are thus formed. Those whose flocks graze together or near each other make a point of meeting and going out together to the flocks. Then news and gossip are exchanged, and arrangements may be made for other co-operative activities. Pastoralist Arab girls who want to learn peasant breadmaking arrange to do so with an older woman, or the wife of a farmer may make inquiries as to who may be interested in joining the reaping crew on her husband's vetch or barley fields in the future.

Shortly after the Halbii waHdii (one milking) began in Tell Ṭoqaan, late in February, 1954, the three wives of Shayx Nuuri devoted a day to braiding a very long shbag rope of black and white strands of wool to be used with his sheep in the east. Not long after, the first wife of the three went east to take charge of the milking of his flocks there; the second wife, who remained in the village, then took charge of the milk from his household flock in Tell Ṭoqaan along with her other responsibilities.

Two series of milk processing are found in Tell Ṭoqaan. One leads to the making of cheese (jibn), kariishii and saman; the second to laban-shnaynii and zibdis-kushuk. Both may be produced in the household, but in general the first is a commercialized production depending on an available surplus, and the second is a household concern which nearly every family can afford.

Each spring, when the cattle and flocks freshen, cheesemakers move into the Tell Ṭoqaan area, set up their tents and utensils, buy up the surplus milk, and process it into cheese and by-products. In 1954 there were such cheesemakers stationed at Resafe, Ras l Ain and Shuuha, but their locations may change each year, depending on the best sources. The one at Shuuha sent an agent to Tell Ṭoqaan to buy milk, but many Tell Ṭoqaaniis preferred to take their surplus to the man at Ras l Ain. He was well known to them personally and was a tribal Arab, a Bu Layl from Osmaniyya. His partner was a merchant in Aleppo who supplied the cash to pay for the milk and who marketed the products there.

The Shuuha cheesemaker was a partner of a merchant in Saraaqab, "Abu Tinikii" (a nickname), who was reported to buy up the milk of many villages around Saraaqab and as far west as the Ghaab marsh; his market was Beirut, Lebanon. At Tell Ṭoqaan the agent set up his measuring utensils and containers in the courtyard of one of the peasant farmers. A son of one of the peasants recorded the quantity received from each seller and noted the date the milk was taken in a notebook, one page for each family. The milk was then taken to Shuuha.

At Ras l Ain the same bookkeeping procedure was followed, but there the milk went immediately into the manufacturing process. The cheesemaker employed six women and girls. The milk was poured into four shallow wooden tubs about 3 feet in diameter and 1 foot deep and one tinned copper container about the same size. Two small cupfuls of majbanna were added to each tub and they were covered with sections of a reed screen. This rennet substance is made from the stomach of a lamb which "has never eaten grass"; and the cheesemaker said it was better than the "Franji" ("French," i.e., foreign) curdling agent. Within 15 minutes the cheese formed.

The contents of the tubs was occasionally tested with a finger. When judged to be the proper consistency, the first tub was uncovered and the surface of the curd was sprinkled with water, rubbed over lightly and pressed down; the pale yellow whey that rose to the surface was dipped off into the second tub and the curd was stirred up vigorously.

Meanwhile a screw press was brought out and a string of handkerchief-sized cloths drying on the tent rope was taken down and tossed into the first tub, after untying them two women took up handfuls of the curd, squeezed it firmly and tied it into the cloths. These were passed to the girls at the press who stacked them in rows and expressed more liquid. The packets of cheese were swept into a sieve scoop, turned out on a reed screen, unwrapped, and the cloths passed back to the women at the tubs for re-use. The whey from all the tubs was collected in the last metal container, cooked down. The curd rising from this was scooped off, packed in coarse baskets, and sent to Aleppo where it would be made into saman (clarified butter),

The cheese made in this process is mild and sweet and does not keep. It will keep indefinitely, however, if it is melted and when cool enough to handle pulled like taffy, tied in knots, and then packed in brine. The Shuuha cheesemaker put up his cheese in this form for the Beirut market.

The household milk processing runs four days from fresh milk the first evening, laban on the second day, shnaynii and zibdis ((butter), on the third day, and on the fourth day the process of making kushuk begins. One day's work includes all steps of the process as long as the milk season lasts, for owing to the heat none of the products keep longer than a day in usable form. No milk or subsequent product of it is ever wasted or needs to be thrown away because of spoiling.

Fresh milk is made into laban the evening it is milked. The bacterial action is "started" with a little of the day's laban. The milk is heated slowly in a container to blood temperature, and left overnight, covered with a felt mat or sheepskin cloak so it will cool very slowly. By morning it is laban, the cultured milk product product which is a characteristic food of the Middle East. Early on the third morning the laban left from the previous day is thinned with water and churned in a goatskin bag. In Tell Ṭoqaan the laban bag is rolled back and forth on a mat for an hour or more. Zibdis (butter) forms and as it is taken from the opening of the skin bag the woman recites the formula, Bismillaah ar RaHmaan ar RaHiim (In the name of Allah the All-merciful). The remaining liquid is shnaynii, a tart, refreshing drink in hot weather. The butter is eaten as a lunch staple, sprinkled heavily with sugar and scooped up with bits of bread.

On the fourth day leftover shnaynii is cooked down with salt until it is very thick, placed in a damp and inflated white cotton sack, and left on a mat in a shady spot to dry out further to a viscous paste. Then it is dropped in small dabs on a mat, usually spread upon a flat roof away from children and animals, and left to dry in the sun into small hard cakes. These are kushuk; they are crumbled as they are picked up and then are stored for use in the seasons when there is no fresh milk. Mixed with water kushuk makes a salty, strong-flavored laban, which is used in winter food dishes that relieve the routine boiled wheat and bread diet. The same preservation technique is applied to tomatoes.

Other Animal Products

Wool, hair, hides, meat.— Very little was observed of techniques and disposition of other animal products, such as hides or meat. Except for wool there is very little production of other items besides milk. Goat clipping and sheep shearing begin in mid-May and are not completed until June. The goats the shepherd clips selectively for the best and longest portions of their hair while they graze. Sheep are sheared, a few at a time, each noon when they were brought into the village for watering and milking. A pair of long-bladed shears are used and the wool is taken off in one piece—a good shearing, I was told, rolls out like a felt mat.

When an animal dies naturally it is flayed and the carcass left to decay in the sun. The meat is never used and open abhorrence is expressed if there is some question as to whether as animal died or had its throat properly cut. Skins, whether of these or butchered animals, are prepared with repeated applications of salt and laban. Hides of goats to be used for the laban churning bags are cured with pomegranate peel.

Meat is an infrequent item in the villager's diet. Calves and yearlings are known to be used for meat, but apparently were never butchered in Tell Ṭoqaan. I was told that Circassians ate horsemeat, but that Arabs did not. Male lambs and kids are occasionally bought and butchered by a shopkeeper if he can arrange ahead of time for five or six purchasers of the meat. But butchering a lamb generally takes place in connection with an important social occasion such as the entertainment of important guests or the honoring of new officers at the gendarme post on their first official visit to the village. The feasts at the end of Ramadaan, the fast month of the Muslims, are also celebrated with the butchering of a lamb. When an animal is slaughtered by one of the wealthy city landlords on a visit to the village, portions are distributed to their dependents in the village.

The head of the household regularly cuts the throat of the animal as he recites the formula, Bismillaah ar RaHmaan or RaHiim. (This is recited even when a father cuts the throat of a small bird snared by his son.) The carcass is usually cut up by a man, though women may take over after he has begun. Since the meat is used in small pieces roasted on spits, or boiled, or minced and pounded, it is not cut into the roasts and chops of Western butchery. Rather, it is cut off the bones in terms of the larger muscle bundles. The head is carefully skinned and the skull is the only bony portion that is cooked whole. The brain and tongue are regarded as the delicacies rather than the eyes. Internal fat and the kidneys are eaten or given to the children to roast. The stomach and intestines are saved and carefully washed and cleaned, and the latter are sold to the itinerant specialists who come each year to fluff up the wool or goat hair stuffing of mattresses with a gut-strung bow.

Manure for fuel.—The use of animal dung for fuel rather than fertilizer is a well known trait of Near Eastern village life. In the Tell Ṭoqaan area only the dung of work animals and cattle is so used. Sheep and goat dung is not used; these animals graze on the fallow fields and the Tell Ṭoqaan farmers realize their dung is beneficial to the fields.[2] Making the fuel involves definite if simple techniques and even styles for drying which have geographical distribution. Regarded as unpleasant labor it is usually done co-operatively by the women and girls, and some aspects of social organization in Tell Ṭoqaan are expressed in the co-operative groups they form.

The dung fuel is made in two forms, jillii haṣaad, summer or harvest fuel, and jillii makbayya, winter fuel. The dung is brought in basket loads from the compound areas to the village midden; straw and water are also brought, and the ingredients are mixed to the necessary plasticity with pitchforks and bare feet. The women of households which do not have animals or access through economic relations to the stables of those that do, often glean the grazing areas of the village herd during the winter to build up a supply.

Summer fuel is molded in hemispherical lumps about a foot in diameter and left in the sun to dry. They are turned up on edge after a few days to complete drying, and they carried to the storage bins near the dwellings. After an adequate supply of summer fuel is made, work begins on the winter fuel.

2. I have been informed by C. Otten that sheep and goat dung is used as fuel in northern Iraq.

In Tell Ṭoqaan the same hemispherical lumps of dung and straw are molded for the winter as for the summer fuel, but when the makbayya, a circular structure, is built these are laid out in a regular pattern of a double circle, each lump overlapping the next. A narrow opening into the center of the circle is left, and the ends of the two walls closed. The makbayya is about 8 feet wide, and walls are built up solidly of overlapping hemispheres to a height of about 3 feet. Bracing walls are built between the two circles. These structures are left until thoroughly dry, then dismantled and stored for winter use.

In the spring near all the villages between Tell Ṭoqaan and Aleppo different styles of jillii makbayya may be seen: meandering walls, labyrinths, open-work walls made of lozenge-shaped lumps, each course set perpendicularly to the one below, and so on. The style appears to be uniform for a whole village and for a number of villages near each other.

Such dung fuel is used for cooking kettles of food which require several hours of simmering and for heating quantities of water for laundry and baths. It is never used in the bread ovens.

From day to day the women of two or three households exchange mutual help in making jillii fuel; each day the group works for one of the families and each day the midden is a busy scene. Most of the village is represented among the groups. The girls and younger women do most of the work, supervised by the older women of the households. The co-operative arrangement is made by the women themselves and does not necessarily reflect other patterns of co-operation or employment which may hold between families in other economic activities. The women of the families of the two largest lineages in Tell Ṭoqaan worked together, however, and not with families outside their lineages or kin groups. But most of the families are single units without local kinsmen, and in these the basis of co-operation appeared rather to be one of social compatibility and similar economic status. Shayx Nuuri's two young sisters and one of his daughters frequently helped a family employed by him as servants; this was said to be part of their training in women's work. They carried water or straw but definitely did not participate in mixing the ingredients.

Poultry

Chickens, geese, and turkeys are the poultry found in Tell Ṭoqaan. The chickens are the local breed; hens are rarely eaten since eggs are a local commodity. The one flock of geese, numbering forty in January, had nearly all been eaten by May. There are about a dozen turkeys; the hen turkeys are used to brood chicken eggs as well as their own. They are valuable enough for the owners to tie a scrap of colored cloth around the leg as a property mark.

Nearly every family keeps chickens and they wander freely about the village during the day, but return to their owner's compounds or dwellings at night. Generally, they forage for themselves, but now and then a little barley is thrown to them. Each chicken is known individually and is remarked upon in terms of its owner, djaj Nuriyya, "Nuriyya's chicken." They are also referred to by names which describe their plumage, ?al-faḍḍii, "the black hen silvered with a little white."

With the exception of a few geese, all fowl are the property of the women and any money they make from selling eggs to the shopkeeper is theirs. Fowl are occasionally purchased from itinerant merchants. Surplus eggs are sold to the local shopkeepers or to itinerant egg merchants. One of the shopkeepers regularly buys up eggs locally, takes them on to Saraaqab, and sells them to the next middleman in a series which leads ultimately to the Beirut markets. An itinerant egg and chicken merchant may cover a wide area on his rounds, and one who visited Tell Ṭoqaan was also seen at Jiinii, about 60 kilometers northwest.

Whenever eggs are added to a nest for hatching, or whenever the nest is inspected or shown to a visitor, it is necessary to recite the formula, Bismillaah ar RaHmaan ar RaHiim.

Bees

Bees are kept for honey and wax by a number of households. If a man has more than half a dozen hives they are placed in a special court walled up with mud brick and without a gate for access; trees and flowers are also planted in the courtyard. The hives are hand-molded sun-dried mud cylinders about 2 feet long and 14 inches in diameter. One end of the hive is closed by mud and has a small aperture for the bees to enter; the other end may be closed with a cloth packing or a round wooden lid. The hives are laid on mud bricks so the first row will be raised a few inches off the ground, and the rest are laid on top of these to three or four rows in height; apertures all face south. Over the whole apiary a layer of mud and reed is plastered to keep the hives cool.

Besides individual ownership of hives a tilit, "one-third," contract may be made in which one party claims two thirds of the hives and his partner claims one third for the keeping of them. The honey, however, is divided half and half. The one-third contract, it should be noted, applies to swarms or hives, and not to the products.

When the bees are about to swarm, early in May, they are carefully watched and new hives prepared by the women. As soon as a new swarm starts out every available person seizes a metal pot and stick or spoon and stations himself so that the noise he makes will cause the swarm to stay between him and the compound. When the swarm alights, a new hive is placed under it and flowering plants laid around it. Grass or green barley is laid thickly on top of the hive and wetted down to keep the hive cool. The swarm is swept into a container and tossed into the new hive. If Allah is willing, the swarm is captured and in the coolness of the hive will settle down. Again, whenever one looks into a hive one must recite the formula, Bismillaah ar RaHmann ar RaHiim.

IX

BUILDINGS AND COMPOUNDS

ECONOMIC DIFFERENCES as well as pastoral and peasant traditions are expressed in the variety of architecture in Tell Ṭoqaan in contrast to the greater homogeneity of peasant or tribal villages in the area. The properties of the tribal shayx display the fullest and best possibilities of construction and furnishing in two respects, traditional features of size and material and workmanship, and ability to afford those items of Western or industrial origin which contribute to the prestige and evidence of his status. The most affluent village families, whether of peasant or pastoralist tradition, are those whose heads are foremen or partners of the major landlords or who posses land, flocks, or monopoly of a locally important craft service, such as carpentry. It is important to note that they are also the larger families, with working sons and their families. These are the families which are able to construct and maintain full compounds in traditional fashion. Finally, the major part of the village population who work as clients or farmhands and shepherds occupy the decaying compounds and are barely able to maintain them from year to year. These are the small families, those with young children or daughters only.

The Compound

When a family begins to build in Tell Ṭoqaan, the minimum essentials of a compound in dwelling room and storage bins are erected first. Many families achieve no more than this. But it can be seen from the range, from partly completed units to full compounds and from the additions made in the spring of 1954, that a building program is not considered complete until a full compound is finished, even though it may take several years. The surrounding wall may even be the last step in the process. The parts a compound has vary according to economic status, and in some details according to whether the family follows shepherd pastoralist or peasant traditions the more closely. Accumulation of property in animals, if not in land, also determines the make-up of the particular compound. Expectations in regard to the marriage of sons may affect the building designs. But foresight, planning, and execution are all contained within the traditional concept of a whole compound with its appropriate parts.

The compound, where complete, consists of a square courtyard surrounded by the various room units and other structures. A wall encloses the whole; for economy of effort and materials it runs between the inner structures and uses their outer surfaces as continuations of the wall. Occasionally in Tell Ṭoqaan and usually in the older villages to the west, the walls of neighboring compounds are shared. Ordinarily there is only one gate, which in Tell Ṭoqaan is often open during the day, but always closed and locked at night. In the older villages, such as Saraaqab and Afess and those west of the highway, the gates to family compounds are closed at all times and the life going on behind them is secluded from all except kinsmen and guests.

Within the compound various arrangements of parts are found. If the head of the household can afford a reception room, it is located close to the gate. In it guests are entertained and usually they do not enter any other dwelling room, particularly if they are not kinsmen or fellow villagers. Next to the reception room is the common living room of the family. There is no door between it and the reception room, but there may be a small window through which the owner communicates his orders for tea or Turkish coffee to his wife. Nowhere in a compound, in fact, are rooms connected with each other by doors or corridors; each room unit has only one exit and that to the courtyard.

If the compound does not have a reception room, the dwelling room is usually located opposite the gate of the courtyard. This room unit is the first structure erected in the building program and it is here that food reserves are stored. The second structure built is the cooking room; after this an oven is built and sometimes enclosed in a domed room of its own. Only families which eat peasant bread, however, build ovens; pastoralist bread does not require them. Immediately outside the compound or incorporated into its walls near the corners are the storage bins. These are tall round structures built up of handfuls of mud or of broken mud brick. They are often fully cone-shaped, or truncated and capped with reeds and mud. In these bins brushwood, straw, and dung fuel are stored.

Additional room units may be required within the compound for the animals, tools, and equipment. The usual order in this event is to build a new dwelling room and to turn the old one over for use as stable or fold. Small mud cones for chicken houses are scattered about in the corners; mangers may be built along the compound walls. The well, covered by a mud brick well house, is preferably located within the compound; trees, flowers, or a vine may be started near it, but very few seem to survive. Nearly every compound has a platform of mud brick 8 or more feet square and 3 to 6 feet high, with a stairway at one side. On this the family sleeps on hot summer nights.

These then are the parts of a villager's completed compound: wall, dwelling room, reception room, cooking room, oven, storage bins, stable or fold, well if water is available, and sleeping platform. But that there is variety in details of construction, building types, and interior furnishings, and possibly additional structures, may be seen from the following.

Construction Types

With few exceptions all of the buildings of Tell Ṭoqaan are based on two simple foundation plans, the rectangle and the square. Only the storage bins are circular. Larger units are simply made by multiplying the basic ground plans linearly. Just one house, that of an urban landlord, had a second-story room reached by an exterior wooden stairway. Architectural diversity, however, is to be found in the roof types and in the use of the corbelled arch. Interior and secondary features, simply added to the basic ground plan, make the difference between a shop, a stable, a cook house, or a dwelling unit.

Apart from the tents and Shayx Nuuri's stone house, all of the buildings are constructed of sun-dried mud brick erected on a minimal foundation of stone rubble laid directly on the surface of the earth. Use of rafter poles, mats, and bundles of reed or woody plants depends on the roof type. Cement is of recent introduction and is used as a surfacing material for roofs or floors, as mud plaster is, and not as an ingredient in wall construction.

Since the roof type to be used determines the structure to be built, these types are discussed with their associated ground and wall plans. There are three major roof types in Tell Ṭoqaan: a low-pitched or gabled roof (ṭaam), a flat roof (xashab, "wood"), and the beehive or corbelled dome (qabbii). The pitched roof has no variants; it is the cheapest and poorest made, except for an "amateur"-built doomed room (qabbii ruummil, see below). Both flat and domed roofs have forms that vary with cost, materials available, the builders' skill, and size of room.

The pitched roof is made on a frame which consists of a ridgepole, three or four pairs of rafters, and one central pole, or post, which supports the ridgepole and is embedded in the earthen floor. Such a roof is usually found only on small rectangular rooms, about 8 by 12 feet in size, that have walls 5 to 6 feet high. A few light sticks are lashed as joists between the rafters. Tightly bound bundles of the dried, woody stalks of asphodel are laid parallel to the rafters and lashed to the joists; they extend raggedly beyond the ridgepole. Over this bundles of dried reed are laid, and the whole is covered with a layer of mud and straw mixed to the same consistency as that for bricks. Only a few such structures are in Tell Ṭoqaan, but the majority of dwellings in Ras l Ain and Jazraaya are of this nature. The ones in Tell Ṭoqaan were occupied by families of low economic status or were used as stables or folds.

Most of the room units in the Tell Ṭoqaan compounds are of "sugar loaf" or pointed dome construction and three variants were distinguished locally. These are: the qabbii ruummii, which is built almost directly from the ground on a very low square foundation and is usually rather crudely constructed and not more than 6 or 8 feet square at the base; the qabbii qarma, which has a large dome which does not rise to a point (tanṭur) but is truncated and roofed over with rafters and reeds and plastered with mud and straw; and the qabbii tayyax described below, which is regarded as superior to the other two.

The qabbii tayyax is built on a square foundation or, when double-domed (jawz qabaab,"pair of domes"), on a long rectangle divided in the middle by the piers of the central arch. Even if a single dome is constructed first, provision for a second one to be added later is always included; that is, the connecting arch between the two will be built but filled in with brick and plastered over until it can be opened and the addition made. For this type of room the foundation walls are raised 4 or 5 feet and on the exterior extend up in a facade around the whole unit. Indentations in the wall at the point where the dome slope begins are fitted with short metal eaves troughs. This facade is the tayyax. It may be straight from corner to corner or be arched in the middle. On the facade of a single-domed room the arch usually covers the filled-in arch on the side where a second domed room will eventually be built. Pendentives to support the dome are made by spanning each corner with a heavy wooden beam or slab of stone. In Tell Ṭoqaan the qabbii tayyax room units are from 8 to 12 feet square; but much larger ones are seen in such older villages as Afess and those west of the highway. Many of the domed structures in Tell Ṭoqaan were said to be 70 to 90 years old and reputedly among the first built at the time of the founding of the village.

The flat roof is laid over a rectangular room 8 to 10 feet wide and often 16 feet long. Walls of the unit are very high, 9 to 11 feet. The roofing material is supported on stout rafter poles spaced at two-foot intervals across the narrow width of the structure. Over them, in the best roofs, reed matting is laid, and over the matting a thatch of dried reed bundles. Less expensive roofs omit the matting. Over the matting is spread a thick layer of mud and straw. This is a common type of roofing found elsewhere in the Near East; in the Lebanon it is necessary to roll the roofs with limestone rollers during the winter rainy seasons to squeeze out the water and pack the mud. None of these rollers were seen in Tell Ṭoqaan and there were many complaints about leaky roofs during the winter. One solution has been, when a family could afford it, to surface the roof with several thin layers of cement.

In most cases only the reception room of the compound is a flat-roofed room. The timbers are expensive and they must, of course, be imported; they are said to come from Turkey. Cement is an added luxury. The flat-roofed unit has more prestige than the domed, and when the head of a peasant household can afford to build a reception room he chooses it rather than the double-domed, a type which he probably already has in his compound.

Although buildings with one or other of these three roof types are in the majority in Tell Ṭoqaan, there are, a few others and a special type, the stable compound, which should be noted. The most arresting building is Shayx Nuuri's stone house, considered the architectural attraction of the village. It is built of dressed limestone blocks with added embellishments of decorative tile and glazed and shuttered windows. Stone masons and materials were imported from Aleppo.

The Nuuri house is divided into two main areas, the public reception rooms and the family rooms. Approached from the front the building appears as a long rectangle. In the center rises a high pointed archway which gives entrance to the open foyer. Above the arch is inscribed a welcome: "Welcome, our guests, and you will find that here we are your guests and you are the owners of this house" (quoted in Shayx MaHmuud's History, Part II). On the right of the foyer a door leads into the formal reception room, a spacious room floored with decorative tiles. Chairs are placed around three walls. In winter a wood-burning stove is placed in one corner and olive wood burned in it, a more expensive fuel than crude oil. Oil stoves are found in the other rooms of the house. On the left of the foyer a door opens on a less formal room; it is barren of furnishings except for reed mats on the cement floor. If luncheons are served here, tables and chairs are brought into it. In cold or cool weather a mat is spread in one corner and a large charcoal brazier placed in the center for the coffee pots. Here informal groups may gather to sip Arab coffee and talk, when the wives of Shayx Nuuri receive visiting kin or men of the village. At the rear of this room a door leads out to the area in the shelter of the building. The building is continued with a line of three rooms along the west side. The first of the family rooms is an elaborately furnished bedroom, carpeted and filled with a Western-style suite of double bed, wardrobes, dressing tables, mirrors, portraits, divans, and cupboards. Here a woman guest may be received and be served coffee after luncheon. Beyond this room are two more family rooms where general household activity takes place in winter or in very hot weather. One room contained a tall white refrigerator.

At Jazraaya a similar though smaller house has been built outside the village for Shayx Nuuri's brother. But at Ras l Ain and Zammaar the shayx of each Bu Layl section residing in these villages occupy houses which are not architecturally as different from those of the rest of the villagers as are Nuuri's and his brother's. At Kuusaniyya, the BuShab^{c}an village shayx occupies a compound like those elsewhere in the village but larger. These differences indicate that in the household as to production activities, the more rich and powerful a family, the more extensive and diversified is the acquisition of goods associated with the diffusion of industrial civilization.

On the southeast corner of Tell Ṭoqaan two families live year-round in the black goat-hair tents of nomad style. The tents face east and are divided into living side and stable side by screens made of reeds and wool cords. Both are banked around the outside with earth and brush to keep out wind. Within the past two or three years two other tent-dwelling families have built double-domed houses and become, as the Shayx MaHmuud's History reads, "half-civilized."

The large storage and stable compounds in Tell Ṭoqaan belong to the landlords or their partners. While the hired farmhands of the owner may sleep in the straw of the storage rooms, no families inhabit them. Here mules and horses, farming and gardening equipment, fodder and straw are kept. Riding mares are stabled separately from the other animals. In these compounds the units are either pairs of domed rooms or single, flat-roofed rooms, and they are built solidly around the courtyard. There are no grain and flour bins, cook houses, ovens, or other structures characteristic of the family compound. These compounds are called generically hawsh dawwaab, ("stable compound"), whereas a family compound is often called hawsh Abdullah, or hawsh YaHya ᶜaarif, and so on, after the owner.

Construction Procedures

Building and renovating activities take place in spring before harvest begins and in late summer after threshing is finished. For the construction of flat-roofed and domed rooms a specialist may be hired.

Brickmaking is completed before the start of construction operations. The bricks are made on the village midden or near the building site from earth in the immediate vicinity. Five thousand was given as the usual number required for a double-domed room. Only one size of brick is used in Tell Ṭoqaan; they measure 18 by 9 inches and are about 3 inches thick. A smaller-sized one is made especially for dome construction in peasant villages along the highway to Aleppo where, as indicated in the larger sizes of dwellings attained, peasant techniques are superior in achievement as well as more pervasive than in the mixed and largely pastoralist area of Tell Ṭoqaan. The bricks are made of a mixture of earth, water, and straw poured into wood forms which have two or three compartments. Mixed in pits where the earth is dug out, the mud is transported in wheelbarrows to the spot where it is poured into the forms. West of the highway in such peasant villages as Jiinii a two-man litter is still used to carry the mud. About two weeks are needed for drying.

Stone foundations for walls are laid directly on the ground. Walls are kept straight by a string stretched horizontally between two pegs. No device was noted for keeping them plumb. Walls are laid either one or one and a half brick lengths thick;

a different pattern of laying the bricks is correlated with thickness and quality of construction. Mortar mud without straw intermixed, is laid between courses but not between bricks; gaps are chinked with brick fragments. Features such as air vents, fireplaces, niches for cupboards, windows, and the salt jar are built into place as the walls rise around them. The tops of window openings are spanned by sticks and boards; in the older villages in the area such as Kuusaniyya or Afess, window openings are spanned by a low arch.

The walls of pitched and flat-roofed rooms are plastered before the roof is raised, but the construction of domes is finished before plastering. All such plastering is done by women. (A specialist may be hired, however, to surface areas with cement.) After the layer of mud and straw plaster dries, whitewash is applied to the interior and around doors and windows on the exterior. The whitewash is made of limestone mined locally and soaked in water. Thin layers of cement are used by those who can afford to do so to surface roofs and floors. The roof surfacing is used only on the flat-roofed rooms as a protection against rain; the floor surfacing is a protection against insects. The order of priority maintained in cement surfacing is first the threshold, then the floor, the roof, and lastly the window sills.

Organization of Labor in Housebuilding

Housebuilding in Tell Ṭoqaan is conducted on a different basis from that in such older villages as Saraaqab or Afess. In those villages, when a man has a house to build all his friends and neighbors on his "side" of the village come to help, and it is finished in a few days. He, in his turn, will go to help them at need, and no money is paid or expected. This was called the "old way," as villagers have done "from the beginning" (min l?awwal), or from "ancient times" (min qadiim). But Tell Ṭoqaan and Tell Suultaan, it was said, are masriyaat ("money") villages; people work only for money. There is a little mutual help arranged among the women and girls and occasionally between two young men who are special friends. Usually, in Tell Ṭoqaan, if a man builds a new room, he depends on his immediate family and kinsmen or he hires help at the rate of two pounds Syrian a day for men to mix and lift libin (mud and straw mixed) and for women to plaster. Three pounds Syrian a day are paid the mason or ma^{c}maar.

Two reasons are given for Tell Ṭoqaan being a "money" village. On the one hand, a peasant said, most of the work in Tell Ṭoqaan is controlled by Shayx Nuuri and the urban landlords; they have money and can hire as they please; they pay for work in money and this has been done in Tell Ṭoqaan for many years. On the other hand, there are several households which are so large, like Bayt Hammuud, Bayt Tell Haanii, and Bayt MHarrak, that they have lots of boys and girls available and each household is self-sufficient. They are even able to send the sons out to work for money which they bring back to the head of the household.

The ma^{c}maar, or mason, is one of the few specialists found in Tell Ṭoqaan. Two men worked part time at the trade, both in Tell Ṭoqaan and outside in other villages. They were said to have learned bricklaying from a mason who had come from Aleppo many years before to build the domes and walls of the Nuuri stable compound. A mason builds all three types of houses, but knows especially how to build the domes.

Among the dozen new room units under construction in Tell Ṭoqaan in the spring of 1954, one local man was employed as mason on two, and he also extended his own dwelling to nearly a full compound. A mason from the village of Shayx Idriis was engaged to build two other houses, but the rest of the building that spring was done by family groups or by the hired hands of the landlords. Only two families exchanged help.

Plastering, which is done by the women, has its specialist aspect, for one or two of the older women in the village did it for pay. The work involves not only the surfacing of walls and floors, but the building of shelves, mantles over fireplaces, and grain and flour bins, and the making of decorative appliques. The latter aspects are considered in the section on interiors.

Interiors of Dwellings

Simplicity and orderliness distinguish the interiors of the villagers' dwelling rooms to a Westerner's eyes. There is no familiar furniture except an occasional low stool. On entering, footwear is left on the threshold. The room, whether square or rectangular, is always arranged in the same manner. One or two rush mats are spread on the floor. A small increment of affluence is indicated if a felt mat is laid over these close to the wall opposite the entrance. This is the "sitting" end of the room.

Across the far end of the room to the right of the entrance stretches the nawl, the grain bin. This is built by the women of mud made with sifted red earth. It is as long as the room is wide and is about 2 feet deep and 4 to 5 feet high. The bin is divided into three or five compartments which are open at the top for filling; a circular access is provided at the base of each for taking out supplies. The middle compartment is the smallest, because there is an opening through the bin in the center about 2-1/2 feet high and 2 feet wide. The bin is not pushed flush against the wall, but a space of about 3 feet in depth is left. Entrance to this area is gained through the opening in the bin, and here belongings are stored in chests or woollen bags well concealed from sight. During the day the sleeping mattresses, quilts, and long bolster pillows are folded and stacked on top of the bin. In some households a curtain of plastic or a rayon figured bedspread is spread over the whole. There may be an additional small one-compartment bin for flour or lentils, the quwayyir, also made of mud, which stands near the grain bin. Both grain bin and flour bin are whitewashed.

On the wall opposite the entrance is a long shelf. It may be made of wood by the carpenter, but more often has been built up of mud, layer by layer, by a woman skilled in this work. A few short sticks thrust into the mud wall serve to reinforce the shelf. On it a number of pewter saucers are laid, always in the same manner, the edge of each overlapping the next from right to left. On the wall nearby hangs a strip of black cloth with several pockets in it for thread and needles.

To the left of the entrance is the fireplace and beside it a few cooking utensils, a tea kettle, and a Primus stove (kerosene pressure stove). One or two cupboard niches in the wall are closed by double wooden doors. There may be also a small wooden chest under a cupboard in which a few staples and dishes are kept. Some households of the peasant tradition had large wooden chests, carved on the front panel and up to 6 feet long; other, poorer families had only small boxes and brillantly painted metal trunks. In these the best dishware and clothing are kept under lock and key. While carved chests are a regular furnishing in dwellings in the older peasant villages, there were very few in Tell Toqaan. In their place some families had large sacks of black wool or hair, woven with white stripes and sewn in red at the side seams. The sacks are standard equipment in the tents of the pastoralists. In an earthen house, they are kept behind the grain bin and rarely seen.

A large water jar of unglazed, porous red clay, pointed at the bottom, stands next to the door in a wooden stand. Beside it, for drinking, is a glass tumbler or a small metal bowl. As usually true of the felt mat, the glass tumbler is an addition that comes with affluence.

Besides the pictures cut from magazines or religious prints of either Muslim or Christian tradition, which are frequently mounted on the walls in a cluster near the shelf, there may be other decorative features. Most frequent are the appliques in plaster relief on the grain bin, around the shelf, and on the fireplace. In these arrangement of motifs is symmetrical, and the number of different motifs seen in Tell Ṭoqaan is very small. Three of them to which names are given are shajara ("tree"), the most common; rasm ṭayr ("picture of a bird"); and rasm ?adamii ("picture of a human"). While nearly every dwelling has some such decoration, they are not found in the abundance reported for the Aramaean villages near Damascus(Reich, 1937: 58-62). The women who know how to make them are of peasant background, but since they will work wherever they will be paid, these appliques also appear in houses whose families are of pastoralist tradition.

Another form of decoration consists of bits of colored cloth cut and applied in the same motifs to wet plaster either on the grain bin or in a band along the wall under the shelf. Human figures are also represented and are called rijal ("men"). Bits of broken mirror are also stuck on the wet plaster, usually as the center motif of such designs.

Circular trays made of wheat straw dyed in several colors are hung high on the walls. But these, while found regularly in the houses of peasant villages to the west, are rare in Tell Ṭoqaan.

In several households is found the mrayya. This is a colorful device made on a light wood frame in the form of an equilateral triangle with a rectangle attached below it. The rectangle is divided into four horizontal panels, each of which is filled with one or two triangles. Purple-dyed balls of wool with centers of white cotton cover the frame, purple- and orange-dyed feather tufts are mounted on the corners; interlaced inside the top triangle and stretched down the length of the rectangle are strings of dyed barley grain, wheat, and corn. These devices are made after harvest is finished, apparently only by the women. While the mrayya and the designs of the plaster and cloth appliques may very likely have magical significance, perhaps believed to promote fertility or protect against the evil eye (cf. Reich, 1937: 59-60), but I was not told so; they were said to be for decoration only. The motif of triangle with appendages is found in other contexts such as the mrayya worn by the lead ewe of a flock and in some of the tattoos worn by women.

If there is a reception room for the entertainment of guests in the compound, this room is similarly arranged to the dwelling room, but there is no grain bin, no chest of household goods, no cooking equipment. Instead, a stove in winter, a gun on the wall, and a radio will be found.

Every cupboard and chest, every door has a lock and key. Locks are bought in the town markets and both padlocks and latch locks are used. The women carry the keys and whenever they are away from the compound for any time at all, every door is securely fastened.

In a large compound the head of the family and his wife have a separate sleeping room from that used by the children. When a son marries, or prepares to, or as soon as he can afterward, he builds a new room in his father's compound. In the few instances of polygynous families in the village, separate compounds or dwellings are maintained for each wife and her children.

Other Structures of the Family Compound

The cooking house, the oven, and the well house are three important structures in the family compound. The cooking house is a small domed room with fireplace in one side or corner and often a bath niche opposite it. Usually both niches for these project from the exterior wall as apses and that covering the fireplace is pierced with several holes for the escape of smoke. The bath niche is floored with large rounded stones and the area is surrounded by a low wall. And a drain channel to the outside is provided. Most food is cooked and laundry and bath water is heated over the fireplaces in this room except in hot weather.

The oven in the household which eats peasant bread is the one piece of household equipment which requires the worker to stand up while using it. All other cooking is done on the low fireplaces or before the small Primus stove set on the floor; brooms are short-handled and are also wielded while squatting or stooping. The oven for baking peasant bread, however, is a large jar-shaped container built into a bench of mud brick about

4 feet high, with the jar part tilted at an angle for easy access. Its lining must be of "white earth" mixed with goat hair. An opening into the base permits ashes to be scraped out. The mouth of the oven is about 16 inches in diameter and the interior expands to over 2 feet. A fire of chopped straw is made in the bottom of the oven and allowed to die down to a bed of coals. To the left of the oven the bank of brick extends to form a work bench where the discs of dough are beaten out before they are slapped against the heated upper surface of the interior of the oven. Many of the ovens are not enclosed in a room and the opening is protected from rain during the winter with a large, shallow, tinned copper pan. Ownership of such an oven indicates either peasant background or a taste for, and the acquisition of skill in making, this type of bread. The prestige for a girl of marriageable age is frequently enhanced by her ability in this respect.

All the wells in Tell Ṭoqaan are covered by a cone-shaped well house built of mud brick and open on one side. To the top of the house is fixed a short bar of wood to which is attached an iron pulley, with rope and small bucket. Occasionally the well houses are whitewashed. Distinctive styles are seen in the villages along the marsh north of Tell Ṭoqaan. If a compound does not have a well, a structure similar to the well house is made for a large water jar of porous red clay set on a base. In this case, the wall of the house is cut out in geometric lattice work to provide air circulation.

Other Buildings in Tell Ṭoqaan

Outwardly, the merchants' shops in Tell Ṭoqaan are pitched- or flat-roofed rooms built against the outer walls of their owners' compounds or standing free at some distance from the dwelling. Their interior arrangements are distinctive, however, and all follow the same plan. Each has a center division across the width of the room made by a wall of plastered mud brick 3 feet high and a foot thick, with an opening left in the center for access to the area behind it. This space is the shop end of the room and all the merchandise is arranged there on shelves around the walls, in niches, or in 5-gallon tins lining the wall under the shelves. Textiles and shoes and garments for sale are hung on ropes from the roof. The floor of the shop is raised 6 to 8 inches above the rest of the room. The opposite end of the room serves as a social gathering place and mats are spread on the floor.

The single carpenter's shop in the village has a pitched roof and is built against the outer face of the wall of the man's compound. The door is at one end of the rectangular room, and wood supplies are stacked at the other. Tools are hung from shelves and racks along the walls. A bellows used in soldering or in heating iron straps and bands is set in a depression in the earthen floor close to the door. This instrument was said to be "foreign," that is, it comes from outside of Syria; it is made entirely of metal and evidently is an industrial factory product. Since it is enclosed in a metal case, the principle of its operation could not be ascertained. The operator, to produce a forced draft on the burning wood chips and charcoal fire, turns a handle mounted over a drum; the air is expelled from a tube directed at the base of one side of the small fire. The same type of instrument is used by the iron-working Qirbaat (Gypsies) who visit the village.

The mosque in Tell Ṭoqaan closely resembles on the exterior an ordinary double-domed room.. Inside the room is whitewashed and reed mats cover the floor from wall to wall. There is no threshold and footwear is left outside the door. In the south wall, opposite the entrance, is the apse-shaped niche of the miHraab which indicates the direction of prayer. In a rectangular recess to the right is kept the copy of the Koran. There is no decoration of either walls or niche.

Ownership of Buildings

In Tell Ṭoqaan, it was said, a man may build a house anywhere in the settlement that he pleases, but in large villages to the west, like Saraaqab, he must secure a permit from the government. In Tell Ṭoqaan the site upon which a building is erected is state property of the same legal category as the rest of the land, but the buildings are private property and are bought, sold, and rented among individuals. There is no tax on them to my knowledge, although, in the case of rent, there may apparently be a percentage claimed by the government through the administrative offices of the district in Idlib, for the muxtaar of Tell Ṭoqaan explained to me that if I had been paying rent to my host, 10 per cent of it would be claimed by the government. The only case of rent cited in the village was a fee of 5 pounds a month that was charged for a shop once provided a man from another village by a local resident. Several houses, however, had been sold by one individual to another for prices that ranged from one to three hundred Syrian pounds. Ownership of a building or compound is ascribed to the head of the family, generally a man. In a few instances of widows with unmarried young children, the house was named as belonging to the widow. One widow, however, had named her house after her five-year-old son.

X

HOUSEHOLD TECHNOLOGY AND ECONOMICS

ECONOMIC LIFE in Tell Ṭoqaan has two spheres of operation, the family household and the local commercial enterprises. Most of the business of life centers upon the support of the family household, and it is this focus which in the Levant States distinguishes village community from town or city. Most economic activities are organized in the village in terms of family needs and they take place in, around, and for the compound and its inhabitants. The dwelling is not the only kind of building in Tell Ṭoqaan, but it is the most important. It is for and by the group of people which the compound shelters that food is procured, processed, stored, preserved, and served. It is to the family compound that the animals return each night, and within its walls that the subsistence harvest is stored. It is within and for the support of the compound that labor is organized. Even when members go out to work or surplus crops are sold in an external market, the proceeds return to the compound. The maintenance of the family in its compound is the first concern of village economic life; its subsistence comes first. The technology and economy of the life of the compound is that of the village.

But economic differences in Tell Ṭoqaan, expressed in the control of land and surplus crops, make some households dominate the village economic life and others dependent upon these. The households of the clients and farmhands are supported by those of the tenant farmers and foremen, and these by the major property holders. Thus the web of economic activity in Tell Ṭoqaan consists of a group of relatively prosperous households, dominated by the independent and locally lavish establishment of the tribal shayx; to these, as satellites, are attached the lesser households. The absence of permanent local household organizations belonging to the urban landlords only emphasizes the preeminence of that of the tribal shayx, and, as future chapters will show, bring home to the observer the completeness with which the life of the household is the life of the village in all its aspects.

The second sphere of economic activity within the village is that which is external to the family organizations, as such, and has none of the integration and organization and distinctiveness that a family compound had. Dispersed in the settlement are the several small stores and on the eastern edge of the village is the carpenter's shop, and toward these activity gravitates from the households. In the milking season the arrival of the cheesemakers attracts business. But none of these compares to the significance of the family households as the centers of village life, and all of them are dependent upon the prosperity and productiveness of the families.

The dominance of household life in Tell Ṭoqaan, and the lack of any others centers of economic and social activity, such as waqf properties associated with the mosque and its upkeep or a market or public oven or coffee house, may be locally determined by the small size of Tell Ṭoqaan and the presence of a paramount tribal shayx. Even so, this situation has the flavor of nomadic pastoral life in which the family group of tents, whereever it may be located, is the nexus of life, social and economic, and contributes to the impression of the strength of the pastoral tradition in Tell Ṭoqaan.

It is the management of the family compound that is the realm of women's activities in Arab village life, as it is among the pastoralists' tents. This "inner" side of village life thus holds the place in the traditional village community that is to be protected, since it is the heart of survival. As such, the status of women in a small traditional community is not "low"; lower than man's status, but the other half of life. The fact that some economic activities, once household centered, are commercialized and taken into the men's sphere of control is suggested in the life of Tell Ṭoqaan (see Division of Labor). Here, however, my concern is with the delineation of household technology and economics as the locus of life in the village.

In the traditional economy of the area all work is manual labor, aided by animals and simple machines in the heaviest farming techniques, and the distinction between men's and women's work is not only a matter of status but primarily that of an ancient dichotomy which has long been reinforced by sentiments having the strength of taboo. The introduction of industrial technology has affected first the spheres of men's labor in the fields and their activities as negotiators between the household and the external world of other households, public market, court, and political system. Industrial farming machinery, transportation, and communication have modified the men's sphere of life, but the manual labor of the household is still largely unrelieved by machines and by the new ideas and possibilities associated with them. Thus, insofar as manual labor declines in prestige in the whole society, the status of women, who have remained manual laborers, declines, or at least does not keep up with the men's sphere of activities.

The work and schedule of life within the compound is still determined by the simplicity of its traditional technology. Intensity is low and increases only with size and multiplication of mouths to feed and hands to labor.

Food

Village households secure their food in three ways: by the productive work of the household organization; by purchase out of salary and wages or, partly, by a wheat allowance included in payment for some farmhand labor; and by the generosity of the employer or patron. However the supply is secured, the bulk of it comes from local agriculture, gardening, poultry, and milk production. In spring an abundance of wild plants are gathered for salads and throughout the year field birds and swallows are trapped and roasted and brought home. Both these supplements provide such welcome change, that they are of some local economic significance. The salad plants are often the object of excursions from nearby villages.

The year-round staples of diet are wheat cooked in various ways in addition to bread, onions, garlic, lentils, saman (clarified butter of sheep milk), laban, and tea. While bread, boiled cracked wheat (burghul), and onions are routine, the peasant wife can combine cooking processes and a limited number of ingredients into a fair number of different dishes. Besides the staples mentioned, corn, red pepper, spices, rice, olive oil, lemons, tomato paste, squash, eggplant, fresh milk, and sugar, and occasionally poultry or lamb, complete the list of foods and condiments that she uses. The diet of a household is restricted more by economic status than by any other factor, although acquired tastes become very evident when Western foods are offered. Dates, cheese, and pastoralist-type bread appear to be far more popular and preferred in households of Circassians and people of pastoralist tradition than among peasants. Most foods are boiled in water, laban, or milk. A few are fried in olive oil or saman. There is no oven for baking pastries. Lamb or kid may be broiled on a spit over the fire in the bread oven, but it, like poultry, is usually boiled.

Tea was said to have been introduced recently, but in the last four or five years, because it is cheap, it has become the poor man's coffee. Brewed like Turkish coffee, but in larger proportions, it is served in small glasses. A handful of tea leaves and a small tumblerful of sugar are placed in an aluminum teakettle of water, brought to boiling three times, and allowed to settle before pouring. A stick of cinnamon may be added if special guests are present. In a group which includes guests from outside the regular household, the tea is made and served by the eldest son present; in the usual family group it is made by the wife. Tea is drunk several times during the day, but not at meals. While the small glasses are usual, on one occasion at a luncheon in a Circassian household, the guests were served tea in Western style teacups during the meal.

Turkish coffee is found only in the more prosperous households and is reserved for the most distinguished guests who may stop at the compound, particularly the gendarmes. Women make the drink from machine-ground coffee powder bought at the town market, Powder, sugar, and water are brought to three boils in a small aluminum or enamelled container specially designed for this type of coffee. The brew is poured into demitasse cups while still boiling.

Only Shayx Nuuri's household served the traditional bitter Arab coffee spiced with cardamon. This was made by the "slave" and is boiled and reboiled down through three copper coffee pots of graduated sizes set in a rectangular brazier of glowing charcoal. In serving, a half teaspoonful is poured with a flourish and clink of cups and pot, into the bottom of a small china cup. (These cups are of Japanese make and import and in form are the usual handleless teacup of the Orient.) After the formal round of three servings in which the full etiquette of greeting and service is followed, a group may settle down to informal talk and coffee sipping.

Shnaynii and lemonade are also prepared beverages. No alcoholic liquors are drunk by the villagers, but the landlords consume arak, the licorice-flavored drink of the Mediterranean area, beer, and other liquors freely.

On a regular work day a light breakfast of bread and tea is eaten on rising; perhaps only tea is available. Lunch may be eaten in the fields between ten and twelve and consists of bread, onions, and leftovers from the meal of the night before. The main meal of the day is served after sunset and after the evening prayer and consists of bread, a main dish, and, in season, salad, green onions, laban, or cheese. The main dish on ordinary days is usually burghul. This consists of wheat (parboiled, dried, and coarsely ground or cracked) cooked with saman, onions, and garlic; sometimes lentils are added, or, in poorer households, corn. A thick lentil soup, flavored with lemon juice if available, is also a common main dish in the winter. In late spring, fresh green beans cooked with sheep butter and garlic replace burghul. When a guest is present or when a luncheon is served for a large number of people, other dishes are added. For the most important luncheons and feasts a lamb is butchered and quantities of rice are cooked.

Fresh fruits or pastries are rarely seen in the village. But occasionally a shopkeeper brings a load of oranges by donkey from Saraaqab, or the head of the household returns from a trip to a village market with treats of pastries or tangerines for the members of the household. Toasted and salted watermelon seeds and popcorn are sometimes prepared for snacks.

Cooking

Almost all cooking is done by women. Men may take charge of roasting lamb on spits over a charcoal brazier in certain contexts of service by the foreman or a servant for a landlord. In the preparation of complex dishes which require several operations and a careful laying of the food in the big copper pot, a woman recites the formula, Bismillaah ar Rahmaan ar RaHiim, before each step.

Cooking is done with a variety of metal utensils. The traditional cooking pots are of tinned, hand-beaten copper; a well-equipped household has several sizes of each kind. In Aleppo these are made chiefly by Armenians in the bazaar shops; in every large market village or town two or three shops of metalworkers are found. Of these, the tanjara is a deep pot, wider at the base than the rim, and with a slightly convex bottom. It is used for making boiled and stewed dishes and the largest ones, equipped with heavy iron loop handles, are used for heating laundry and bath water. The muqlii is a round shallow pan, with curved sides and two handles standing up from the rim, that is used for frying. It varies in size from 8 to 14 inches in diameter. The tusht is also a round, shallow pan but with straight sides and a flanged rim. Some are 3 feet in diameter and about 8 inches deep. They serve a variety of household purposes; bread dough, particularly, is mixed in them. In the smaller sizes, all of these containers are also found in aluminum and are imported from

Europe. They reproduce the forms of the copper vessels quite closely and are regarded with favor and acceptance by the women, although few have been acquired.

A metal mortar and pestle are used for pounding up spices and meat. Occasionally glass is pulverized in the mortar, mixed with bread dough, and put out for mice and rats. A cutting board, either round with a short handle, or a smooth length of board, finds many uses in preparing vegetables, greens, or bread. Long-handled wooden spoons are used in cooking. The "kitchen knife" is the muus, a jackknife with a three-and one-half-inch blade and a handle of the black horn of the water buffalo. These knives are made by the Qirbaat.

Frying and brewing tea or Turkish coffee are done on Primus stoves. These are European imports of Swedish or German manufacture and found in all households. They are started with alcohol and burn kerosene vapor under pressure. Boiling and simmering are done over the mud-brick fireplaces in the cooking houses or over portable and outdoor fireplaces. In the fireplaces the jillii, or dried manure fuel, is burned. Preparation of the main dishes for most meals and luncheons takes three to six hours.

Grinding wheat for burghul or bread flour is a daily task in a few households, but probably not more than five or six. By some people the method is looked on as pastoralist and old-fashioned, and associated with parties that lead to drinking and other undesirable activities between boys and girls. It is preferable, I was told, to take one's wheat to the mill at Osmaniyya or Saraaqab where it is machine ground and clean. An expedition of this nature takes all day and boys, about twelve or older, are sent on such errands, riding the family donkey, and bringing back news and gossip as well as the flour.

The grindstones in the village are of black stone and cost about twelve pounds for a small one; the nearest specialist in their manufacture is at Maar Shuuriin. They consist of two disks, with holes in the center. A wood peg fits tightly in the center hole of the lower stone and loosely into that of the upper. Near the outer rim of the upper stone is a peg handle— by which it is turned. The grain is fed slowly down the center hole and comes out around the edges between the stones as the stone is revolved. Lentils are also split by a few turns in the grindstone.

Besides dried laban cakes (kushuk) and tomato paste, parboiled wheat and corn, the other foods preserved for use in winter were red pepper, squash, and eggplant. These were dried whole and hung on strings from an arch or rafter.

Eating

At family meals and those at which a friend may be informally entertained, a circular mat is placed on the floor, the pot or dish of food is placed in the center, and several pieces of bread and a metal tablespoon put at each place. Men and older boys eat first. They kneel around the mat; each recites the formula, Bismillaah ar Rahmaan ar RaHiim, before he begins to eat, but he does so for himself and not in unison with others. If one of the men wants water, the oldest son brings it at request. Eating is done directly from the pot in which the food is cooked. Bread is torn in pieces and eaten with the right hand only, since the left is "unclean." A very conventional person never touches the bread with his left hand. When one is finished eating he recites the opening line of the Koran, l Hamdulillah rabb il ^{c}alamiin ("Praise be to Allah, Lord of the Worlds"), and moves away from the tray. As a guest it is proper to eat only part of a dish of food.

Coffee or tea are served after the meal if a guest is entertained. Shortly after the coffee is the correct time for the guest to leave.

When a luncheon is served for important guests, such as the gendarme officers or wealthy landlords from other villages, the resources of several households in tables, chairs, chinaware, tableware, may need to be pooled. Such luncheons are served on tables and for a large group three or four are placed end to end down the length of the room. The most important guests sit opposite the door. Food is heaped on platters, which are placed down the center of the table, and each place is provided with a plate, spoon, stack of bread and individual dish of sauce or gravy made of meat, fat, potatoes, onions, and sheep butter cooked with tomato paste.

The host does not eat but stands behind the most important guests and, with sleeves rolled back, tears the choicest pieces of meat from the bones and puts them on the guests' plates. He also cracks the lamb's skull open and places brains, tongue, and cheek morsels on the guests' plates or on top of the rice directly before them. Each guest eats directly into the rice on the platter before him and whatever portions of the meat spread over the crest of the mound of rice fall into his excavation are his.

Each person leaves the table when satisfied; outside the door an attendant hands him a piece of soap, pours water over his hands, and hands him a towel. After the guests and chief household heads of the village have left, other men of the village eat. And after them the host, his wife, and the people who have helped prepare the luncheon sit down together over the remainder.

In Tell Ṭoqaan only three households were of the status and affluence to give luncheons to which the heads of all households as well as other guests were invited. One, a peasant farmer, as grandson of the founder of the village and first cousin of the two largest landholders in the village, as well as the holder of two faddaan of land, had some access to help from his cousins; the other two men were each head of the largest lineages in the village. None of them was of pastoralist background. Two of the landlords who were often in the village frequently entertained guests at luncheons and card parties. Their guests included the officer of the gendarme post at Saraaqab (outranking the men at the Tell Suultaan post), other landlords, government officials, and city men. Villagers never participated in these, though it was the duty of the foremen, chauffeur, and any kinsmen to be in attendance. The landlords might attend, or send a representative in their foreman, luncheons given by the village men if the other guests were distinguished.

Bread

If one drops a piece of bread on the ground or floor, one must pick it up immediately, kiss it, press it three times to one's forehead, and eat it. When hot bread fresh from the oven is offered, one replies not only ᶜaysht (village equivalent for "Thank you") but fil baarak ("your blessing"). Both bread and coffee are from Allah and require special treatment and respect.

Bread is made regularly every third day. The dough is leavened with a handful left over from the previous baking; this is called the xamiirii ("leaven"). If a woman has no leaven she borrows a little from a neighbor, or it can be made by letting a little fresh dough stand for six to ten days. Freshly ground whole wheat flour, water, a little salt, and the leaven are the only ingredients in bread.

Two kinds of bread are made in Tell Ṭoqaan, the oven bread (xubz tannuura) of peasant households and xubz ṣaaj of the pastoralist-tradition households. The kind of bread made in a household is a good indicator of both economic status and affiliation. Greater prestige is attached to peasant bread. The half-dozen girls of pastoralist background and of marriageable age had all sought out peasant women to teach them how to make peasant bread, but none of the peasant girls or women learned the pastoralist's style of bread. If a peasant household wants xubz ṣaaj, a girl of pastoralist background is asked in to make some. Both kinds of bread, once the making is under way, demand a steady pace and practiced, rhythmic movements. The work is done in an hour or two. The dough is prepared early in the morning and baking starts late in the morning.

For the peasant bread, xubz tannura, a woman puts on an apron or an old gown. The dough is taken from the mixing pan and molded into fist-sized balls on a flour-sprinkled board. A small dish of oil or water is placed nearby to put on her hands so the dough will not stick. The first dough ball is beaten out with a rapid tattoo of the hands, turning it at the same time, until it forms a flat disk about 10 inches in diameter. Then it is lifted and rotated as it is tossed from hand to hand so the disk is enlarged to 14 or 16 inches across. It is then dropped over a velvet-covered pillow with a pocket in the back for the hand. With the first piece to go against the heated oven wall, the formula, "Bismillaah . . . " is recited. Nearly as soon as the next disk of dough is ready, the previous one is cooked and beginning to come away from the oven wall. After the supply of plain bread is made, another kind may be made which are smaller disks sprinkled with red pepper and spice. When the new type of bread is started the "Bismillaah . . . " is again recited.

Pastoralist bread, xubz ṣaaj, is made on a convex iron griddle over a small fire of twigs and straw. The disk of dough is started as for peasant bread, but the final stretching operation of tossing and turning from arm to arm draws the dough out to a thin tissue and the result is a ragged, paper-thin sheet, pliable when hot and very brittle when dry. The last disk of dough is punctured with several holes before it is stretched and thrown on the hot iron. This piece is called the fulaaHa and was said to be "for the children." The technique of enlarging the disks of dough is of particular interest and concern to women of both peasant and pastoralist tradition and they are freely critical of each other's styles. The iron griddle can be purchased in sizes which range from 14 to 30 inches in diameter in village and city markets. Prices range from three to seven pounds.

In the area the pastoralist bread is associated with the shepherd pastoralists and Bedouin, all people who live in hair tents and nomadize, but it is found elsewhere in the Near East. In the Lebanon and among the Kurds it is called "mountaineers bread."

Household Work and Crafts

Most of the maintenance work, in a peasant household which farms, gardens, and has some product animals, poultry, and beehives, is done entirely by women. In order for such a household to function as an economic unit and continue as an organization, the following tasks are necessary: manufacture of storage bins for the year's supply of wheat and other grains, building of storage bins or silos for straw and other fuel, milk processing, grain cleaning, food preservation, wool washing and preparation, and fuel making. They are all performed by the women, who also exercise certain handcrafts for household use—the making of beehives, trays, and mats, and sewing.

Households which have little or no property of subtenures in land or animals and depend on wages or salaries from outside labor require many but not all of these same tasks. A number of handcraft skills of women are utilized not only in and for the peasant households, but, like sewing and plastering, are marketable both within Tell Ṭoqaan and in the village markets outside. Since these are available to laborers, the interiors of their houses often are embellished with the decorative details of peasant dwellings. Common to both types of establishment are the seasonal renovating, cooking, laundering, cleaning, sewing, and fuel-making which keep a household going. All of them are women's work and hand labor.

On the basis of peasant organization of the houshold as compared to that of the wage laborer, 16 of the families in Tell Ṭoqaan live chiefly within the peasant system, 29 are laborers' households, and 8 share the characteristics of both. The two families of tent dwellers do not fit well into the classifiction, but since they are self-sufficient units which control the tools or knowledge of their economic activities, they are more comparable to the peasant households. Only one man, of the adults of the peasant households, was known to work outside; only a few of the younger members do. And on the whole, most of the women of these households are occupied full time at home.

The following operations and handcrafts, not described elsewhere, deserve further comment. Barley cleaning is done by wielding a large sieve. In six hours one woman will clean the contents of a large burlap sack, an amount equal to one shimbal. As a dry measure of grain, it appears equivalent to about 4 bushels; the sack stands nearly 4 feet high when filled and is rated as half a camel load locally. Such a sack of cleaned barley is worth ten pounds to the household. Endurance, skill, and control of the sieve are evidenced in the steady swinging and tossing which separates chaff and dirt from grain.

Among the skills in clay work which the women practice is the manufacture of portable fireplaces. These are made in three or four days in spare-time moments and all follow the same basic design. The sides of the fireplaces are built up with blobs and heavy coils of red clay. After drying in the open a few days a fire is built in them to test their strength. Their manufacture, and that of beehives, and the interior plastering are the only crafts which may be said to be related to pottery work. All household china is purchased in the markets or from peddlers and is a cheap, imported ware, probably from Japan or Europe. Only the water jars appear to be Syrian made.

Baskets and trays are made by all the village women for household use. The only tool needed is an awl made by the carpenter for half a pound; it is a stout nail hafted in a wooden handle. Coil technique is used exclusively and the material is wheat straw. The binding straws, some of which are dyed green or yellow, are kept damp for pliability in a wrapping of wet cloth.

One pastoralist woman in the village was observed making a reed screen (zurb). This was for the Nuuri household and it was designed for the tent set up on the threshing ground for any transient group moving east with its flocks for the spring grazing. The zurb is the partition screen used in nomads' tents to separate the women's side from the men's. The kind made for a bride and groom is the largest and most elaborate, woven closely of colored yarns, and was said to cost a hundred pounds. An ordinary zurb may cost only five or ten pounds; the woman making this particular screen said Shayx Nuuri would pay her five pounds for it. They can also be purchased in the "Bedouin" market in Aleppo.

Three or four days were spent spinning the wool strings with which the reeds of the screen were bound together.

Weaving the screen took one day. The equipment consisted of a stout pole about 3 inches in diameter and 10 feet long laid across two 5-gallon kerosene tins, a pillow under each end so it would not roll off. The wool strings were wound on fourteen ovate stones which had been brought from the spring the day before. Beside the weaver was a stack of straight, dried reeds about half an inch in diameter and 5 feet long. The screen was half done when I saw it. As the woman continued, each new reed was laid on top of the pole and one each of the seven pairs of stones carrying the wool strings were swung over from one side to the other; their weights on the strings held the reed in place. As she worked two strands intertwined down each end of the screen and another pair down the middle. On either side of the midline strings, two pairs are worked diagonally one from the center and one from the end until they meet, and then are worked diagonally away from each other again so that a symmetrical pattern is repeated on each side between the end strings. Each reed is not set the same as the next, however. Two settings alternate, one for the three pairs of end and middle strings, and one for the four pairs of strings worked diagonally. Thus, the fastening twists pick up two reeds at a time.

A Day in a Peasant Household

In mid-March in Tell Ṭoqaan when the young lambs, kids, and calves have begun to graze, when the heaviest rains of late winter are over, when the wheat is well up and seedling beds and vegetable gardens are being planted, when the days are long and pleasant with mild weather, warm sun, and scattered showers, before insects have begun to multiply and the dust of summer to blow and drift, life in a peasant household is at its most agreeable. To narrate the day's routine in a peasant compound at this time is to give some idea of the pace and concerns of daily living at its "best". What the Tell Ṭoqaaniis remember as "best" from past years, of course, are the unusual and outstanding events, the great feasts and celebrations, the special favors from Allah or from the wealthy and powerful, and the seasons of unusual harvests. Here the "best" is conceived of as a typical good day, when the weather is clear, the work is accomplished without mishap, minor problems are solved or settled, hopeful plans are made, and no unusual events mark the day.

In the early darkness just before dawn the household begins to stir; the father and head of the household is heard reciting the first prayer of the day in the courtyard. Shortly afterward he and his eldest son release the animals from the stables —the two mules and the young horse, the cow and her calf from their small stable at the end of the far courtyard, and the seven black nanny goats and their seven kids from the former dwelling room, now assigned to animals, which opens off the near courtyard. Around this space the reception room, dwelling room, and kitchen room are also and here most of the social life of the day takes place, in the sun or in the shadow given by the walls, as comfort demands. In the kitchen room the wife spends a few minutes mixing bread dough for baking later in the morning. The two mules nibble at the remains of green barley lying in the mangers along one wall of the courtyard; the eldest son and his father throw the light halters over the mules' heads and the collars around their necks. Then, the youth, with a bag of bread for lunch tied to his belt, drives the team out to plow. He will begin where he left off the day before, the place marked by his plow slanted back on the handle, plow beam high in the air, and the yoke supporting it. He is working on a fallow plot near the tell, plowing it for the third time since January. And he carries a couple of homemade bird traps to set, for spring has brought many birds to the village lands. Other plowmen of the village are moving out to neighboring plots and elsewhere on the fallow lands and call greetings to each other.

The second son, a boy of thirteen or fourteen, follows the cow, calf, and young horse out of the courtyard, watching sleepily until he sees that they join the village herd of similar animals which is moving under the care of the village herdsman's sons slowly toward the grazing on the far slope of the great tell near the border of the marsh. The seven nanny goats are separated from their kids by the mother and her youngest son and the adult animals are driven out of the compound to join those of the carpenter's family with which this household co-operates in herding their small flock of product animals. The combined flock of the two households number 17 nanny goats, 16 of which are giving milk, two bucks, and a ewe giving milk. The carpenter's second son leads the small flock in the direction of the low limestone ridge on the southwest side of the village where he and the shepherd for the local tribal shayx will graze the animals of their flocks near each other. Far along the ridge which encircles the village, the shepherds of the two major lineages of the village are moving with their flocks to the day's grazing.

After the goats and the ewe are well on their way the carpenter's ten-year old daughter and her small brother arrive in an erratic and disorderly rush with the flock of kids; the seven kids of the peasant household are shooed out to join them. The young animals are just learning to graze a little, but most of the day they will lead the two children a chase from the field borders where they nibble a little, cluster in a group to sleep briefly in the sun, then are up and away through the village, leaping and clambering by way of half-ruined walls to the roofs of stable compounds. Then nearby adults must go to the rescue of both children and animals. "They are little devils."

Once the animals are taken care of, the remaining members of the household breakfast quickly on tea and bread and leftovers from supper the night before. The two younger boys set out for school, held in a room the Shayx has taken in the compound, across the village, of an old shepherd partner of Shayx Nuuri. The father of the household begins to clean the mule-stable floor; his wife carries out the dung and straw in loads on a broad round tray to the spot outside the compound and among the storage bins where previous loads have been dumped. Between trips she complains to her husband that their client's wife, who is supposed to come every other day to help her around the compound, rarely comes more than twice in a week. When their client is home in the village, she tells him, he sees to it that his wife comes regularly, but now that he is away for a while she never turns up, just like all the Hadiidiin women from Tell Qelbi—no brains for their obligations. This morning, she goes on, she expects one of the widows in the village to come and help her instead. Her husband listens and grunts in more or less agreement.

When the widow arrives she is put to work rolling the churning bag of laban and water. She squats on a mat in the chill shadow of the compound wall and as she churns the laban the two women carry on a conversation that begins with formal greetings, the widow respectfully addressing the peasant and his wife Abu Adnaan and Umm Adnaan after their eldest son. The conversation continues with brief comments, and when the husband leaves, warms slowly to a cautious exchange of gossip and information between the two women. In the sixteen years each has been in the village (their two eldest children are nearly the same age), the widow has visited this compound only half a dozen times, for medications for herself or her children for earache, in the treatment of which the peasant has some special reputation,

The peasant's wife has never been in the widow's house, for the two women are of different tribal groups, but more significantly, the widow is a Bu Layl who lives to some extent on the generosity of Shayx Nuuri, since her only boy is still a child of five. The peasant's wife, on the other hand, came to Tell Ṭoqaan from Saraaqab, a much larger village. She is a member of a large and powerful family there, a poor branch of it, but nevertheless, a member; and her husband is a grandson of the founder of Tell Ṭoqaan, perhaps, it has been rumored, an illegitimate son, but in any event locally recognized as a descendant of the founder and acknowledged by his cousins, the legitimate descendants, as a kinsman. And the cousins are urban landlords, educated men, effendiis, who own automobiles, tractors, and residences in Aleppo. In part, the conversation of the two women skirts these subjects and alludes to these facts and rumors; together they get the work done. The peasant's wife hears that the widow's daughter does not know how to make peasant bread since they do not have peasant oven, but she has learned to sew well. It is generally known that of the four or five marriageable girls in the village, her daughter is regarded as one of the best in comportment and ability. The widow hears that, yes, the peasant's oldest son is interested in finding a wife, but has not settled on anyone yet. The laban is churned, the compound is swept, the peasant's wife shakes out the sleeping mattresses and quilts, folds and stacks them on the rack above the wooden bride's chest at the end of the long dwelling room. The widow sweeps the room and shakes the mat in the courtyard while midmorning tea is brewed.

The husband, who had gone out to watch once more the way the old mule worked at the plow, scarcely able to finish a furrow, returns for tea. The mule won't last, he comments. Already all he wants to do is to lie down at the end of a furrow; he might go on a while if he could rest and eat grass every other day, but the plow must work every day to get even half their land cultivated. One of the men in the village whose property is in sheep and and who has no land to cultivate has a white mare that is pregnant. She might be a good buy and Allah might bring them a mare, a horse, or at least a strong mule. The peasant leaves for the carpenter's shop or the small store next to the mosque; the man who owns the white mare will be in either place. His wife asks the widow to pick over some lentils while she bakes the bread. A fire of coarse chopped straw is started at the base of the big oven jar and, while the fire burns down to a bank of coals, the peasant's wife prepares the working space and dough.

The widow sits outside the door of the small domed room in which the oven is located; while the two continue working and talking a young girl strides gracefully into the courtyard bearing a tinned copper pan filled with freshly collected and peeled down thistle stalks, a favorite green eaten raw or cooked in laban. At the instruction of the peasant's wife she tips the greens, nearly half a bushel, out on a tray in the kitchen room and leaves. The widow asks why the girl had brought the greens, but the wife declares that indeed she doesn't know. Probably her husband bought them. However, both of them know the girl is the muxtaar's daughter, the next to the eldest and another of the eligible. After the breadmaking is finished it is approaching noon and time to go out to the first milking. The widow's work is finished, so the peasant's wife pours several handfuls of the dry lentils into a small pan the widow brought with her and adds over them a generous portion of the greens. She picks up the wooden container for the milk, locks dwelling room door and compound gate, as they leave together.

The trip out to and back from the place on the ridge where the goats are grazing takes nearly an hour; as she moves across the village she is joined by the wives of several employees of Shayx Nuuri, who will milk the sheep of his flock, and the carpenter's wife and oldest daughter. When they return to the village the carpenter's wife and the peasant's wife take their milk to the compound where the cheesemaker's agent, who comes each day to buy their milk, has his containers and measuring utensil's arranged. The peasant's wife returns alone to her compound, pausing at the house of their client to ask the client's wife why she has not come to work on the days she is expected. The client's wife says she will come the next day certainly, but she had heard that her husband and oldest son were returning from their trip and she wanted to have her husband's small shop freshly white-washed for him. The peasant's wife, on her return to the compound, puts out bread, onions, and laban for her husband and two youngest sons for lunch. She mentions to her husband that their client's wife says she will come tomorrow. The youngest son comes first from school and tells his mother that his brother was beaten on the soles of his feet by the Shayx because he did not know his lesson, but his brother denies the whole event and is evidently in a bad mood for he throws clods of dirt at the young dog. After lunch there is time for the peasant to take a brief nap in the sun in the courtyard and for his wife to chat with an old shepherd while she adds another layer of mud to the new beehive she is making. He has come in to ask if they could use a little green fodder he would glean for them. Perhaps tomorrow, she puts him off. About mid-afternoon the oldest son returns from plowing with the team; he unharnesses them, waters them at the stone trough in the stable courtyard, and leaves the animals in the courtyard. The second son returns from school soon and takes the plow team out to graze near the spring until sunset. The oldest son eats, then changes his plowman's gown and heavy boots for the striped gown and long coat of a peasant farmer, and goes to join his friends at one of the shops.

The peasant's wife starts the kettle of burghul for the evening meal simmering soon after her eldest son returns from the fields. Sewing, repairing a broken basket occupy her for an hour or so. Villagers may come in to talk, some to ask what to do about a sore that is not healing, or perhaps a girl of pastoralist background who is learning to embroider a gown in the pattern like that the peasant woman wears.

Late in the afternoon the peasant's wife again goes out to milk the goats grazing west of the village. Along the way she meets again the group of women who went out together at noon. After the milking the women, shepherds, and the flocks move slowly back toward the village together. The lambs and kids have been brought part way from the village and held behind a rise of ground until called for. When they are turned loose within sight of the mother animals there is a brief pandemonium as the two groups of animals come together and parent seeks offspring, and the young take the last milk that was left for them. It is just sunset as the people and animals slowly re-enter the village. From the hillock in front of the mosque the shopkeeper, as muezzin, chants the evening call to prayer. The animals of the village herd are walking slowly toward their owner's compounds, finding their own ways from the edge of the village.

In the compound, after all the animals have been stabled by the boys, the members of the family go in to eat in the dwelling room. The father of the household has brought a friend who came to the village this day, in itinerant shoemaker returning with a caravan from selling his services among the shepherds nomadizing in the eastern grazing steppe. Two or three times each season, when the caravan returns to its starting point at Idlib, he drops out at Tell Ṭoqaan to visit this household, as his father did before him. He has been among the Harraamshii shepherds, who will return after reaping, to camp at Tell Ṭoqaan and pasture their flocks on the fallow fields during the dry summer, and he has seen the shepherd who cares for the two young ewes which the peasant owns. He relays greetings from the shepherd and assurances that the animals are well. After performing the sunset prayer the men and sons of the peasant gather around the supper tray. They are served bread, burghul, the fresh greens brought that day, fresh green onions, and sugared fresh butter from the morning's churning. After the meal the men smoke, drink sweet tea, talk and play a few games of cards. The visitor fits a pair of sandals to the youngest son's feet, He will leave them as a gift the next morning. Two or three men who usually work for the peasant come in for the evening's talk. News heard on the shopkeeper's radio is repeated, news from the grazing areas, the condition of the barley growing in the vicinity of the ridge is reported by the wife. The peasant speculates on the possibility of borrowing money to buy an irrigation wheel this year. And where he will place it and how he will lay out the garden around it. His wife prepares the evening's milk production for the next day's laban while the men talk.

Late in the evening, when the callers are gone, the family retires one by one. The mattresses are placed in a line along the floor. The one nearest the door is occupied by the head of the household; next is his wife. Her youngest son sleeps beside her, then the second son. The eldest son, who must be up and plowing again at dawn, long since retired on the far mattress while the men were still talking. Before retiring, stable doors, compound gate, and dwelling room door are securely locked. Just before he come in for the last time, the father of the household scans the sky and predicts the next day's weather to be fair, if God is willing.

XI

DISTRIBUTION AND COMMERCE

Noncommercial Distribution and Exchange

TWO LEVELS OF NONCOMMERCIAL dealings in goods, tools, or economic aid are distinguished by the villagers in Tell Ṭoqaan: that among families of a lineage and that between unrelated families. The head of the household, within the single family unit, controls all the resources and stores and does all the major buying and selling. It is he who goes out of the village to the market towns and he who makes contracts or enters into obligations in the interests of the household. All money earned by sons and daughters is contributed to a common fund under his control. What the wife receives from eggs is excepted, but as a matter of fact any money she earns goes to fulfill family needs, particularly clothing for the children.

Among the families of a lineage economic aid should be given as needed and requested: li ᶜindii ᶜinduu u lᶜinduu ᶜindii ("what is mine is his, and what is his is mine"). Thus, a peasant farmer could use his landlord cousin's automobile or tractor without paying the fee required of nonkin, and had only to supply his own fuel. And when a work animal fell sick and could not be used, a man could borrow one from a brother or cousin; if it were injured, no compensation would be required. Between patrilineally related families, bread and other food were freely interchanged; repayment was not expected, rather, there was the obligation to give. But between families related only through marriage of the mother there was no such evidence of economic sharing except as incidental gifts, clothing or trinkets, passed from uncles and aunts to children. In a few instances boys and girls helped their maternal aunts in chores.

Between unrelated families, qurda ("debt"), the custom of reciprocity in kind, holds. Bread given one day was promptly returned on the next baking day. The same equivalence held for other items: money for money, tobacco for tobacco, flour for flour; money could never be substituted for the item originally borrowed. Beside the obligation of reciprocity, it was said there was also the obligation of generosity, to give if one has the needed or requested item, and not to refuse. This latter obligation was said to be honored more by the people of pastoralist background than by peasants or landlord. In the few instances cited as examples the situations seemed too unusual, except the one involving the ethnographer ,[1] for one to believe that this obligation remains as a valid practice in the area. To the contrary, both concealment of goods (sugar) to avoid requests and refusal when it was known supplies (straw) were available were observed.

Loaning and borrowing of tools and animals occurred among friends after discussion of expected use. There was also a custom, practiced in a joking manner, in which one person, seeing that another possessed something he needed or wanted, could lay his hand on the other's arm, say mbaarak ("Blessed"), ask for the item, and the other was obliged to give it up. In this way new items of clothing or accessories, such as headcloths or shoehorns, sometimes passed from hand to hand among friends, or by this means a woman might get a hen from her sister. It was not observed, however, that any extensive economic sharing or exchange by noncommercial means took place beteen the villagers. Those instances that occurred were on a small scale, such as borrowing bread when running short one day, and served, merely to relieve emergency situations. In a village, of course, this scale, "small" to western eyes, is the usual scale of life.

Distribution of food on social or religious occasions within the patterns of traditional hospitality or ritual occurs occasionally. The social events that I observed were the luncheons given for new gendarme officers installed at the Tell Suultaan post. These had their political purpose in establishing good relations with the gendarmarie as well as an element of conspicuous consumption. The cost and quantity of food served are topics of general discussion and comparison and contribute to the reputation of the host.

1. It was well known in the village that among my supplies there was a case of canned milk. When the mother of a month-old child died, attempts were made to place the child with a foster mother and to persuade men who owned sheep or goats with newborn young to let the child be fed with a little milk from these animals. These requests were refused. The mothers with nursing children said their own children needed their milk; the men said that the lambs and kids needed that of the mother animals. These arguments were presented to me and after consultation with my host I agreed to give the necessary milk from my tinned milk supply. No debt was to be added up. The obligation of generosity had been previously described; when it was discussed again my gift was the only example that was not hypothetical.

Funeral services include distribution of food "to the poor," and the death of kin calls for contribution of food by kin to the bereaved household.

Feast days of the religious calendar were said also to require the head of a household to provide a meal to which he must invite whomsoever he met in the village.

Commercial Distribution

While barter of wheat for vegetables was reported to be carried on to some extent in Tell Ṭoqaan, most exchange of supplies and goods appears to operate on a monetary basis.

The staple food supplies are produced locally and payment for labor in many contract cases, includes all food or a wheat allowance. Peasant households are able to produce the major part of their subsistence diet, but landless laborers' households are not. Although the standard of living in Tell Ṭoqaan, provides minimum survival needs for the poorest families, the import of a number of items is required, and no one can survive on local production only. These are: all clothing or textiles, tools, utensils, lamp and Primus stove fuel (alcohol and kerosene), and articles of diet not locally produced (olive oil, spices, sugar, tea, coffee, and fruits). Most of them are brought into Tell Ṭoqaan and are either sold by the local shopkeepers or by itinerant merchants. Individuals also travel to the nearby market villages to purchase directly.

Of the six men who are called shopkeepers or who are concerned with selling goods, four actually have shops; three of them are flourishing. These three shops were the primary economic activity of their owners. Two were owned by older men without local kinsmen and they were fully engaged in commercial operations as the source of support for their families. The third and best shop was owned by a young man who was a member of one of the large lineages in Tell Ṭoqaan. His time was fully occupied with his store and he was in the process of separating his own residence from his father's compound to the rooms added to the shop built only the year before. Presumably he was supported in his enterprise by his father.

The three men whose shops were not flourishing actually spent most of their time in client, gardening, or peddling activities. They opened for business when they had the chance to visit a town market and lay in a small supply of a quick selling commodity

—oranges, for example, which they knew was in short supply in the villages. The display of merchandise in these is very similar, although one shop has more to offer in clothing and shoes. In another, the shopkeeper specializes in buying up eggs, which he sells in Saraaqab, and in the spring his son acts as a middleman in the lamb market, buying in Abu Duhuur and selling in Saraaqab. Local people also sell their vegetables and eggs to the shopkeepers, who in turn resell them to the nonproducing villagers. It is a local joke that from time to time when a woman has sold all her eggs to a shopkeeper, she has to buy some back (at the shopkeeper's price) when her family demands eggs to eat.

The merchandise in the shops typically includes many small items, easily transported and cheap, which indicate the range of diffusion of goods from urban to rural areas; for example, matches, cigarette lighters with fuel and flints, shoe polish, elastic cord, belts, thread, cologne, gum, soap, mirrors, razor blades, binding tape, face and hand creams, tobacco and cigarette paper, snaps for clothing. Among the tools and utensils are metal sieves, pliers, scissors, and padlocks. Clothing includes shoes of the tuwasiim type (the peasant slipper), a few jackets of Western cut and evidently second hand, and headcloths for both men and women. Foods to be found are dibis (a raisin molasses), rice, salted watermelon seeds, dates, sugar, tea, eggs, chick peas, tomato paste, dried apricots, and many kinds of hard candy. Very small stocks of all these, except the candies, are on hand at any one time.

Credit accounts are carried by all the shopkeepers. Examples of the prices quoted indicate that the customary practice is to charge one price cash in the winter; but if credit is extended the price is nearly doubled on yawm l baydar ("threshing ground day"),[2] Thus, a bedspread that costs six pounds in March when it is taken costs ten pounds when it is paid for. Of course, this is not to be considered an interest or carrying charge, but simply a change in price!

One local man whose shop has only nominal existence is a peddler of "notions" to nearby villages. When he cannot find day labor in the village during the winter, he peddles his small supply of trinkets to two villages a day in the immediate area. In two boxes carried by his donkey he keeps such small items for sale as needles and thread, pepper and other spices, beads, gum, charms, and candy. During the summer he works as a partner in gardening for one of the landlords.

2. The traditional day of settlement of debts.

To the village come many itinerant merchants, each specializing in one commodity or line of goods. Prices for their goods are regularly higher than in the village or city markets and the villagers do not seem to buy unless the goods are needed immediately. The merchants most frequently seen are dealers in cloth and ready-to-wear gowns. One, well known in the village and a Bu Layl tribesman from Zammaar, had free access to many of the compounds as a kinsman, but others spread their wares in a convenient spot in a village path. Besides the cloth merchants there are chicken and egg, olive oil, and raisin merchants.

A number of the men in the village, are said to buy up portions of the cotton and grain crops in season, to sell in the village markets to the west. At harvest time grain merchants also come to the village to buy the crops. The business of selling the surplus crops upon which the local economy is based was said to be complicated by many circumstances, such as debts owed money lenders against the crop, prices offered in different markets, transportation problems, and crop abundance or scarcity. Unfortunately, the selling season, which lasts from the middle of August to the end of cotton harvest late in the autumn, fell outside the period of my residence in the village.

Weekly markets are held in the larger villages and towns, and local men attend them regularly. Women very rarely leave the village except to visit kinsmen or a doctor. The markets most often attended are at Idlib (Wednesday), Saraaqab (Sunday), and Abu Duhuur (Monday).

XII

DIVISION OF LABOR

IN TELL ṬOQAAN an intricate combination of customs determining the division of labor is associated with the heterogenous character of the village and the economic differences among the 56 households which comprise the foci of village economic activity. There are not as many kinds of work to be done in Tell Ṭoqaan as there are ways to allocate them. The same activities recur in different contexts, and these different contexts are reflections not only of economic or class inequalities, but persistance of traditional customs, such as the sex dichotomy, or subcultural distinctions between agrarian peasant and shepherd pastoralist traditions. Three contexts or systems of economic relations are involved, the peasant household organization, the landlord-hired labor organization, and the tribal shayx organization.

Even within peasant households traditional rules of division of labor, along sex, age, specialization, and subcultural lines, are cross-cut by a class division. For landless men form the predominate part of the Tell Ṭoqaan labor force, and many men work for peasants as clients or contract laborers, as well as those who contribute their work in traditional fashion as members of extended families or lineages.

The control of resources in property, tools and equipment, and of work and services distinguish the three systems. The positions of the landlord, tribal shayx, peasant, and laborer with respect to this control are summarized in Table VI.

Characteristic of all the systems is a distinction between the management or supervision of an activity and its performance. Another common trait, the breakdown of an activity into component jobs, will vary in division with the system. For example, plowing and sowing can be two different jobs. In the landlord-hired labor system, for example, plowmen and sowers are hired under separate kinds of contracts—but a peasant, farming his own land, may delegate performance of both to his son. Again, breadmaking in the peasant system is allocated to women as a part of the general division of labor along sex lines within the household economic unit. In the tribal-shayx unit it is a specialist job for which a woman is hired. The allocation of the same categories

TABLE VI
CONTROL OF RESOURCES IN PROPERTY, TOOLS, AND LABOR
AMONG LANDLORDS, TRIBAL SHAYX, PEASANTS, AND LABORERS IN TELL ṬOQAAN

Resource	Landlord	Tribal Shayx	Peasant	Laborer
Property:				
Land	Controls large holdings	Same as landlord	Controls small holdings	No control
	Controlling partner in subtenures	No subtenures (in Tell Ṭoqaan)	Junior partner in subtenures	
Product animals	Large flocks, both local and in pastoral zone	Same as landlord	Local flocks (wide range in size)	Local or household flock, or none
	Controlling partner in joint-owned flocks	Same as landlord	Junior partner in joint-owned local flocks	
Tools:				
Work animals	Owns	Same as landlord	Owns	Does not own
Peasant equipment	Owns	Same as landlord	Owns	Does not own
Industrial equipment	Owns	Same as landlord	Does not own	Does not own
Labor	Employs wage labor	Same as landlord	Uses family primarily Employs	Sells labor
	Purchases specialist services	Same as landlord	Purchases and sells specialist services	Purchases household and personal services
	No clients	Takes clients Owns "slave" labor	Takes clients	"Skilled" labor (foremen, drivers)
			Assumes client status to tribal shayx	Assumes client status to peasants

of jobs may differ among the three systems, particularly with regard to those which in the peasant system are assigned along sex lines. And finally, a few jobs are found in the tribal shayx unit that are not in the other systems, for instance, the bread-maker, body-guard "slave," and coffeemaker "slave."

Landlord-Hired Hand System

Within the system of landlord-hired labor economic relations the division of labor by class predominates. The urban land-holders constitute the employer class. Decision, judgment, and ultimate supervision are their prerogatives. They do no manual labor themselves. The women of this class rarely visit the village; when they do, they do not participate in any way in village life except to visit kinsmen. In comparison to laborers, the landlords control all land, working animals, and tools and equipment for pursuing agriculture and gardening in Tell Ṭoqaan. The laborers own no land or working animals or tools and sell their labor to the landlords for wages or salaries. All contracts for labor are subject to the decision of the landlord to renew when the period of agreement is ended.

Labor in this system is wholly concerned with agriculture and gardening and no household servants or attendants are regularly employed in the village. The work is divided into the job categories of foreman (wakiil), several types of farmhands (?ijara; singular, ?ijiir), field guards, harvesters, day laborers, and tractor drivers. The harvesters may be migratory workers who come in season to the village from the west.

The foreman and farmhand categories are not recent developments in Tell Ṭoqaan. Formerly, the position of foreman or overseer was similar to that of a peasant partner of a landlord and tenure was customarily secure; two of the oldest men in the village had been foremen for the same landlords for twenty and thirty years, respectively. But with the introduction of cotton and industrial agricultural machinery, many responsibilities traditionally associated with the foreman have changed. The old foremen, in consequence, have been dismissed and younger men who know the new crops and the handling of tractors and plows and irrigation pumps have been hired in their places. There has been considerable turnover in foremen in the village in the past ten years.

The foreman supervises the work of the farmhands and day laborers and is responsible for seeing that the fields are plowed and planted as the landlord directs. He is responsible for seeing that the farmhands perform the care and upkeep of tools and work animals. While the landlords of Tell Ṭoqaan spend little time in the village, they do come and maintain closer personal control over the farming of their lands than the traditional absentee landlord is reported to do. During the winter the foremen also make regular visits to the landlords in the city. In Tell Ṭoqaan, the foreman no longer wields the authority he did in the past. The yearly salary of one of the foremen was 300 Syrian pounds and 4 shimbal of wheat.

Depending on which of the several categories of each farmhand is subject to a contract, or daily wage agreement, made before the work begins. The ?ijiir masnaawii is on a year's contract to do all kinds of labor concerned with farming and gardening which is assigned to him by the foreman. The salary in money was not given, but the wheat allowance was, in general, 4 shimbal of wheat and in one special case fifteen. The ?ijiir mshaharjii works on a monthly contract. The ?ijiir yawmiyyii is on a contract for plowing only, and is paid three Syrian pounds for each day that he plows. There are also temporary jobs such as sowers, reservoir diggers, fodder gatherers, which pay three pounds a day or less.

The agricultural calendar is given by tradition; the village population provides the year-round labor supply. Carrying out the extra-job hiring, assigning of jobs, and arranging the procedure, through each step of the economic cycle is the major preoccupation of the daily social intercourse among men of the village.

Tribal Shayx Unit

As a landholder, the economic relations of Shayx Nuuri in Tell Ṭoqaan correspond in many respects to those of the urban landlords. All of his fields are worked by hired farmhands under the supervision of a foreman. He does not, however, have any farming partners or tenants as do they (see Table II). His irrigated gardens are worked under the same "one-third" contract as are those of the city men. But the presence of his household in Tell Ṭoqaan provides many additional economic relations which have no counterparts in the others' dwellings. The Shayx's household is a permanent residence; those of the urban landlords are used for brief visits in spring, for business, for the hunting season.

Servants and attendants are hired by Shayx Nuuri from among the villagers. One category of laborer, ?ijiir faa^{c}il, a day laborer hired for service work in the compound, reception room, or house as demanded, is found only in his organization. One or two youths serve thus as messengers and attendants.

The families of his farmhands also work for the Nuuri household: the wives of his plowmen and fieldguards milk his local household flock or do other household work. In contrast, the families of farmhands who work for an urban landlord do not usually perform any work for him.

The position and activities of the wives, sisters, and daughters of Shayx Nuuri also differ from those of members of the landlords' families. In his establishment, the responsibilities of the household organization are divided among his three wives: The first wife maintains general command over the household activities and oversees the flocks and milking in the east in spring; the second wife is in charge of the household when the first is absent and manages the processing of milk from the local household flock. The third wife and the youngest takes charge of matters when the other two are absent; she occasionally disclaims knowing much about work and it is said of her that she eats but does not work. It is she who receives many of the village guests and clients. All three wives direct and supervise the work of both men and women; a farmhand's own housebuilding was observed to be directed by one of the wives. Minor or incidental household tasks such as fetching water and personal services which, in the peasant household, are done by women, in the Shayx's are performed by men. Broiling lamb on skewers over a charcoal brazier or in the bread oven is done by women in a peasant household; but for both landlord and tribal shayx it is performed by a man, usually the foreman.

There remain three special positions which are found in Tell Ṭoqaan only as part of Shayx Nuuri's household, and which are reported also in the households of other tribal or sectional shayxs in the area. These are the Negro "slave," who acts as bodyguard or coffeemaker, and the breadmaker (xabbaazii). The two Negroes with whom I came in contact were both said to have been "slaves" purchased by their owners, and it was said that every shayx should have one or two. The one was Shayx Nuuri's "slave," a very old man who acted as coffeemaker and attended the women of the household when they made calls in the village. The other, Maṭar, the bodyguard for Shayx Nuuri's brother, was said to be paid fifty pounds a month salary. The description of his position recalls the many tales of the slave as the trusted aide of his master among the Bedouin: he acts as his owner's policeman and at his direction will beat or shoot whomever it is necessary to so treat; and he always rides beside his owner. Both men are cordially received by the villagers; in the socially significant gesture of offering or making a cigarette it is always, however, the slave who passes his tobacco case to the host rather than the other way around in the usual manner of entertaining a guest.

Shayx Nuuri's household employs one of the village women as breadmaker. She is married to her second husband, a local shopkeeper, and is paid for her work in money. The new household which she has joined is not further obligated to Shayx Nuuri's household, although occasional "favors" asked cannot be refused.

Peasant System

The peasant system of economic relationship obtains among the small landholders, tenant farmers, contract gardeners, and local specialists of the village (carpenter, mason, shopkeeper, and herdsman). The position of the peasants in regard to control of property, tools, and work is given in Table VI. As freeholders of small amounts of land, they may be economically independent of the landlords; as tenant or farming partners with the landlords, they retain control of the peasant tools and equipment and working animals, even though their status in relation to land tenure is the subordinate one.

A prosperous peasant may hire a few farmhands under the same type of contracts used by the landlords, but it appears to be characteristic of the peasant system in Tell Ṭoqaan that (1) the source of labor is first the family, second the clients (see below), and lastly hired labor, and (2) that the customary rules of division of labor by sex and age are followed. The peasant technological and economic activity is organized around the maintenance of the household and family as an independent unit in the village. Within its economic organization social relationships predominate over commercial. Jobs which are allocated in one way by sex and age, or both, within the peasant system are allocated differently in the landlord-hired labor system. The differences will be pointed out in following sections.

The "client" is a distinctive feature of the peasant system, but a similar relationship appeared to be held between some peasants and Shayx Nuuri. None was known to be associated with the urban landlords. Each year certain of the peasants, make an arrangement called salaf ᶜala Hasaad ("advance on the harvest") with the head of a household. These are the "clients." They agree to associate themselves and their families with the patron and work for him in return for food and for loans during the year or payment on yawm l baydar ("threshing ground day"). The contract is not only economic but sociopolitical as well and implies that the client is a supporter and follower of the household head. He spends much of his free time with his patron. His agreement does not, however, prevent him from finding temporary jobs elsewhere from time to time, or even from leaving the village for several months. The patron takes care of his family while he is gone. All the older and more prosperous heads of households are said to have such clients from among the poor men of the village, and the number a man has contributes to his prestige and power. But an agreement must satisfy a client or he will join another household the following year.

Division of Labor by Sex

In Tell Ṭoqaan the division of labor between the sexes is in most respects quite marked and has two dimensions, that concerned with wage-paid jobs within the landlord-laborer system and that concerned with the peasant household. Only men, for example, hold foreman and farmhand contracts in connection with agricultural and gardening work. Women work at some of the same jobs (sowing and reaping) done by a contract farmhand but only on a daily job basis. Again, only men take paid jobs with landlord employers as well diggers, reservoir diggers, in instances where the same projects are performed within the peasant's or laborer's household, however, women also take their turns in the well or reservoir.

From the traditional point of view, in activities connected with agriculture only men plow, or drive tractors, and sow broadcast. Only men direct gangs of field workers. Both men and women sow with the seed tube, reap, and winnow. In connection with animals only men herd the work animals, care for them, deliver the young. In flock management and milking, only men are shepherds, but both men and women milk. Men shear sheep and clip goats; only men slaughter animals.

All commercial activities are engaged in or managed by men: shopkeeping, itinerant peddling, the middleman's role in merchanting. Women, however, sell eggs or poultry within the village and, in villages to the west, women are seen selling their own handcraft products (mats, trays, water jars) in the markets.

All planning and directing of building operations are done by men; all mixing of mud and straw for bricks is done by men. Both men and women make bricks, but only women plaster and make interior furnishings of clay and do household projects of cement surfacing. When a cement specialist is hired, however, he is a man.

Men also control all property in land or animals. They control all political activities and all but one of the religious. The religious event which women instigate and in which they figure largely is the zuwaara or pilgrimage to a saint's tomb.

Within the household, whether a shayx's, peasant's, or laborer's, the division of labor between the sexes is equally marked. Women manage, supervise, and do all the work in household maintenance: cooking, laundering, cleaning, preserving food, grinding grain, renovating. Men, however, control one aspect of major importance, that of hospitality. The entertainment of guests in the reception room or, lacking one, the dwelling room, is a major sociopolitical activity which involves traditional Arab etiquette. Making and serving tea or Arab coffee for guests is done by men only; Turkish or sweet coffee is made by women. Serving food at a luncheon for guests is performed by the host only; the women of his household never appear.

For clarification of the division of labor between the sexes, three systems may be distinguished. First, there are a number of ancient conventions by which certain activities are allocated to only one of the sexes and which the other may not do in any situation. Plowing, sowing broadcast, making bitter Arab coffee are thus men's work and prohibited to women. Making bread, carrying burdens, making fuel or manure and straw, working in clay are, equally distinctively, women's work. Second, there is the system by which men control property and do the major economic activities, hold the top jobs, and know the specializations and professions, while women participate only at the unskilled, handcraft, and subordinate levels. Thirdly, there is the system by which contract and some wage labor is taken over by men; once such jobs are taken out of the context of the peasant system of activities, they become part of the landlord-hired labor system.

Division of Labor by Age

Children begin to participate in work as soon as they can follow directions, and responsibility begins at six or seven. A child of three will be sent to drive a troop of young goats out of the green wheat and can do so with the proper call. At six to eight children run errands, mind the household flocks of lambs and kids, care for younger brothers and sisters and help in household activities. At twelve or so, according to their sex, they begin to learn and practice their respective tasks. Boys plow, care for animals and deliver the young, go on errands that take them to other villages. Girls learn all their household tasks, work in the fields, and learn or do profitable specialties in sewing. By fourteen or fifteen, both boys and girls, are contributing in paid labor or skill to the household.

Certain prerogatives are withheld from men until they have established households and have children. A man works until he has sons to do men's work; he then retires to the full status of adulthood in which management and direction are his responsibilities. If for economic or personality reasons he does not succeed to the senior position as head of a family or lineage, he remains in a subordinate position to the brother or cousin who has outranked him, unless he can detach himself from his superior kin and establish himself on equal basis. It is at this point that it is said that a man (rijaal) is one who prays; the term rijaal ("man") is not merely biological in meaning, but also sociological. Young men, still responsible for the daily labor on which the family depends, do not pray and are not expected to observe Ramadaan fasting, or attend Friday services at the mosque if these are held. They are not called men or regarded as men, but as shabaab, youths. The acquisition of property in land or animals is also a man's responsibility; only those, for example, who have land or animals can participate in the choice of muxtaar or herdsman, or in any other villagewide concern.

Women also reach in adulthood, when they have daughters-in-law or daughters, a privileged supervisory status, when they can order the events of the household and perform a minimum of the labor involved.

Old age brings variable roles depending on economic status and sex. A man of a prosperous household conveys his prerogatives to the most able son and retires from active life to one of prayer and relative ease. Depending on his personality he continues to command respect and is sought out as an advisor. A woman, if she practices a handcraft, continues active as long as she can.

Division of Labor by Ethnic Group

The ethnic diversity of the population of Tell Ṭoqaan has been pointed out in (Chapter III). Both tribal and nontribal people are found in the village; ethnic categories such as Kurd, Circassian, Turk are recognized. But the major distinction made by the villagers, and clearly to be observed in language, familial background, and in many customs, traits, and behavior, is that between people of agricultural peasant background and people of nomadic pastoralist background. To some extent these distinctions, locally recognized, are also found in the division of labor.

In agricultural work there are no ethnic distinctions drawn between any group in general field labor. Most plowmen and sowers appear to belong to the peasant category, however, for to these activities some special knowledge and skill are attributed. None of the positions of foreman were or had been filled by people of pastoralist background.

On the other hand all the positions of professional shepherds were held by men of pastoralist background and tribal affiliation; special knowledge of sheep and goats were claimed by men of pastoralist tradition in contrast to their lack of experience with cattle. Knowledge of the handling of camels, handcraft work in wool, particularly the making of animal harnesses, and the processing of milk were all regarded as crafts and skills properly belonging to the pastoralist tradition and best exercised by people of that background.

Of the several ethnic groups represented, only the Circassians were singled out; to them were attributed greater skill, industry, and honesty. One man was hired as a foreman because, as a Circassian, he could be expected to know and do the work properly. The two other Circassians were specialists, one the carpenter and the other a tractor driver.

In housebuilding, the professional masons were peasants, but several domed houses were personally built in 1954 by men who only a few years before had lived in tents.

The general impression was that most of the work done in Tell Toqaan was unskilled in the sense that it could be learned easily without lengthy training, but that the better performance was ascribed to and expected from people whose cultural background was associated with specialization in agriculture and gardening as opposed to shepherding and associated activities. The older men, whose experiences had been concentrated on shepherding or agriculture, retained the attitude of specialists toward them. For instance, an old shepherd would state specifically that he knew sheep but not much about cattle, and he would disdain knowledge of farming or gardening.

Division of Labor for Village as a Unit

Only one matter came to my attention for which the village as a whole was responsible; this was the repair and maintenance of the telephone line within the boundaries of Tell Toqaan lands. If the village does not provide the labor and materials needed for any repairs, it must pay the equivalent in money. Arrangements for repair are made between the muxtaar and gendarmes from the post at Tell Suultaan.

Specialists and Specialization

There are few specialists in Tell Toqaan whose work carries the same weight of special knowledge and professionalism as does that of the teacher. Rather, the various ones present seem to secure most of the local market for a particular type of work either by virtue of owning the tools of the trade they practice or by establishing residence and reputation in the village. Such categories as shepherd, shoe repairman, and tractor driver come, perhaps, closer to specialist in knowledge and training than do those of herdsmen, carpenter, and brick mason.

Moreover, Tell Ṭoqaan is serviced by a number of itinerant specialists who visit the village regularly and who lay claim to all the local work in their trade. Other itinerant tradesmen are less closely associated with the village and simply include Tell Ṭoqaan as one of the villages visited in their rounds in the area. At the time of the field session Tell Ṭoqaan did not have a resident barber; two brothers from Idlib shared the trade. One or the other came every two weeks or so and visited each household that requested his services. Before these two men took over the local work there had been a resident barber, and his son remained in the village and worked as a farmhand for one of the landlords.

Early each spring a circumciser visited the village. He was a Kurd of the "ᶜAbasiyyiin tribe" and said that all the men of his tribe were circumcisers.[1] In addition, he was a barber, but he did not perform this function in Tell Ṭoqaan, because the trade was already claimed by the two brothers from Idlib. This man carried a surgical kit, which included gauze and cotton dressings, disinfectants, and sulfa powder, and, when called upon, dressed wounds and pulled teeth. His clothing was distinctive, particularly his headwear, so that, as he said, people would know from afar who he was. His long coat was brown, as were his Turkish trousers; on his head he wore a brown wool peaked cap wrapped turbanwise with a yellow and white headcloth; and he carried a cane.

From time to time Tell Ṭoqaan is visited by professional doctors from Idlib or Aleppo. Whether they came by request or not I do not know; but when one who was reputed to specialize in eye ailments came, he was called upon by anyone who had any kind of a disability which was not responding to local methods of treatment.

A blacksmith to shoe horses and mules comes at intervals to the village from Osmaniyya (see also Chap. VIII, p. 97).

All of the above specialists maintain close relations with the villagers, are known by name and personal history, and are entertained as friends or, in the case of city doctors, as guests, Others generally come in small groups and ply their trade in the village paths rather than in the compounds. These are the repairers of Primus stoves and kerosene lamps and the shoe repairmen. In the summer, I was told, there also come men who make felt mats out of wool provided for them in the village and others who fluff up mattress fillings with special gut-strung bows.

The local specialists in Tell Ṭoqaan are the shepherd, herdsman, and mason, previously described, and the carpenter, shoe repairman, teacher, and tractor drivers. These seven may be considered the full- or nearly full-time "professionals" of the village.

The carpenter is an elderly man, a Circassian. Before moving to Tell Ṭoqaan he worked as a foreman for a landlord in another village and had been a soldier in the Turkish army in the First World War. He had had no special training in carpentry,

1. All members of this "tribe" are circumcisers and barber-surgeons and are dispersed widely in rural Levant society. The circumciser who visited Tell Ṭoqaan stated that his "tribe" received official confirmation of the profession from the Ottoman sultan and under the Ottoman regime received compensation for each male circumcised. Their evidence and claim for payment was based on the number of foreskins they presented the Ottoman official to whom they annually reported.

but what he had picked up he had passed on to his eldest son, who then did most of the actual work under the father's supervision. In supplying carpentry for houses, he serviced only the villagers; the landlords import such items as city-made windows or bring more skilled artisans for anything they want done.

All work in wood, that is, plow making and repairing, seed-tube making, the manufacture of wooden shelves, shutters, and doors falls to the carpenter or his son. The son has also learned, independently, to solder and do a little metalsmithing. A small supply of lumber is kept in the shop, and a wide range of tools—saws, chisels, hammers, adzes, bit and brace hang in racks on the walls. The only carpentry tools in the village are in his shop. All toolmaking and repairing takes place in the shop, but any installations in houses are made on location and each set of shutters, door, or frame is built to fit the particular space. Upon occasion the carpenter, or his son, as well as the circumciser will pull teeth.

The present carpenter was said to have lived and worked in Tell Ṭoqaan for 17 or 18 years. Before he settled in the village, it had been serviced by a series of itinerant carpenters from Sermiin or Idlib; these came and stayed four or five days at a time in the village until their work was done. Like the shopkeepers and other specialists, the carpenter works on credit and collects his payment after harvest on threshing ground day (yawm l baydar) .

There is one shoe repairman in the village. He does not make shoes. Apparently he only does this repairing and his son, although old enough to work, does not appear to be learning his father's trade. The charge is three pounds for resoling a pair of peasant shoes with rubber soles and reinforcing the side seams with leather patches, and it is considered exorbitant. The tool kit includes hammers, awls, beeswax, heavy shears, wire and nail cutters, long curved needles, cord, and scraps of leather. Socially, the man appeared to be something of an outsider and had come only recently to the village from Azmariin.

In the person of the shayx are combined the roles of teacher, prayer leader in the mosque (?imaam), clerk, and curer.[2] Shayx MaHmuud AHmad Chawlak (see Chap. V, p. 36) had held this position in Tell Ṭoqaan for three years. Before him a young man from Sermiin had served as leader of worship and teacher in the village.

2. This category of shayx is, of course, to be distinguished from the position of shayx as political head of the Bu Layl tribe held by Shayx Nuuri Shwatiyya .

As teacher, Shayx MaHmuud's primary work is to teach the boys in his school a traditional course in reading the Koran and Hadiith. With the father of each child he arranges a contract for the type of training the student will receive. He charges fifty pounds a year to teach reading, writing, arithmetic and the Koran; thirty-five pounds a year to teach just reading, writing and arithmetic; and fifteen pounds a year for the smaller children who attend sporadically. Boys who were in the Koran class bring their own reading stands, made of scrap lumber, on which to place the Koran. Some eighteen or twenty children were enrolled in his school, and fifteen attended regularly. The class included four or five girls, three of them from Shayx Nuuri's household. Shayx Nuuri's second son also came.

Besides the Koran, a few government texts and volumes of classical Arab poetry constitute the Shayx's library. A window shutter smoothed off and painted black serves as a blackboard. A table and chair made by the carpenter and painted green was his seat of authority whenever he was teaching.

Shayx MaHmuud also acts as kaatib (clerk) for villagers who are illiterate; and in this capacity he reads and writes letters, witnesses documents, and records accounts.

As a religious leader Shayx MaHmuud sometimes conducts Friday services in the mosque and he reads the Koran on the occasions of death in the village or at ceremonies for the sick. In close connection with his special attributes as a trained religious shayx, goes a belief in Shayx MaHmuud's greater capacity than that of ordinary men to cure some ills by massage or written charms. He is not, however, a jidduu shayx and does not conduct the ẓikr (meeting of a religious fraternity) or the curing sessions which are said to follow them. There is no religious fraternity in Tell Ṭoqaan (see Chap. XIV).

In an altogether different category of specialist than the foregoing are the tractor drivers or chauffeurs (the French term is always used). This relatively skilled occupation has come in with automobiles, trucks, buses, and tractors, and in Tell Ṭoqaan only young men hold the positions. Two of these are full-time chauffeurs and a third was learning from one of the others. It is worth noting that the dwellings of the drivers were decorated with pictures of tractors and other agricultural machines as well as the customary pictures.

Sewing and embroidery are becoming a profitable business for the women. One woman supplements the family income by sewing men's Turkish trousers and other garments. The most expensive item, however, is the Saraaqab kab, or woman's black outer gown, which is elaborately embroidered in scarlet cross-stitch design over shoulders, front, and back above the waist, and down the seams. The design of this gown is associated with the women of the large village of Saraaqab, for it is their characteristic dress. By outmarriage, it has appeared also in Afess and a few other places, but up until recently was worn only by women from the parent village. An expertly embroidered gown costs one hundred pounds; those less extensively embroidered may be purchased for less. Women other than those from Saraaqab are beginning to buy them, and several young girls of pastoralist background in Tell Ṭoqaan are learning to embroider them. They follow the pattern of the gowns worn by the two Saraaqab women who live in Tell Ṭoqaan.

To the specialists and specializations described above should be added two others found in the villages of the area but not in Tell Ṭoqaan. Wherever water is difficult to obtain and only deep wells are available, a well operator is found who owns and operates the well equipment and exchanges water drawing for wheat. Maar Shuriin has one such well operator; Saraaqab, a dual-organized village, has two, one servicing each "side" of the village. Some villages in the area employ a watchman or policeman (Haaris) on the same basis as the herdsman. But in Tell Ṭoqaan, it was said, each man is his own watchman. When the new gendarme officers asked the assembled men of the community why Tell Ṭoqaan did not have a watchman, the muxtaar could only reply that the urban landlords and Shayx Nuuri did not want one.

XIII

SOCIAL STRUCTURE

THE PEOPLE OF TELL ṬOQAAN are linked to each other by social ties of kinship and marriage and communal association as well as by economic relations. These relationships also reflect the diverse origins of the members of the community, the mixture of peasant and pastoral cultural traditions, and changes which the diffusion of industrial technology and a period of French rule have brought to Syria. All of these factors influence the forms of the family in Tell Ṭoqaan, the extent to which ancient customs of marriage are practiced, and the extent to which the village is divided into factions or may act as a unit. Besides these structural features the social life of the village in games and parties and the social significance of clothing are considered in this chapter.

Kinship

Nearly every person in Tell Ṭoqaan has some kinsman in the village. Only ten people are without relatives; these are the teacher, five farmhands, three childless wives from other villages, and an irrational woman. Kin relationships are recognized on both father's side (ᶜamm, the father's patrikin), and mother's side (xwaal, mother's patrikin). The functions of these relationships operate through the kinship groupings of family households, of the lineages, and, to a lesser extent, of the tribe.

Arab descent is reckoned patrilineally. Inheritance of property, exercise of authority, economic aid, defense, marriage, and residence are defined according to the father's connections. In the traditional peasant village, in general, the functions of patrilineal kinship relations are presumed to predominate in the organization of the village into lineage or "clan" segments. But in Tell Ṭoqaan such functions do not cover all the relations of a family household. For example, only 22 of the 55 are linked through the father to other families in the village,[1] and are so linked by brother-brother, father-son, paternal uncle-nephew relationships.

1. See list of families in Tell Ṭoqaan (Appendix B, Table XIII, Nos. 2-17, 33-38).

The remaining 33 households are without local patrilineal kin. Between some of them, however, there are ties through the mother's kin. Most of these families are recent immigrants, but a few are "remnants ", that is, households with a lineage history in Tell Ṭoqaan. Although, within the village as a whole, economic relationships distinguish and divide the society between laborer and landlord, peasant farmer and client, rich and poor, peasant and pastoralist more than is true in typical Arab villages, nevertheless, kinship is important.

Social status in Tell Ṭoqaan, as in most Arab villages, is to a considerable extent defined by the position of a man among his own patrilineal kin. Thus, the heads of the two largest lineages in the village are also important men in its affairs. One peasant (and a household head) stands in an anomalous position. As grandson of the founder of the village and as a peasant farmer with land, animals, and sons, he ranks high among the villagers. It is his second cousin, the largest landholder and an urban landlord, that is the head of the lineage, however, and to his status the peasant cousin shows deference.

Connections through mother's kin between families and lineages are quite numerous in Tell Ṭoqaan and are of historical interest to the villagers, although they have little apparent effect on social life other than the fact that easier relationships hold between an individual and his mother's kin than do those between him and his patrilineal kin. The matrilateral relationship was expressed as xafiif ("light") as compared to the weight of authority of the patrilineal kin. For example, three local lineages were linked at one time because three men, now deceased, married the three daughters of an early settler in Tell Ṭoqaan. When a daughter of one of these lineages died in another village, because of the matrilineal connection between them the wife of the head of another expressed the desire to kill a lamb for the bereft lineage.

The Family

The population of an Arab village is usually organized into a number of patrilineal extended families which are linked together into a smaller number of lineages. This pattern does not prevail in Tell Ṭoqaan, even though a part of the community does consist of a group of lineages. The types of social groupings in Tell Ṭoqaan that are based on kinship relations are the local lineages, a tribal unit (the Bu Layl), and a few isolated families without local patrilineal connections. The local lineages are further divided into the "old" lineages, to which length of residence or connection by marriage into old families gives greater prestige, and "new" lineages, members of which have moved into the village recently. An old family or lineage in Tell Ṭoqaan is either one whose presence dates from the founding of the village[2] or one whose immigrant generation is now deceased and whose first-generation sons are now the family heads.[3]

A "family", as the term is used here, consists of two or more persons connected by kinship or marriage who live in their own dwelling. Excluded, by definition, are single men without dwellings and widowers without kin, but included are widows with children and siblings who reside in one dwelling. Three kinds of families are found in the village: (1) the nuclear, (2) the polygynous, and (3) the extended or joint. Distribution of the 55 families in Tell Ṭoqaan among the three types is given in Table VII.

TABLE VII

DISTRIBUTION OF 56 FAMILIES IN TELL ṬOQAAN ACCORDING TO TYPE

Type of Family	Old Lineage	New Lineage	Total
Nuclear	17	21	38
Polygynous	0	4	4
Extended or Joint	8	6	14
Total	25	30	56

Nuclear.--Although the nuclear is the simplest, there is considerable variation in size among the 38 of this form. The smallest family consists of a widower and his son, the largest of a widow, her six sons and one daughter. These two families, of Baggara and Bu Layl tribal affiliation respectively, have not been fully accepted as village residents by members of the old lineages because the

2. See Appendix B, Table XIII, Nos. 2-4, 5-10.

3. See Ibid., Nos. 20, 40.

oldest generation member is the one who moved to Tell Ṭoqaan. But an example of a nuclear family which belongs to a local lineage is furnished by the household of one of the shopkeepers, his wife, and his two children. Both husband and wife, as patrilineal parallel cousins, belong to the Bayt Tell Haanii lineage (see p. 171), but live in their shop separately from their kinsmen's compounds. Since the husband's father is head of the lineage the young man does not yet rank as "head of a house" (ṣaaHib l bayt, see p. 167).

Most of the nuclear families in Tell Ṭoqaan are landless laborers and have few supplementary resources in flocks; most of them have no patrikin in the community, and these are the poorest families. The specialists and shopkeepers, who are somewhat better off economically, also fall into the nuclear family category, although the men with sons nearly old enough to marry were clearly looking forward to becoming heads of extended family households.

Polygynous.—Except for tribal membership, the four families of this type have no other patrilineal kin in the village. Three are headed by older village men, and the fourth by Shayx Nuuri. Each of the village men has two wives and each wife has her own compound, so that ranking was not apparent between any two. Two of these men are regarded as "head of a house" and the third is a Bu Layl tribesman. None of these have been fully accepted as village residents by members of the old lineages.

Shayx Nuuri's large household includes his three wives and their children, all living in the same complex of buildings. This group, ranking above all the village and area in property and social status, presents more clearly than the other three, traits of polygynous family organization traditional in Arab society. The first two wives of the Shayx are clearly ranked, the first taking priority over the second in prerogatives of household management as well as in terms of seniority. Had she been blessed with a son rather than daughters, that son would have outranked his brothers born of other wives. Both these two marriages were kin endogamous, but the first wife was regarded as "closer" to the Shayx's own lineage than the second wife. The third wife was acquired in a political marriage linking Shayx Nuuri's family as the ruling family of the Bu Layl to the ruling family of the Hadiidiin tribe.

Extended or Joint.—Families of this category may comprise one or both spouses of the oldest parent generation, any married son or sons and their offspring, any unmarried sons and daughters of the senior pair, and any unmarried brothers and sisters of the father of the whole household. The 14 extended families in Tell Ṭoqaan vary in composition, but all retain the characteristics of joint residence and economic contribution by the members to the household. The head of an extended family is usually the oldest male and the father. One such family, that of one of the shopkeepers, consists of the elderly shopkeeper and his second wife, two sons and their wives, an unmarried daughter, and a dependent female cousin who is the mother of one of his daughters-in-law. The head of the family and his oldest son both keep separate shops just outside the walls of the family compound.

Each family, regardless of economic or social status, has a recognized head and the dwelling is named after that person. Generally, the head is the oldest male in the family, if he is a young adult or older. In two instances widows are the heads of families and their houses are named after them. When a young son is old enough, he will in each case take over the responsibilities of family head. Rarely, the oldest brother of two or more siblings is the head of the family, and the house is named after him. Thus, the household and its ownership defines the family; those who share shelter and food as kin are of one family or one bayt. Clients and employees may live under the same roof and share meals, but they are not kin and do not inherit.

Many but not all, of the family heads in Tell Toqaan are regarded as "heads of houses" (singular, saaHib l 'bayt, "the owner of the house"). Those who are "heads of houses" are older men with property or subtenure in land, property in sheep, or business in a shop or specialization. Usually, there are working sons in their families, whether these are married or not. The heads of houses are the oldest men, the fathers, in their households. And they belong to the "old" families of Tell Ṭoqaan, whether of tribal, peasant, or ethnic-group derivation.

Family heads who are not ranked as "heads of houses" are more often of pastoralist background, of laborer status, or of recent immigration. One peasant was apparently excluded on the basis of his youth, for he owned a faddaan of land, had a large compound, and supported a household which included a brother and his mother as well as his own wife and small children. His family was, moreover, one of the old families in the village. He moved, however, in the society of the young unmarried men of the village, and joined them in games on the threshing ground rather than standing on the sidelines with the "heads of houses."

Within the family the father is the authority in all matters of decision and discipline. Economic enterprises are planned by him; hiring laborers or making client arrangements are his responsibility; all money earned by other members of the family at labor outside the household is turned over to him. He gives or refuses his daughter to a prospective groom. He slaughters the lambs or kids that are eaten on special occasions. He is the host to guests. If he is a mature adult, he is the one member of the family, at least, who prays and observes the fast month of Islam.

A woman who marries into the family from outside the husband's patrilineal kin is always something of an outsider. If she can, she visits her own paternal kin occasionally, even if it means a trip by foot or donkey to a distant village. She does not take her husband's name, although a village woman may be briefly identified to a landlord as belonging to the house to which her husband belongs, if it does not go under his name. She retains her own tribal or ethnic identification in her affinal home. She may be addressed by her own name coupled with that of her grandfather or father, as well as by a teknonymous term. To bear children, and especially sons, gives a woman status in her affinal family and among other families in the village. To be known for maintaining a household properly, for good cooking, especially breadmaking, and perhaps for some extra skill in a handcraft or folk medicine promotes her reputation in her husband's family and village.

Sons are expected to show respect toward their fathers, to serve them in errands, to address them by the kin term, ya ?ab, "Oh Father," and not by personal name. In a social gathering, the sons in the order of their seniority, are responsible for making and serving the glasses of tea. The younger son takes the responsibility if an older is not present. Smoking is a prerogative of "men," and a boy is careful not to be caught smoking by his parents. This concealment is considered a respectful act toward one's father. Drinking coffee is also a prerogative of "men," and children do not participate. Children do join in tea drinking.

In the household in which I lived there was evidence that boys are eager to push ahead to the work and activities, dress, and mannerisms of men. A boy will initiate learning to deliver goats or to plant a crop he has not yet tried. And there is also frequent talk between the adults as to which of the sons is showing the greatest ability, but I never heard this discussed before the children.

Relations between a mother and her sons are in general warm and affectionate, but several instances of public outbursts of temper, tongue-lashing, and chastising occurred. Effective discipline, however, comes from the father; but occasions of beating or spitting in the face of the misbehaving son appeared very rare. The youngest children receive the greatest affection from all adults.

Rivalry between brothers over the small things they possess is strong, and from time to time they maliciouly destroy each others' toys. Sisters appear to be more co-operatively inclined toward each other than brothers. They often work together on household tasks such as fuel making and plastering. When separated by marriage they visit each other whenever opportunity allows.

Nephews and paternal uncles, from observation, behave rather formally toward each other, particularly if the uncle is economically and socially superior to the nephew's father. Between nephews and maternal uncles and aunts much greater affection is shown than on the patrilineal side.

Solidarity of the family in its contacts with the members of other families is marked. Confidence and informality diminish with distance or absence of kinship or economic connections. Even the purpose for which two brothers and a cousin are sifting dirt outside the compound wall will not be told a villager from outside the family. And the concealment of family goods and stores from those not in the family circle is a regular habit. The clients of a peasant farmer share the affairs of the peasant family circle, although some enjoy more confidence than others.

Lineages

Less than half the families in Tell Ṭoqaan are linked to any others by patrilineal connections. Among those which are linked, the oldest and largest form "segments " which are similar to each other in structure. While below the level of control exercised by the wealthy landlords, the segments are the centers of political and social strength and prestige in the community. It is these segments that are the lineages.

Local opinion divides the people of Tell Ṭoqaan between the newcomers and the "old" families and lineages whose households furnish in their heads the "men" of the village. Although these might be called the "elders" or the "council," there is not, to my knowledge, any specific term for the group. If a man holds land or if he ranks as head of a house, he has achieved full adult status in the community.

My host named 11 families or lineages as being the important ones in Tell Ṭoqaan. Most of these were made up of descendants of men who had settled in the village as followers of his grandfather, the founder. All the rest were "small" families, "weak" families, laborers, or newcomers. Among the important families were the three largest lineages of the village: two of them had three men who were heads of households; one was represented by three family households, only one of which was headed by a man of sufficient age and status to be regarded as a head of a household.

A number of the characteristics of patrilineal kin groups in Tell Ṭoqaan are illustrated by these three lineages. All three bear a lineage name different from that of any living individual. One is named for the village from which two brothers came to Tell Ṭoqaan; the other two after the men who first settled in Tell Ṭoqaan. Each of these lineages now boasts a large number of descendants and households (it is customary to evaluate a lineage by the number of men in it, including small boys): one has 20 living male descendants, one has 14, and one has 10.

While these three lineages are the largest in Tell Ṭoqaan only one, Bayt Tell Haanii,[4] includes kinsmen beyond the range of second cousins. This lineage is given in Figure 5. The head of the lineage and the two other senior men of the lineage are grandsons of two brothers who came to Tell Ṭoqaan at the time of its founding. Five lineage-endogamous marriages (see Fig. 5) seem to assure the lineage of solidarity; two of them are traditional parallel patrilineal cousin marriages. The other two lineages used as examples here do not have such lineage-endogamous marriages in their local history.

Each lineage is headed by one man called the ?abu l kabiir ("the elder father") of the group; in each of the three cases he is the most prosperous, but not necessarily the eldest. The lineage head of Bayt Tell Taanii is a partner in farming and sheep raising with an urban landlord, and this appears to be the wealthiest of the households in this lineage. His cousins are also partners in farming with urban landlords, but for smaller amounts of land.

Abdullah Hammuud is the lineage head of Bayt Hammuud.[5] His father, who is still alive, is the oldest and most respected man in the village. Formerly he headed the lineage and for many years was foreman for all the lands of the village founder's descendants. Now he has turned over the authority of head of the Hammuud lineage to his only son. Two cousins of the lineage head comprise the other households of this lineage group, and it is now economically associated with Shayx Nuuri.

4. Appendix B, Table XIII, Nos. 5-10. 5. Ibid, Nos. 2-4.

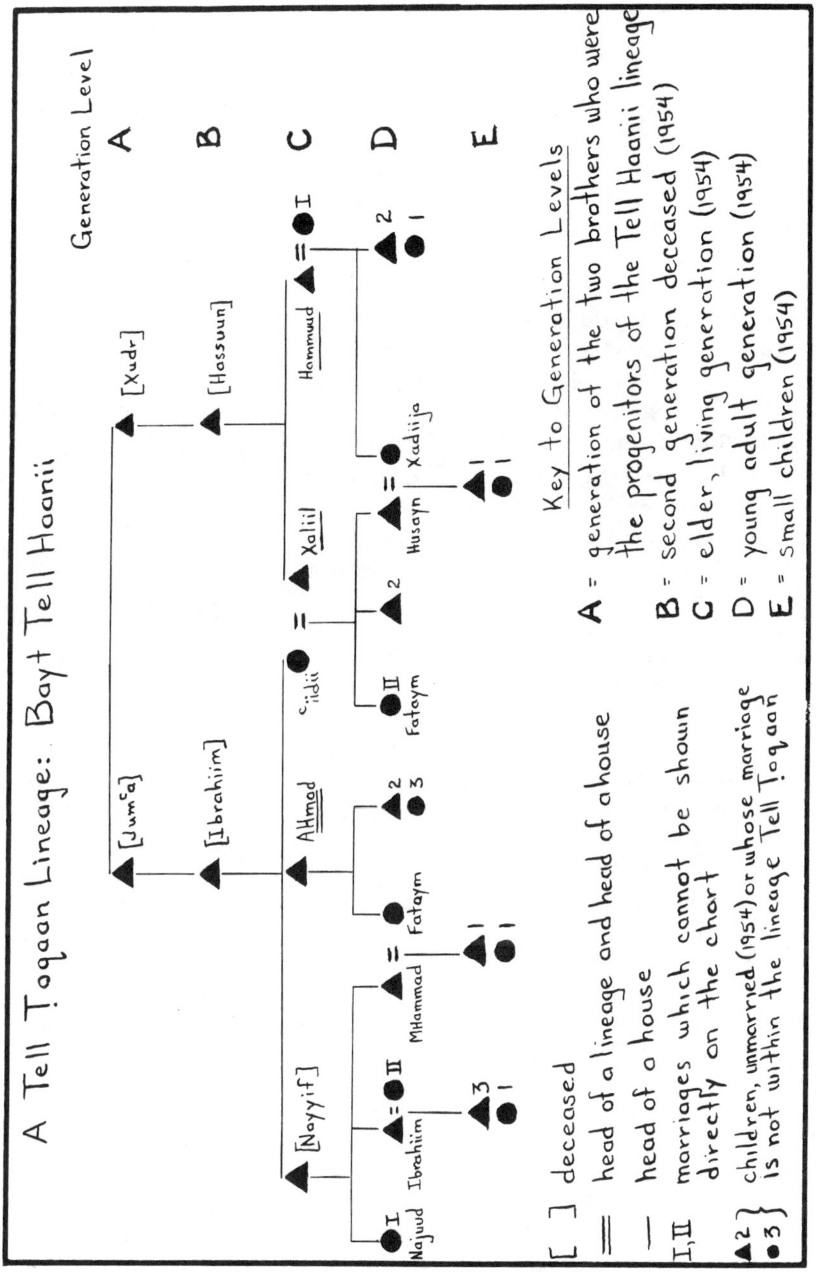

Fig. 5. A Tell Ṭoqaan lineage: Bayt Tell Haanii.

Lineage head of Bayt Mabruuk is Shayx Qadduur,[6] now resident in the village of Shuuha and considered a wealthy partner in farming there. He owns a compound in Tell Ṭoqaan in which one of his nephews lives. He is a shayx "of learṅing, of books," not a religious shayx, and is an accomplished reciter of classical Arab poetry. In Tell Ṭoqaan a shopkeeper and nephew of Shayx Qadduur is the only older man who ranks as head of a house in this lineage. The other nephews of Shayx Qadduur are all laborers and young men; one works as tractor driver for an urban landlord.

Bayt Tell Haanii is a peasant lineage; Bayt Hammuud is sedentarized tribal Bu Shayx in affiliation; and Bayt Mabruuk is sedentarized tribal Hanaadii. For all three, the local lineage group appears to be of primary importance.

During my stay few events other than the giving of luncheons for gendarmes demonstrated the functioning of a lineage group as a distinct unit in Tell Ṭoqaan. None of the lineages which held land or tenures held or worked them in common; but the men of junior households in the Tell Haanii lineage worked for their fathers or uncles who did hold tenures. The women of the large lineages worked together rather than with other women in the village.

It was obvious that the lineage head was free to pass judgment on the activities and projects of a junior member. One lineage head, an urban landlord, spent a dinner hour calling his first cousin, a peasant farmer, to task for various reasons. Another advised his cousin, a mason, on how he should build his house and apparently convinced him that he should change his plans and build a flat-roofed room instead of a double-domed room. In each instance the junior member observed some subservience. One account of a murder some 8 years previous indicated that the head of the lineage, who was also the father of the murderer, was responsible for a fifth of the blood price, and the remainder was collected from the rest of the lineage. Had any member refused to contribute his share, I was told, he would have been ostracised from the lineage. Qurḍa reciprocity does not, of course, operate within such a kin group, but sharing is expected. This distinction was several times pointed out to me as the difference in relations between patrilineally related and unrelated households.

Social contacts are more freely and casually maintained among men within a lineage than between men of different lineages. Men enter the compounds and dwelling rooms of their kin <u>on either father</u>'s or mother's side without formality other than

6. Appendix B, Table XIII, Nos. 11-13.

greeting. But a man calls for the person he wants at the gate or courtyard of a family to which he is not related; he does not enter without invitation. If a woman of the household replies, she often extends a kin term to him, calling out, "fuut, ya cammii!" ("Come in, my uncle"). The heads of households and the lineage heads follow more closely, perhaps, than do their juniors, the etiquette which rules that a man should not visit the compound of a man outside his lineage except on business. The propriety and dignity of those family heads who did conform to this rule was pointed out to me in contrast to the reputation of one or two men who did not. It is within his lineage that a man of status and head of a household should find his social life. The only nonkin men who attend a man's reception room regularly are his clients and employees, or the single men in the village who do not have local patrilineal connections.

The leisure time of winter afternoons and evenings are times when the reception rooms of the heads of lineages in Tell Ṭoqaan are gathering places for card games and talk. The heads of families who do not have patrilineal kin in the village apparently "should" remain with their families in the evenings; one man was criticised, for leaving his compound and going around to the reception rooms of the lineage heads, even when his wife and children were visiting kin in another village.

This is enough, perhaps, to suggest that Tell Ṭoqaan is segmented by the local lineage groups as well as divided by economic classes. Some smaller or remnant lineages in Tell Ṭoqaan have histories of more affluent days. Bayt Hawraanii and Bayt Darwiish, which are both now reduced in size and economic status, formerly shared as partners in farming or as foremen to landlords a peasant status in the exploitation of Tell Ṭoqaan lands. Both Bayt Hammuud and Bayt Mabruuk have also been reduced and most of their members now work on wage contracts for the landlords. It seems likely, then, that the old social and economic order of Tell Ṭoqaan was based much more extensively on segmentation into a group of lineages than it is at present, and that the acquisition of property and farming machinery by a few landholders, and the reduction of tenures to laborers' contracts finds Tell Ṭoqaan divided between class and lineage organization. Very few matters of decision concerning the whole village, in farming or relations with the state, appear to remain in the control of the men of the village and the powerful lineages.

Marriage

Patterns.—Peasants or peoples of diverse ethnic origin comprise about one-third of the village population, tribal peoples two-thirds. There is opportunity for intermarriage among them. But lineage endogamy and particularly the preference for marriage to a parallel patrilineal cousin are important features of the Muslim Arab marriage. It would be expected that, in spite of proximity, the effect of these marriage and kinship customs would be to maintain distinctions between tribal, peasant, and ethnic groups and at the same time support lineage and family structure, (Patai, 1952, 1955:361; Barth, 1954: 164-71). From the material available on marriages in Tell Ṭoqaan it is possible to suggest in quantitative terms whether or not there is a significant amount of intermarriage crossing the lineage and tribal boundaries set by the culture.

From the genealogical charts of families dwelling in the village in the period from January to June, 1954, 122 "marriage sets" (one male and one female recognized as spouses) were collected and listed with data describing them in several respects. The 122 marriages cover nearly the whole history of Tell Ṭoqaan and include marriages in families which have been there since its founding as well as very recent arrivals. In most cases it was possible to state whether the marriage took place before or after the residence of one member was established in Tell Ṭoqaan. Three other kinds of information have less complete coverage: presence or absence of kinship endogamy, village endogamy or exogamy, and ethnic (including tribal) affiliation of each member of a marriage set.

Kinship endogamy.—When it was said that a tribally affiliated individual had married a "bint ^{c}amm" or "?ibn ^{c}amm," this did not necessarily mean a genealogically defined parallel patrilineal cousin, for the terms were sometimes used by peasants when the exact genealogical connection was unknown. It meant, primarily, that the spouse was from the same tribe and tribal section. The category "kin by reputation" in Table VIII, therefore, includes all marriages which were ascribed to this kind of "cousin," but which could not be verified from the family charts as a lineage cousin.

It appeared that the villagers were more concerned with distinguishing genealogical cousins in giving peasant lineages than when discussing tribal families. That is, the "?ibn ^{c}amm" referred to by a peasant was much more likely to be a patrilineal parallel cousin from his patrilineage than an "?ibn ^{c}amm" referred to by a tribally affiliated villager. This must be regarded more as an impression than as a generalization, owing to time and linguistic difficulties in the field. In any event there appear to be two dimensions or culture traits of "cousin kinship," one of which, associated with peasant lineages, is more concerned with exact genealogical position as a criterion than the other.

TABLE VIII

KINSHIP AND SOCIOCULTURAL SEGMENT ENDOGAMY AND EXOGAMY IN 73 MARRIAGES

Kind of Marriage by Segment	Number of Marriages						
	Kin					Nonkin	Total
	Kin by Repu-tation	Cousin					
		Father's Kin			Mother's Kin		
		FBD	FSiD*	FFBSoD			
t x t	12	4	0	0	1	0	17
T x T	0	0	0	0	0	11	11
p x p	22	2	1	1	0	6	12
Out of segment	0	0	0	0	0	21	21
One spouse unknown †	0	0	0	0	0	12	12
Total	14	6	1	1	1	50	73

*Marriage II in the Bayt Tell Haanii lineage (see Fig. 5).

†Precise sociocultural category of one spouse in the marriage set is unknown, except that he or she is not considered to be kin.

The following symbols are used to indicate kind of marriage:

t x t: marriage between members of the same tribe.

T x T: marriage between members of different tribes.

p x p: marriage between two peasants, nontribal, without ethnic identification.

Out of segment: "Segment" refers to any sociocultural category and includes peasant, tribesman, and the ethnic categories of Turk, Kurd, Circassian, Alowite.

The data on 73 marriages for which there is information on kinship endogamy or exogamy are summarized above(Table VIII). Of these, a third are endogamous within the Tell Ṭoqaan definitions of kinship. Kinship endogamy can thus be considered one of the marriage patterns, if not the prevailing one, in the Tell Ṭoqaan population. Peasants and tribal people are about equal in the proportion of marriage which is with kin. Marriages of the Nuuri lineage are included in Tables VIII and IX.

Village endogamy and exogamy.—In Table IX two kinds of information are combined. For 54 marriages the sociocultural affiliation of each spouse has been entered together with information on whether the marriage is village endogamous or exogamous. Twenty-nine, or 53.7 per cent, of these marriages, represent marriages between two members of the same tribe or between two peasants (t x t, p x p); 25, or 48.1 per cent, represent marriages across subdivisions of the community. But the distribution of the second group suggests that local circumstances of ethnic diversity in a small population necessitates such marriages. This is in contrast to the opinion of the old woman that Hadiidiin should marry Hadiidiin and Mawali marry Mawali. A comment that came closer to the actual situation was, "The son of a laborer takes the daughter of a laborer, and the son of a shayx takes the daughter of a shayx."

In the village, marriages of local men to Alowite women were explained on the basis of the bride price. Alowite women cost only four or five hundred pounds compared to the prices of one thousand pounds or more demanded for pastoralist or peasant girls in the local area.

The Circassian (C) category, like the Alowite (A), is a more distinct sociocultural subdivision than either Kurd (K) or Turk (Tu). Both the former are distinguished by linguistic or religious differences from pastoralists and peasants. But the Kurds and Turks in Tell Ṭoqaan could be classed as peasants except for the fact that the ethnic difference is locally remembered. The data in Table IX show that no cross-tribal marriages occur within the village, although fourteen tribes are represented by individuals in Tell Ṭoqaan (see p. 27). On the basis of these totals in Tables VIII and IX, it may be said that both kinship endogamy in a broad sense and sociocultural subdivision endogamy are distinct marriage patterns in Tell Ṭoqaan.

The totals in Table IX (28 village-endogamous and 26 village-exogamous marriages) appear to suggest that there is not a strong preference for either pattern in Tell Ṭoqaan. If the different sociocultural categories involved, however, are considered separately, a definite preference for village endogamy is apparent.

TABLE IX

KIND OF MARRIAGE BY SOCIOCULTURAL SEGMENT AND VILLAGE ENDOGAMY OR EXOGAMY IN 54 MARRIAGES

Kind of Marriage by Segment	Number of Village Marriages		Total
	Endogamous	Exogamous	
t x t	8	9	17
p x p	8	4	12
T x T	0	8	8
p x t	2	0	2
t x p	6	0	6
K x A	0	1	1
p x C	1	0	1
t x A	0	1	1
t x K	0	1	1
Tu x T	1	1	2
K x p	1	0	1
Tu x p	0	1	1
C x T	1	0	1
Total	28	26	54

The following symbols are used to indicate kind of marriage:

___ x ___: represents a marriage, male x female.
t : tribal affiliation; t x t: marriage between two members of the same tribe.
T : different tribes; T x T: marriage between members of different tribes.
p : peasant, nontribal without ethnic identification.
K : Kurd
A : Alowite
C : Circassian
Tu : Turk

Eight out of 12 peasant males have married in the village. Only 14 of 31 marriages of tribal men are village endogamous, but 9 of the village-exogamous marriages of tribal men are tribally endogamous. The ethnic-segment males also exhibit the tendency for village endogamy in 3 out of 6 marriages. . Hence, it may be concluded that the peasant group does show a definite pattern of village endogamy. This pattern is also present in the tribal group but is reduced by the tendency for tribal endogamy. Thus, although endogamy in kinship, sociocultural segment, and village are present as marriage patterns of the tribal and peasant residents of Tell Ṭoqaan, they are obscured somewhat by the conflicting units themselves. The ethnic units, presumably because of their small size, show only some tendency to village endogamy. Thus traditional customs of preference for a spouse from one's own smaller social group within a larger one tend to outweigh simple proximity in Tell Ṭoqaan, but it is not at first apparent because of the diversity of this small population.

Residence.—Patrilocal residence in extended family units is considered to be the rule among Near Eastern families (Patai, 1952: 8). There are 14 such families in Tell Ṭoqaan, including 5 immigrant families. Only two men of the old families of Tell Ṭoqaan established separate residences while their fathers were still alive.

Thirty-one of the present 56 families in Tell Ṭoqaan immigrated to the village. Neolocal residence is twice as common among these families as it is among the older residents. Of these, Bayt Abu Umar represents the settling of a peasant from the Latakia area who had previously come to Tell Toqaan for several years as a harvest worker. Another man from Howaarii married a daughter of a Tell Ṭoqaan lineage head and took her to his village. Three years later he returned and built a house near his father-in-law. The explanation was that there was no work in Howaarii. Even among the older immigrants to Tell Ṭoqaan there were some men who came to the village to work and who married women of Tell Ṭoqaan families. On the other hand, a few men who settled in Tell Ṭoqaan have sought wives for themselves and their sons from their villages of origin or have brought them from other villages. The five local Bu Layl families of the village are of recent settlement and are said to have followed their tribal shayx and employer, Hajj Mustafa Shwatiyya, when he moved the tribal headquarters from Jazraaya to Tell Ṭoqaan about 1944. These Bu Layl families, moreover, have come from different villages of the Bu Layl enclave and do not represent one section of the tribe. One may conclude, from these examples, that the traditional rules of residence have broken down under the impact of increased mobility.

The traditional pattern of splitting up an extended household and its property or tenure rights, into as many units as there are sons, has less chance to be observed in a community whose members are mostly landless and tenureless laborers than in a village the lands of which are farmed wholly under peasant freehold or stable tenures. It may be pointed out, however, that, although many men and families have settled in Tell Ṭoqaan in the present adult generation and these appear to be cases of neolocal residence, in each case when the children of these immigrants have married their residence has conformed to the patrilocal rule.

Tribe: the Bu Layl and Shayx Nuuri.--In Tell Ṭoqaan the terms ᶜashiirii and faxuḍ are used to describe "tribe" and "section of a tribe," respectively. It was also said that ᶜashiirii can be applied to a large lineage group like that of Bayt Tell Haanii or to even the larger ones that are to be found in the village of Saraaqab. To emphasize the solidarity of the patrilineal group my informant equated the terms ᶜamm (patrilineal kin) and ᶜashiirii, and in other contexts it was pointed out that in a one-ᶜashiirii village all the residents consider each other as ?ibn ᶜamm (patrilineal cousin), regardless of the exact genealogical connection.

The Bu Layl constitute the only organized tribal group in Tell Ṭoqaan. Numerous individuals in the village were identified as members of other tribes (Hadiidiin, Mawali, Bu Harb, and so on), but in Tell Ṭoqaan, outside of their families, there is little apparent solidarity between the two or three households of men of the same tribe. When Mawali and Hadiidiin meet in the same room during a discussion of tribes, they may refer jokingly to the fact that they are supposed to be enemies. But as soon as the point is made it is dropped as no longer significant in their daily interactions.—they are now all Tell Ṭoqaaniis, whether of pastoralist or peasant background. There is peace now, it was said, and people of one tribe marry into another, ordinary man and shayx alike.

The history of the Bu Layl has been treated briefly (Chap. V) and a little can be added here to the information given by Von Oppenheim (1939: 322-23). Most of the Bu Layl appear now to be sedentarized and are said to occupy wholly the villages of Tell Aaluush, Zammaar, Osmaniyya, Jazraaya, and Ras l Ain, and, in part, Tell Ṭoqaan. The paramount shayx of the tribe,

Nuuri Shwatiyya, succeeded his father, Hajj Mustafa Shwatiyya, about 1951, on the death of the latter. Shayx Nuuri is at once Shayx of the tribe and of one section or faxuḍ, the Fawadla.

Table X lists the villages, sections, shayxs, and number of men attributed to the Bu Layl according to my informants in 1954.

TABLE X

THE AGHAYDAAT-BU LAYL

Village	Section	Shayx	No. of men
Tell Ṭoqaan	mixed	Nuuri Shwatiyya	. . .
Osmaniyya	Hallahil	Nuuri Dalbash	200
	^{c}abaḍii	Hamaadii	. . .
Jazraaya	Fawadla	Nuuri Shwatiyya	300
	Bu ^{c}ajiil	Husayn Hajj Diyaah	150
Zammaar	Udrayfaat	AHmad Hajj Slaymaan	300
Ras l Ain	Harramshii	MHammad Arbayya	200
Tell Aaluush (?)	Bu Layl	MHammad Abayḍ	170

In Tell Ṭoqaan the Harramshii are reckoned a separate tribe and are counted as followers or clients of Shayx Nuuri. Most of them are tent dwellers at Ras l Ain and move east with the sheep in spring. A few families camp at Tell Toqaan. The ^{c}abaḍii at Osmaniyya are also apparently a separate client group or lineage and are the same group cited by Von Oppenheim (1939: 323) as the Al Bu Ṭaamer. The "Al Bu Djemaa^{c}a" section given by Von Oppenheim (1939: 323) I cannot identify. Shayx MaHmuud's history also adds a number of nomadic "followers" from the Bu Seraya and Al Balahiish tribes and locates them at Tell Ṭoqaan and Ras l Ain.

Shayx Nuuri maintains his headquarters at Tell Ṭoqaan. Shayx MaHmuud's history contains a number of passages on Shayx Nuuri and his predecessors of which the following is typical:

> If generosity dies, he revives it; if benevolence lacks, he creates it. I have never seen such a generous man, neither before nor after. His yearly expenditure on guests amounts to a hundred thousand pounds. He has built a modern-styled guesthouse, with a sitting room, a reception room, and a drawing room (I, 103).

Generosity, wise advice and judgment, uniting the sections, and protecting his people are the virtues and work of a tribal shayx, according to Shayx MaHmuud's history.

Shayx Nuuri's household in Tell Ṭoqaan includes his three wives and their children (in all, thirteen), his two half sisters, and the four young children of his deceased brother, Faysal. In attendance at all times are ^{c}ali Sa^{c}iid, the slave," his foreman and family, several "servant" families, and his clients and day laborers. Guests and visiting kinsmen are always present. Shayx MaHmuud's phrases do not seem exaggerated for the village scene.

The two elder wives of Shayx Nuuri are his cousins from his patrilineage and, the third is a daughter of Nawwaf es-Salah, paramount shayx of the Hadiidiin tribe and one of the powerful men among the tribes in Syria. Other marriages in the Shayx's lineage are instructive of other political ties. Nuuri's brother Mahya is also married to a daughter of Nawwaf; one sister is married to the son of the shayx of the Al Bu Shabadiin section of the Hadiidiin in Tell Qelbii; another sister is married to the son of the shayx of the Bu Sha^{c}baan l Waldah at Kuusaniyya. Two of Nuuri's many daughters have married the sons of section shayxs of the Bu Layl. Although the Bu Layl are counted as allies of the Mawali, the marriages above are links to tribes formerly at war with the Mawali.

The influence of Nuuri in the village may be gathered from two other aspects, the proportion of the laborers of Tell Ṭoqaan who work for him and the nature and extent of contact between the members of his household and the villagers in daily life. Seventeen households and half a dozen other individuals find their employment under Nuuri. Thirteen households are distributed among the urban landlords or their partners. The second group is further segmented among the different landholders and are not under a single organization. Nevertheless, the factioning of the village tends to draw the latter group together. They "belong to" the urban landlord group; the others "belong to" Nuuri.

In many aspects of daily life the Bayt Nuuri influence is found in the village. Nuuri's half sisters are young girls who move freely in the village and work with the girls of their age groups. All his children play and grow up with the village children. His daughters and second son attend Shayx MaHmuud's school. His second wife often appears in a dependent household to supervise work done there; or she comes to manage and direct a wedding and dress the bride, because the family are Nuuri servants and the groom is a Nuuri employee. His sister is the belle of the burghul-grinding bee, a winter evening's entertainment for many villagers. His eldest son, Husayn, returns often to the village from school in Aleppo, changes his city clothes for the gown and coat and headcloth of a pastoralist, and joins the young men of his own age. He may even be called upon to perform a shayx's duties in the absence of his father and to settle a dispute. In the jiil, "generation" relationship of "special friends" who were born in the same year, Shayx Nuuri and his household are joined with villagers.

However regular and frequent the contact between the Nuuris and the villagers, the difference in rank is never forgotten. His children are allowed to win the games and praise, are served tea first, and are never reprimanded. But on their side, they do not forget either and are courteous, well-mannered, and use the terms of respect in addressing adults. Between the adults the difference is more marked and the line of authority is clear. When a Nuuri enters a dwelling everyone rises; and when a Nuuri commands, it is done. When a Nuuri sees something he or she wants, it is given or taken—a lemon, a toy, a pack of cards, and, during the war, land.

The character of these social relationships between Shayx Nuuri's family and his household and the villagers seems feudal in the sense of the lord of the manor. The Nuuris are the local aristocracy. But, although some aspects of local justice are under Shayx Nuuri's jurisdiction (see p. 193) and the social relationships described above indicate the status of his family within the village, military or police control of the area rests with the state, and economic relations follow a pattern of class division in which the Nuuris are members of the landlord class and act in apparent mutual agreement and regular contact with the urban landlords.

Kinship Terms and Usage

Kinship terms collected in Tell Ṭoqaan are shown in Table XI, where they are grouped under the kind of informant because of vocabulary or dialect differences.

As it may be seen from these data, Arabic terminology for consanguineal kin is based on 12 elementary terms, or it may also be said that these are 6 pairs of terms which distinguish the sex of denoted kin. They designate the closest male and female kin of four generations, including Ego's: grandparent's, parent's, Ego's own, and Ego's children's generation, and on the parent generation, the father's patrilineal and mother's patrilineal lines are distinguished by the paternal uncle/aunt and the maternal uncle/aunt terms. But on the grandparents' generation this distinction is not made. From the twelve all other consanguineal kin may be designated by combination of the appropriate elementary terms into the required descriptive appellation term. Any relative as far as kinship is recognized may thus be described precisely by Ego and the system can extend indefinitely. Seniority of siblings is not distinguished and mother's kin are separated from her generation only.

The twelve elementary terms for consanguineal kin are as follows:

1. jiddii: my grandfather
2. jiddatii: my grandmother[7]
3. ?abii: my father
4. ?ummii: my mother
5. ?axii: my brother
6. ?uxtii: my sister
7. ?ibnii: my son
8. bintii: my daughter
9. ^{c}ammii: my paternal uncle
10. ^{c}ammtii: my paternal aunt
11. xaalii: my maternal uncle
12. xaaltii: my maternal aunt

Some of these terms, or the descriptive ones made from them for other relatives, have synonyms which are in more common usage than either the elementary or descriptive term. For example, sittii, "my lady," was used by peasants to designate "my grandmother" rather than jiddatii, which was cited, and the tribesmen preferred Habaabtii. There are also several terms of collective reference by which a group of kin may be designated; in these, distinctions are also made between father's and mother's patrilineages (Table XI, Nos. 1, 19, 35, 46, 49-50).

According to my village informants, jiddii, "grandfather," is properly extended in address to all brothers of either grandfather, but the paternal grandfather's sisters should be addressed by the father's sister term, ^{c}ammtii. However, sittii, "grandmother," is extended to the grandmother's sisters on the mother's side. Courtesy and respect for the person addressed by these terms was the explanation given. Such extension has the effect of a classificatory system which draws kinsmen closer together rather than dispersing them by distinguishing their distance.

7. Cited by the villagers but not used; sittii is the usual term.

The Hadiidiin term (No. 52), chantii, "son's wife," is evidently the same as kinntii/kunntii reported by Davies in his list of Palestinian and Syrian terms and shows the pastoralist dialect ch replacing the Kaf (Davies, 1949: 246, 248). The several differences between Mawali, Hadiidiin, and village terms shows a preference by the tribal informants for Hurumtii, "my wife," for the villagers' martii. The former may be considered a more "conservative" term among a people who avoid referring to the wife (Davies, 1949: 252).

I did not hear reciprocals used at all among the Tell Ṭoqaan adults and their children, but Hamuudii, the Mawali informant, gave two, ya ᶜammii Hamuudii, "Oh uncle Hamuudii," by which he would address his brother's children, and ya xaalii Hamuudii, "Oh uncle Hamuudii," for his sister's children. These usages are similar to that which was employed by a gendarme in addressing his young son as "ya baba," "Oh Father," or "Daddy." Davies (1949: 251) also reports such usages between aunts or uncles and their nieces and nephews.

In the Hadiidiin list Nos. 37, 38, and 39 are placed in parentheses to indicate that these were collected in the course of conversation about the members of the informant's family. They are descriptive of the actual situation of a marriage of parallel patrilineal cousins and the informant is referring to his own daughter. Other terms in this list were obtained from a comparative discussion of kin terms among villagers and a Hadiidiin and a Mawali tribesman.

In Table XI the prefixed ya, "oh," indicates specifically a term of address. There is no distinction made in Arabic between male and female speaking. The pronomial suffix, –ii, "my" has been retained in all terms (the term sitt, for example, means "lady," but as sittii, means "my grandmother").

Kinship terms for reference and address.—An individual in the Tell Ṭoqaan area, may be identified in two ways, by the village of residence and by kinship, usually tribal affiliation. The context of the conversation usually decides which shall be used. But conflict between the two principles was well illustrated on one occasion when a Bu Shaᶜbaan woman, living in Tell Toqaan visited in the Bu Shaᶜbaan village Kusaniyya. She was asked where she came from and she replied, "From Tell Ṭoqaan." She described her dilemma to her family on her return. "I am Bu Shaᶜbaanii, but I said, 'From Tell Ṭoqaan.' I didn't know what I should say (ma ᶜarift shuu laazim)." On this occasion she had identified herself as of her husband's village rather than of her own, Saraaqab, though in Tell Ṭoqaan, as other women in her

TABLE XI

KINSHIP TERMS

Term	Peasant (Village)	Hadiidiin (Pastoralist)	Mawali (Pastoralist)
1. Paternal kin	bayt ^{c}ammii; ^{c}amaamii		
2. Father	?abii; ya ?ab; ya baba	?abuyyii	?ab; ?abuuii; ya yuuba
3. Father's brother	^{c}ammii; jiddii	^{c}ammii	^{c}ammii
4. FB's wife	mart ^{c}ammii	mart ^{c}ammii	
5. FB's son	?ibn ^{c}ammii	?ibn ^{c}ammii	walid ^{c}ammii
6. FB's daughter	bint ^{c}ammii	bint ^{c}ammii	bint ^{c}ammii
7. Father's sister	^{c}ammtii	^{c}ammtii	^{c}ammtii
8. FSi's husband	jawz ^{c}ammtii		
9. FSi's son	?ibn ^{c}ammtii	walid ^{c}ammtii	walid ^{c}ammtii
10. FSi's daughter	bint ^{c}ammtii		bint ^{c}ammtii
11. Father's father	jiddii	jiddii	jiddii
12. FF's wife	sittii; jiddatii	mart jiddii; Habaabtii	Habaabtii
13. FF's brother	jiddii		jiddii
14. FF's brother's wife			Habaabtii
15. FF's sister	^{c}ammtii		^{c}ammtii
16. Father's father's F	?abu jiddii		
17. FB's son's son	?ibn ?ibn ^{c}ammii	walid ibn ^{c}ammii	walid walid ^{c}ammii
18. FB's son's daughter	bint ?ibn ^{c}ammii	bint ?ibn ^{c}ammii	bint walid ^{c}ammii
19. Maternal kin	bayt xaalii; xwaal; xaalaat		

TABLE XI (Cont'd)

Term	Peasant (Village)	Hadiidiin (Pastoralist)	Mawali (Pastoralist)
20. Mother	?ummii; ya yawm	?ummwii	?umm; ya yumma
21. M's brother	xaalii	xaalii	xaalii; jiddii
22. MB's wife	mart xaalii		
23. MB's son	?ibn xaalii	?ibn xaalii	walid xaalii
24. MB's daughter	bint xaalii	bint xaalii	bint xaalii
25. MB's daughter's husband		jawwaz bint xaalii	
26. M's sister	xaaltii	xaaltii	xaaltii; ya xaala
27. M's sister's son	?ibn xaaltii	?ibn xaaltii	
28. M's sister's daughter	bint xaaltii	bint xaaltii	
29. M's father	jiddii	jiddii	jiddii
30. MF's brother	jiddii	jiddii	jiddii
31. M's mother	sittii	mart jiddii	sittii; ᶜammtii
32. MM's sister	sittii		
33. Brother	?axii; ?axuuyii	?axuwii	?axii; ya ?xayyuu
34. B's wife		mart ?axuuya	Hurmit ?axuwii
35. B's children	?axuutii	?ulaad ?axuwii	ya ᶜammii Hmuudii; ya jiddii
36. B's son	ibn ?axuwii	?ibn ?axuwii; wald ?axuuyii	wald?axuwii
37. B's son's wife		(bintii)	Hurmit wald ?axuwii
38. B's son's son		(walid bintii)	
39. B's son's daughter		(bint bintii)	

TABLE XI (Cont'd)

Term	Peasant (Village)	Hadiidiin (Pastoralist)	Mawali (Pastoralist)
40. B's daughter	bint ?axuwii		bint ?axuwii
41. B's daughter's husband			rajil bint ?axuwii
42. B's daughter's son	?ibn bint ?axuwii		
43. B's daughter's daughter	bint bint ?axuwii		
44. Sister	?uxtii		?uxtii
45. Sister's husband	jawz ?uxtii	nasiibii	rajil ?uxtii
46. Sister's children	xawaatii	?ulaad ?uxtii	
47. Sister's son	?ibn ?uxtii	?ibn ?uxtii; walid ?uxtii	walid ?uxtii; ya xaalii Hmuudii
48. Sister's daughter	bint ?uxtii	bint ?uxtii	bint ?uxtii; ya xaalii Hmuudii
49. Sister's male descendants	Hafiid ?uxtii		
50. Female descendants of sister	Hafiidit ?uxtii		
51. Son	?ibnii	?ibnii	?ulidii; ?ibnii
52. Son's wife		chantii	Hurmit ?ulidii
53. Son's son			wald ?ulidii
54. Son's daughter			bint ?ulidii
55. Daughter	bintii	bintii	
56. D's husband	jawz bintii	?ibn ?axuuyii; wald ?axuuyii	rajil bintii; ya rajlii
57. D's son		walid bintii	wald bintii
58. D's son's wife			Hurmit walid bintii

TABLE XI (Cont'd)

Terms	Peasant (Village)	Hadiidiin (Pastoralist)	Mawali (Pastoralist)
59. Wife	martii	ya Hurma	martii; ya Hurumtii
60. Wife's F		^{c}ammii	^{c}ammii
61. Wife's M		^{c}ammtii	ya ^{c}amma
62. Wife's B		nasiibii	nasiibii
63. Wife's kin	nisbaatii	^{c}amaamii	^{c}amaamii
64. Husband	jawzii		
65. Husband's B			Hamay

position did, she repeatedly pointed out that she was not a Tell Ṭoqaanii.

Within Tell Ṭoqaan itself individuals are identified by economic status or by kinship affiliation. Young men and men without lineage or other patrilineal kin in the village (except for their immediate families) are identified, for example, as, "Hakmat is a farmhand; he works for the muxtaar," or "MHarrak is head of a household; he has sheep." But when there is a kin-group affiliation a man is identified, for example, as "the son of Xaliil, head of the household, and he belongs to Bayt Tell Haanii (lineage)," instead of by his occupation, storekeeper.

Family and lineage are the means of identifying individuals more often than tribe, with the exception of the Bu Layl. Women are always identified or identify themselves as belonging to such and such a house, and are not designated by economic position. After these categories follow the socioeconomic and ethnic ones, "Hakmiyya is ^{c}araab (of pastoral background)," or "Amiin is Circassian from Xan Aasser."

The extension of kin terms of address to nonkin is an occasional usage which promoted friendly relations. The older men occasionally address other men as their patrilineal cousins, ya ?ibn ^{c}ammii. Once the term used was, ya ?ibn ^{c}ammtii (son of my paternal aunt). One young woman talking the village with a youth of her own age addressed him as ya ^{c}ammii ("Oh my uncle ") although they were not related. Occasionally guests who were not kinsmen to the speaker were addressed by the kin terms describing their relation to their host; men to whom one petitioned for advice were called, "ya ^{c}ammii" (Oh my uncle).

In ordinary conversation in which there is no shade of special pleading or etiquette for which a kin term might be found useful, adults frequently address each other by teknonymous names: Abu Adnaan, "father of Adnaan," or "Umm Mustafa," "mother of Mustafa." More respect is indicated by these terms than by the use of the personal name. The personal name is general between friends or from superior to inferior.

Village Organization

There is little in the everyday life of the people which formally organizes Tell Ṭoqaan on the village level—there is little of what may be called village government aside from the control exerted by the landlords.

The agricultural system which once may have been a major concern of the local peasant farmers, the "elders," in planting the divisions of land, in harvesting, in guarding the herd, has changed in pattern and come under the active control of the landlords.

A village custom called locally ^{c}aadat ^{c}araab, "Arab custom," whereby in time of need or according to the opinion of the "men" of the village a needy person was given support, or a young man was told he should find a wife and the older men would unite to put up the bride price, was discussed at some length. An attempt was made to bring it into play to insure the support and upbringing of a newborn child whose mother died. But it failed and father and children left the village. There were no cases remembered in which the custom had been used effectively in Tell Ṭoqaan.

Even the school cannot be called a village institution; its inception began in one household and the enterprise of Shayx MaHmuud enlarged it to include the children of a number of households. This caused some resentment in his original employer who had brought the Shayx to educate his sons, as he said, and not half the village. And even with the enlargement, the Shayx's school was not wholly acceptable to those men in the village who were of a different school of Muslim law from his, or who, in fact, were not on good terms with the teacher and used this difference as argument against his school.

Only the choice of village herdsman and of muxtaar and the village responsibility for the telephone line were matters which called the "elders" together for decisions and action. Other occasions which united the village—the funeral, the hyena hunt, the wedding dance—are of a different order of events. All else was subject to the landlords.

Bias from the ethnographer's position as a woman and a foreigner and the brevity of the field session may well distort the account at this point, but I feel reasonably certain that it does not. There is the general evidence that the landlords and, especially Shayx Nuuri, controlled the village as they saw fit; there is the express public statement made by the muxtaar to the gendarmes that the village did not have a watchman or village guard because Nuuri and the landlords did not want one. And there was a footnote to the history of the village given by my chief informant, a peasant farmer, to the effect that before the office of muxtaar was introduced, the village was controlled by his uncle who succeeded his grandfather, the founder, as head of Ṣalaah ad-Diin lineage, and the Ottoman gendarmarie.

The muxtaar holds the only political office in Tell Ṭoqaan. He is described as the "policeman" or mayor of the village. In large villages with dual organization there are two. The muxtaar is chosen annually by and from among those who hold "much land." In Tell Ṭoqaan, I was told, electors are the urban landlords, Shayx Nuuri, the peasant freeholders, the elder peasant tenants, and and the lineage heads. This list does not, in fact, include all the men in Tell Ṭoqaan who are ranked as heads of households, and it was implied in another context that these, too, participated. The choice must be unanimously agreed to and is made each yawm l baydar, "threshing ground day."

The muxtaar's is a paid position and his salary is made up by those who hold or sharecrop land and by the shopkeepers. Under the first muxtaars (three heads of households or lineages who served for 8, 5, and 3 years each) reimbursement was in wheat. The contribution varied from a kayl to half a kayl of wheat for each unit measure (marrasii) of land.[8] Where there were partners these paid half and the landlord half. Shopkeepers are now also assessed five pounds each. As a reflection of the extended family, one shopkeeper is assessed double because his son has a shop. The present muxtaar wanted money, not wheat, and his pay was said to be 200 pounds a year. He also collects one pound for each document he stamps with his seal.

---

8. Twenty-seven kilograms, about 60 lbs., is given as the metric measure equivalent for a kayl of wheat in the Aleppo area by Latron (1936: 245).

Nearly every adult man carries, if he cannot read and write, a personal seal, as well as an identity card. This, with settling in a house, according to the Shayx's history, indicates the process of "civilizing" a pastoralist. The muxtaar also carries a seal of office.

The muxtaar is the liaison between the national government of Syria and the village. He must turn over men wanted by the police; he is apparently responsible for seeing that the villagers contribute labor or materials for maintenance of the telephone line. To judge by one occasion, when the village men sit in session with the gendarmes, it is he who speaks for the village in answer to their questions. Any legal papers, such as gun licenses or summonses to court, he stamps with his seals. He goes often on village business to the government offices at Idlib, but the nature of all his duties are not known to me.

Relations with the State

From time to time there were discussions of the different central governments in control of the area and how Tell Ṭoqaan was affected by them. It was said that under the Ottomans the central government was weak and many villages near Tell Ṭoqaan and to the south and west paid the xuwa, "tribute," to the amirs and leaders of the Mawali. But the villages to the north and east (Bu Layl, Hadiidiin, and Hadiidiin allies) did not pay to the Mawali. Tell Ṭoqaan never paid the xuwa because the founder of the village became on good terms with the amirs; he had once arranged for the release from prison of a son of the Mawali amir. The nearby village of Islamiin paid the tribute to Amir Fayad ?ibn Genij, Kfer Amiin paid first to two brothers and ?ibn ^{c}amm (patrilineal cousins) of Amir Shayyish and later to two other brothers and cousins of this amir. Shayx Idriis paid to Amir Shayyish, present chief of all Mawali; Ma^{c}aaret Saraan to Amir Abdul Rezzak; and Maar Dibsii to Amir Turki.

Another form of tribute was described, the surrat. It was said, when an amir came to a village which did not or had not paid the xuwa, he demanded the surrat. From each man in the village a contribution was dropped into a covered container, no one "knew" how much. It was taken to the amir. If he were satisfied when he looked at it he said, "Hajj," "Enough"; if not "Yalla!", "Go! " and more had to be produced.

But under the French mandate and the Syrian government, it was said, no tribute was collected by the tribes from the villages.

At the present time the villagers are well aware of their status as citizens of a national state; they are Suriyyiin, "Syrians," as well as fallaaHiin (peasants), ^{c}araab (Arabs, i.e., nomadic pastoralists), and Mislimiin, "Muslims." They hear and listen regularly to news of national affairs on the several radios in the village, although only rarely is a newspaper seen and read aloud to others. A flood in the Ghaab marsh which drove many people away from their villages, a trade agreement between Syria and America, the announcement of several American students living in Syrian villages, the fall of the Shishekly regime were among the events they heard, discussed, and reported to me. Children in one of their games which uses terms of the Ottoman state structure, Sultan and Vizir (waziir), substituted the personal names of Syrian political leaders. Shayx MaHmuud, who gave occasional evidence of strong nationalist feelings, taught the school children the Syrian oath of allegiance and proper elocutionary manner of reciting it.

Contact with the state structure is maintained chiefly through the weekly visits to the village by a contingent of gendarmes from the Tell Suultaan post. These state police, always uniformed and armed and mounted on well-kept horses, appear regularly. Often, when a number of transactions are involved, they hold their meeting at Shayx Nuuri's.

The villagers are careful to maintain good relations with the gendarmes, and a slight must be rectified by a luncheon. The rule of reception appears to be that the first man, (i.e., first head of a household or lineage) who meets or sees the gendarmes arriving must invite them into his reception room for coffee, provide a place for them to do their business with the villagers, bring the muxtaar, and send a son or client for anyone they wish to see.

Upon one occasion the leader of the post came to one peasant's compound, although it was later insisted that one of the other lineage heads had seen him first. He was not served tea and the social situation was patently awkward. Immediately after his departure, there was an argument and anxiety was expressed. The solution of a luncheon was planned. Three days later amenities were restored by a formal luncheon at the peasant's, which received due praise from the gendarme officer.

The personnel of the state gendarmarie and army appears to be drawn from the general settled population by draft. Only one or two youths in Tell Ṭoqaan had served in the army; one returned early in the field session. My host's household was upset for several days when the gendarmes brought a summons for him to appear in Idlib and explain why his son ^{c}Aarif had not reported for military duty with his class. ^{c}Aarif was a boy of about thirteen. It was finally made clear that the son meant was a child of my host's first wife and had died in infancy many years before. To support his word before the government officials in Idlib my host took with him the personal seals of several men in the village as well as his living son ^{c}Aarif.

It was said in the village that under the French the gendarmes at the state posts were Christians or some non-Muslim group, but that under the Syrian government the small garrisons were mixed. One young man at the Tell Suultaan post was a Syrian Orthodox Christian from the village of Mashta Halou in the southern Alowite Mountain area. This village I had visited previous to residence in Tell Ṭoqaan. Since the name of the Halou family translates directly into that of my surname, pseudo-kinship relations were established with that family in the mountain village. These had the effect in Tell Ṭoqaan, on the one hand, of giving me a social link among Syrians and making me less a foreigner, and on the other hand, apparently, of giving the young gendarme a small and unexpected increment of prestige. It was also of advantage to the villagers and the gendarme was henceforth served tea immediately after his superior officer.

Although these accounts are anecdotal, they serve to illustrate the insecurity of relations between village and state and the means seized upon or used to relieve apprehension.

Both state and tribal law are said to function in the Tell Ṭoqaan area. The law of the Syrian state applies to cases which do not involve members of tribes. When a case of theft, injury, or murder involve one nontribal and one tribal person, evidently a choice can be made whether to settle the matter in the state court or by tribal custom. And if a case involves only members of tribes a similar choice can be made.

All cases of theft that came to my attention, however, were prosecuted or pending trail in the state courts and had been so handled by the plaintiff, Shayx Nuuri. One young man spent a few weeks in jail in Aleppo for stealing a chicken from another peasant villager. Theft was an individual act and to my knowledge there were no raids or feuds in the area, either between villages or kin groups. However, an informant indicated that the attitude of the tribesman still held among some people; that is, an individual could at once be a "man," rijaal, and a thief, Haraamiyyii, if he stole from others not of his tribe. But the attitude was also present that successful thieving or raiding from nonkin did not contribute to a man's prestige and, in fact, lowered it.

An informant gave as an example of the choice between state or tribal law an incident which happened during the Mandate Period. He had once shot and wounded a Mawali thief in his uncle's compound, and the man's kin demanded payment of 10 gold pounds for the loss of the man's foot. His uncle, however, went to the government and put the case under state law. Pressure thus went against the Mawali and they came to the uncle crying for mercy and kissing his hand, because the thief had become an evildoer. So everything was cancelled out, finished. The case was dropped by both parties.

Matters which were said still to be decided by tribal law locally are murder, property disputes, and, apparently, adultery and elopement.

Tribal law (qaanuun ᶜashiirii) is concerned with the killing of a man of one tribe by a man of another tribe. The blood price is demanded for murder and the arrangement is made by the shayxs of the two tribes. The price is 100 gold pounds; 20 pounds is paid by the brothers of the murderer and the remainder is collected from the rest of the kin or ᶜashiirii. Any member of the ᶜashiirii who does not contribute his share is ostracized. Decision by tribal law in murder cases was preferred to state law, because a convicted murderer is hanged by the state. Thus, in this area, the blood price settlement is preferred to vengence and protracted feuding.

Customary law (qaanuun ᶜaarfii) is concerned with property disputes and adultery or elopements. If the case is only a "small" one it is decided by the local shayx. In Tell Ṭoqaan this is Shayx Nuuri. If it is a more serious case it is taken before the judge or court of the tribes. The present local "judge," a Mawali, lives in Bighass. Before him, Dalbash, shayx of a Bu Layl section in Osmaniyya, was judge.

The linguistic obstacle made it impossible for me to get a clearer idea than this on the status and operation of law in the Tell Ṭoqaan area. But the presence of both systems, manipulated to the best advantage, is apparent. It is also clear that law and legal process does not have a village level of operation or institutional organization other than the muxtaar-gendarme tie with the state and the feudal aspect of Shayx Nuuri as judge of local disputes.

Social Life and Occasions

Games.—Winter affords more leisure time than any other season of the year and it is during this season that the long evenings are spent at card games and story telling. When there is no work because the fields are too wet for plowing, but the day is clear, the young men play kura, "ball," or other active games on the threshing ground. As spring comes on more and more of the social, recreational, and housekeeping activities are taken out of doors. Guests come and go. And for a few days in March masked clowns appear to beg for treats. The children play hopscotch, roll hoops, play running tag games, make miniature plows and reed screens, convert small boxes into buses, automobiles, and garages and generally re-create in play the adult activities that interest them. But as the tempo of economic activities increases in late spring, less play is in evidence and from the beginning of harvest until late autumn every day is "all work."

Twice during the late winter in 1954 an evening was devoted to what might be called burghul-grinding bees. One, at least, was held as a village party of the young people for Shayx Nuuri's eldest son when he visited the village during a vacation period from school in Aleppo. At these occasions the largest grindstones available in the village are set up in the middle of a long dwelling room. The boys and girls gather about them and at one end of the room. A boy and girl sit opposite each other at each stone and a steady tempo of grinding or cracking the wheat is kept up accompanied by singing. General teasing and taunting goes on around the room among the crowd of young people. At the other end of the room the adults and old people observe which girl attracts the most attention and who is talking to whom. The avowed purpose is to do the work of cracking wheat for the kibbii dish as well as to have a good time.

While many games fill the local repertoire, shaddii is the most popular among the adults. This is a card game played with the standard pack familiar to Americans and resembles a combination of bridge and rummy. Two or four play. In a family gathering such as I regularly saw and participated in, the wife of the household played with the men. Once when she won the onlookers said she and the loser must exchange headwear and she take the man's headcloth and he her turban. While the landlords gamble heavily at this game, the villagers do not.

Card tricks and other card games and board games such as dammii, a game similar to checkers were demonstrated; ṣiniyya, a game played with a seal concealed under one of nine coffee cups; and munqallii, a game played with pebbles and fourteen pockets scooped in the earth. Ṣiniyya can be played by two or many and it was said that whole villages might gamble at this game for sheep, rice, and the like.

The younger boys played a forfeit game, makruu^{c}a, in which a match box was flipped and rotation of roles and forfeits in the game depended upon how the box fell. The desired roles are Sultan and Vizir, and players try with a successful toss to take over first the Vizir's and then move on automatically to the Sultan's role when a new player wins the toss. The Vizir holds a belt to punish a losing player. The Sultan has the authority to determine the punishment for losing a toss and permission to try a second toss. When a player loses at a toss Sultan and Vizir exchange a formula: "What do you desire, oh Sultan?" (the Sultan names the punishment which is executed by the Vizir). "What else do you desire, oh Sultan?" (He usually replies, "Enough.")

Besides simple punishments thought up on the spur of the moment, as bring a cup of water or sweep the floor, there are a number of conventional ones. For xubz ("bread") the Vizir mimics the tossing of a sheet of bread dough from hand to hand and then slaps the imaginary disk against the cheek of the victim. Then he hands the imaginary bread to the Sultan and the two pretend to eat. For tibin ("straw,") the victim turns his back to the Vizir, who scrubs it with his fist roughly and then thumps his elbow down and then his fist. For diik hindii ("turkey") the player's wrists are tied together with a headcloth, his feet put through his arms, and a tail made with another headcloth. In this position he must move around the room; a stool is put out and he is invited to sit down several times until it is pulled from under him.

Others are ba^{c}d ("expel,"?), in which the player puffs out his cheeks with a mouthful of air and the Vizir, with a quick jab of his fingers, makes him expel the air noisily. For Hashiish ("grass") the Vizir siezes the victim's hair, pulls it forward, and pretends to cut it off roughly with the edge of his hand. In minshaan hisaan ("for a horse") the Vizir holds the victim's nose while he must hum, then with a quick blow of his other hand strikes his grasp loose so the victim snorts.

A specified number of blows with a belt on the hands or soles of feet may also be ordered by the Sultan, and once a mock prayer had to be performed. But the boys said of the prayer that, "muu laazim," this should not be done. The ba^{c}d, menshaan hisaan, and mock prayer forfeits result in vulgar or improper behavior, and the others are humiliations appropriate to low status.

The team games played on the threshing ground in winter by the young men are kura, ?ajarib, and ta^{c}abii. There does not appear to be any formality in team selection reflecting any factions in the village. Visitors from other villages participate. In kura ("ball") a leather-covered ball is knocked up and down the length of the threshing ground with sticks and mallets. Scoring, if any is kept, was not clear to me; the action resembles field hockey. The game sometimes leads to fights and injuries which bring interference from the elders and muxtaar.

In ?ajarib one team gathers in the center and moves on hands and knees. The other team attacks on foot. The intent seems to be no more than for one man to trip and lay flat a member of the other team, and then the two may change places and stance.

Ta^{c}abii is played with a batting stick and ball, with one team at bat and running, and the other in the field. The pitcher stands close to the batter and merely tosses the ball up so he can hit it. The field of play is long and narrow; when a batter has made a successful hit he runs to the far end of the field beyond the members of the other team. A hit by another teammate brings him back. Sides change when a fly ball is caught. (This game bears some resemblance to cricket but moves more rapidly.) Of all active field games and tag games played by the children, a peasant commented, that these are the things that young men and boys should do when there was no work. It made them strong. They should not stay in the house all day and do nothing.

Masked clowns.—On three occasions early in spring my host's house was visited by youths of the village costumed and masked. Certain women in the village were reported to be frightened by these apparitions, and one of the wives of Shayx Nuuri, who was present during one visit, even confessed to this.

One clown, "Hajuuj Majuuj" was dressed as a misshapen dancing dwarf. A tray balanced horizontally on the head of the carrier made the frame for an enormous head made of a woman's black gown pulled over it and the body of the carrier. A sheepskin cloak, inside out, was belted at the level of his knees for the waist line. A stick through the shoulders made the short arms of the cloak stand out grotesquely on each side at normal waistline level. "Hajuuj Majuuj" danced clumsily for the audience, received a handful of candies, and went on to other houses in the village, followed by the boys present.

Twice the shayyib visited. These wore turbans, false faces, and hunchbacks, and each carried a heavy stick. The masks are made of a rectangle of leather with slits cut for eyes and mouth. Goat-hair moustaches were affixed, and a nose of dough. They answered questions with grunts and head movements, but would not speak. They were teased and threatened with sticks until they danced. They came as a pair, dressed alike, and were said to represent father and son. When they were given oranges they left to visit other houses.

The appearance of the clowns came soon after the first of spring and they visited not only other houses in the village, but those of the landlords. While they were said to alarm some women, they did not appear to be associated with any other purpose than entertainment, and accounts were given later of men from one village setting out to frighten another village by this means as a "practical joke." The men and boys participated in the play, and most of the women seemed to regard it as horseplay.

In enlarging upon the practice of disguises, accounts were given by an informant of boys dressing as girls when there is a celebration with evening dancing. Other men and youths compete for their attention at the dance, but after it is over the masqueraders disappear. On one occasion a poor man was promised a cheap bride by the men of the village, but when the time came for the two to be left alone to consummate the marriage, the man discovered that a local youth had been dressed as a bride. He threw the youth down and fled from the village.

Clothing and Its Social Significance [9]

In northwestern Syria the clothing an individual wears often indicates his or her social status, ethnic affiliation, and locality or even village of residence or birth. The styles of dress seem to have the weight of long tradition and custom and do not appear, at first observation, to be influenced by cyclic changes in fashion. Jouin and De Boucheman, however, have both shown that styles have changed fundamentally both in city and rural areas in recent centuries, as a result of introductions, chiefly from Turkey, and that modes appear and disappear even among the pastoralists. (Jouin, 1935: 481-505; De Boucheman, 1935).

Although a few examples can be found in Tell Ṭoqaan of both style change and fashion, as well as of the breaking down of

9. See figures, after page 256.

customary social identifications associated with clothing, nevertheless, the rather stable sociological distinctions in clothing are more marked there. The first distinction to be made among styles of clothing in this region is that between urban and rural costumes. In the city, both Western and urban Arab dress is found. In Aleppo and Idlib, men are often seen in urban Arab gowns and women in the traditional ground-length black skirts, cloaks, and veils. The Western styles worn by men are more varied than the short black dresses and black veils which city women adopt, and which represent fundamental departure from Arab custom. In rural areas, however, the people have clung to the long gowns and sirwaal (full "Turkish" trousers, of heavy black, brown, or white cotton); neither Western trousers for men nor short skirts for women are worn. Western or European garments for the upper part of the body are widely employed, however, and sweaters, Navy blouses, suit jackets, coats are added for warmth in winter. Knitted cotton undergarments are also used.

Most noticeable is the difference in dress between the people of Tell Ṭoqaan and its area and those of the older peasant villages west of the highway. The long yellow cotton gowns of the pastoralists prevail in the Tell Ṭoqaan area in contrast to the heavy black Turkish trousers of the peasant men to the west. Likewise, the black gown and headdress of the pastoralist women, found south and east of Aleppo, are preferred to the tunic and simply tied headcloth of the peasant women.

This is the first impression of contrast in clothing that strikes one, between the beginning of the Ma^{c}mura and the old sedentary zone to the west. With closer acquaintance the many significant differences in costume detail and their application to the varying categories of socioeconomic status, age, ethnic affiliation, and occupation which cross-cut one another in bewildering fashion, become apparent. Once these cues have been learned, farmhand or household head, peasant or pastoralist, married or unmarried woman, and so on, can usually be identified by their clothing. Moreover, working clothes and "proper" wear are clearly distinguished and so great is the sensitivity on this point that I was asked to emphasize this when showing photographs in America.

Quality of make and of material is also stressed. The price, city of manufacture, and reputation for quality in clothing are closely associated, much in the same fashion that certain tools are said to be better made in one place than another, or that the sheep's-milk butter (saman) produced by one shepherd tribe, the Hadiidiin, is better than that produced by other tribes. Upper- or landlord-class members occasionally remarked that the villagers did not know quality; peasants occasionally said the same of the pastoralists, particularly the Bedouin. For example, the light-weight summer cloak woven of camel wool, a pastoralist's garment worn by men, can be purchased according to city of manufacture, quality, and price in the following order of desirability: the best come from Baghdad and cost seventy to eighty Syrian pounds; the next best, from Damascus and Deir ez-Zor, forty to fifty pounds; then, Aleppo, twenty to twenty-five pounds; and finally, Homs, fifteen to seventeen pounds. Similar rankings were given other articles of clothing of indigenous styles and make included those of "silk" and the different wools. English cotton, however, was regarded as the best cotton cloth.

One depreciatory generalization was made, and this with reference to women's gowns only: some villagers classified pastoralists' clothing as "handmade" and, therefore, as of less prestige than that of machine-sewn city make. Other villagers, however, attached greater prestige to the pastoralist work because of the skill that is involved, particularly in a wool craft.

Among the garments worn in the Tell Ṭoqaan area only men's coats and cloaks and footwear are made for wear in one season only. The sheepskin or lambskin farwii is particularly a winter garment both of peasant and pastoralist and depending on the quality, prices range from ten to fifty Syrian pounds; the best, according to a peasant, are made of matched lambskins from "newborn" or "stillborn" animals that "have not eaten grass," and one may select combinations of brown, black, and white.

In winter footwear is usually worn, socks and wooden clogs or rubber boots. Within the village people usually go barefoot in summer, but often put on red or black peasant slippers or sandals if they have far to walk. Extra undergowns are added for warmth in cold weather, and the number worn is reduced in summer.

In general, women wear only cotton or "silk" (actually rayon). Men's garments, especially the matched gowns and long-skirted, tailored coats of the peasant farmers, are of wool or even of wool suiting which appears to be of European manufacture. Those of the laborers are cotton. In Tell Ṭoqaan both men and women wear the same style yellow, or saffron yellow (when new), long-sleeved outer gown. It is full-cut and has an opening from the collarless neckband nearly to the waist. A deep yoke panel in front and back is sometimes decorated with red-and-black checks printed on the cloth.

The basic and socially significant garments of a man consist of the headcloth and hair ropes. Various materials and styles of headcloths are worn under the ropes. Peasants wear a heavy white or a rust-colored cloth of cotton, with a very short knotted fringe. A man who is head of a house may wear a yellow-and-white plaid one of a cotton and "silk" mixture. A red-and-white checked headcloth with long fringes is associated both with pastoralists and young men. A fine white marquisette headcloth is worn by men "who do not plow," that is, landholders of large estates, shayxs, and city men who exchange their fez for Arab headdress when they visit the village.

A man is rarely seen without hair ropes holding the headcloth in place. If instead he merely wears a folded cloth tied around his head, it may signify he is a recent widower or the subject of some other distress. This is said to be a shepherd custom (De Boucheman, 1935: 17) and it was called pastoralist by the Tell Ṭoqaaniis.

A yellow, white, or black cotton gown is worn by most working men in Tell Ṭoqaan. It is usually belted and when a man is working he may tuck it inside the full Turkish trousers he wears under the gown. But a household head or lineage head wears a long-sleeved gown of light wool suiting or wool and cotton mixture, often pin-striped, which opens on the left from narrow neckband to hem and is rarely belted. Under either style is worn a white, print, or striped gown of light-weight cotton patterned after the shepherd or laborer's gown. Heavy cotton peasant trousers, always black in the Tell Ṭoqaan area, are worn by a few men under their long gowns. Others wear homemade, less full trousers of unbleached muslin. Only two men, a peasant from the west and a farmhand, regularly wore them in the peasant fashion, with shirt and jacket. Over these garments men wear a variety of jackets and coats.

Older men, heads of families, customarily wore a farwii, sheepskin cloak, or a light cloak, both very full capelike garments with short sleeves. The light cloak is of fine wool, with gold braid around the neck opening and down the front edges. It may be of black or brown wool and in very lightest weight is very sheer. A white cloak is occasionally seen on a very wealthy and conservative Arab. Shopkeepers wear European-style suit jackets. Working men, if they do not have a sheepskin cloak, may wear the "crusader jacket" of the pastoralists, a three-quarter-length jacket of dark blue wool trimmed with black braid. But such a jacket generally identifies a pastoralist. A tunic woven of heavy cotton cord in vertical brown-and-white stripes and tightly belted is also a working garment of the pastoralists, and is worn over their outer gown. Many poor men buy the second-hand Western style coats and jackets which are to be found in quantities in the village and city bazaars.

Plowmen's leather boots of indigenous make are worn by some farmhands, but rubber boots are more frequent and better liked. In hot weather the villager's leather slipper may be worn by men and women alike, but shoes of Western style were preferred by heads of households. Most men and women had a pair of Western shoes, which were saved for "good," and many young men wore a brightly polished shoehorn on their belts at all times, probably to signify they had shoes, even if they did not wear them. Women walking from one village to the next usually marched barefoot or in slippers and carried their "good" shoes on the package of belongings balanced on their heads.

A woman's basic garments are headdress, gamp, outer gown, one or two undergowns, and women's trousers. Married women and unmarried girls may generally be distinguished by their headwear. In the Tell Ṭoqaan area the pastoralist headdress prevails for married women. A large square of black cotton is so folded and wrapped around the head that a "peak" somewhat like an overseas cap is made which tilts slightly to the right. Chains of gold coins from the bride price should be attached at the right side, if any of the gold remains. Only one villager in Tell Ṭoqaan was observed to have one small gold coin on her headdress. Bu Layl women, or women attached to the Bu Layl, wound a white or pink chiffon scarf around the headdress. Many married women wore the properly folded headdress only when at leisure and visiting in the village. When they were working, the black cotton square was worn as a kerchief and tied with an additional cloth. Unmarried girls wore a simple square headcloth tied with a folded chiffon, rayon, or print cloth. Two women in Tell Ṭoqaan are from Saraaqab, and the women of Saraaqab and Afeṣs wear a distinctive turban made of a large black "silk" or rayon cloth with bands of red and metallic thread along the borders. Again, chains of gold coin hang down the back from each side, if these remain from the bride price.

Every married woman, peasant or pastoralist, is expected to wear the shambar or "gamp" of black crepe. This is a triangular over-collar that hangs over the breast, with a silver ornament dangling from the tip. In the presence of strange men it is pulled up over the mouth. The gamp hangs down the back in a long tail to the waist.

The women's outer gown, like the men's, is very full and sweeps the ground. It is regularly of black cotton, although a city-bought kind with machine-stitched embroidery is worn by a few girls. The two Saraaqab women wear the hand-embroidered gown originally characteristic of that village. The gown is often turned inside out when working. A leather belt is worn with the plain black pastoralist gown and black belts with white plastic eyelets were much in fashion among both men and women in 1954.

Boys and girls wear the same styles of clothing that their parents do, except for the men's gown and coat of wool suiting. Boys go bareheaded until eight or nine years of age when they begin to wear a headcloth and occasionally hair ropes. Girls' heads are always (and should always) be covered after they are five or six years old.

Infants are closely swaddled soon after birth and appear to be kept in this wrapping until they are six or eight months old. It was said that a swaddled infant should be changed six times a day, twice a night and four times during the day. It was also said that a baby should be bathed in warm water and soap every third day in order to grow up strong. One household at least practiced this.

The urban landlords, members of their families, and guests wore Western-style clothing in the village. But Shayx Nuuri and members of his family wore Arab dress. Upon one occasion visitors passing through the village to the eastern grazing grounds stopped to visit me briefly. The party included the English-speaking Beirut wife of a member of the wealthy landholding family of Saraaqab. She and her young daughter were dressed in the embroidered gowns of Saraaqab women, because, she said, when they were in the country they liked to wear the customary clothing of the common people. Soon after her departure the two Saraaqab women in Tell Ṭoqaan expressed their opinion that she should not have worn the Saraaqab gown and they did not like to see it.

Accessories to men's and women's clothing include the polished shoehorn or nail clippers which dangle from a young man's belt and the household keys and a small "white" jackknife made by the Qirbaat (Gypsies) that the women carry. The small knife in particular is regarded as a woman's tool. Young men, especially those of pastoralist tradition, occasionally wear the curved dagger, xanjar, of the nomads. Two kinds are distinguished. A "real" xanjar, that is, one for war, is supposed to have a magnetized blade, but the one actually found does not and is said to be only good to cut meat.

The women and girls of pastoralist tradition have the right nasal flange and both ear lobes pierced for gold rings. Most peasant women do not wear a nose ring. Women of pastoralist tradition are also extensively tattooed on face, throat, chest, and forearms, and occasionally on the right foot. The tattoos are cosmetic or "love charm" in purpose; therapeutic tattoos are also acquired and are discussed in the next chapter. Peasant women usually wear only the therapeutic tattoos.

Tattooing is done by the Qirbaat (Gypsy) women. A girl begins to acquire the customary designs in early adolescence. The "?ibn ^{c}amm" design ("father's brother's son," the preferred husband) is tattooed on the inner surface of the right forearm. It consists of the triangle with appendages which is found as a design in other contexts—the device hung on the lead ewe in spring, the wall decoration (mrayya) made of dyed wheat and cotton. The girls say of the ?ibn ^{c}amm tattooed design that when a girl sleeps with her head on the design she will dream of her future husband (see Fig. 52).

All women lengthen their two hair braids with dark red or green wool yarn; they may attach their "white" knife and the household keys to the ends of the braids.

Most adult men and some older women smoke hand-rolled cigarettes. Each carries a small metal case for tobacco and papers. To roll a cigarette is a gesture of courtesy, or to pass one's tobacco case to another. The latter is always done for a visitor or guest who has just joined a circle of people. Commercially manufactured cigarettes are kept for the gendarmes or other distinguished guests.

XIV

IDEOLOGY AND RITUAL

BECAUSE LENGTHY DISCUSSIONS of practices and of beliefs, in particular, could not be pressed, most of the information on life-cycle ceremonies, medical beliefs and practices, and religious beliefs and practices that follows is based largely upon observation. During the period from January 4 to May 20 several babies were born, one circumcision was observed, there was one marriage and one funeral. Little, if any celebration or ritual attended these events, except for the wedding and funeral. A number of treatments for the sick were observed. Mosque services were held only three or four times and that soon after I settled in the village. Ramadaan, the Muslin fast month, began at moonrise on May 3, 1954, and there was considerable discussion of fasting during the early days of the month, which ended after I left the village. It was my impression, however, that celebrations and festivals, rituals and practices in Tell Ṭoqaan were much less elaborate than west of the Aleppo-Damascus highway.

My host pointed out that the celebrations like those of past times were no longer held. Now only rich men like Shayx Nuuri could provide the food for a feast to celebrate a son's birth, a circumcision, or the bringing home of a bride. Now everything was done hastily—the bride was brought by taxi and taken quickly into the house and the door shut. There were no longer the procession, the music and dancing, the exhibition riding, the dressing up in fine clothes, and general feasting for the whole village.

Although in part the reduction of local ritualistic practices may be owing to the widening gap in economy between villagers and landholders, it may also be due to emigration or disappearance of peasant families and lineages. Perhaps the increase in proportion to the peasant population, of sedentarized tribal shepherd families with different folkways account for some of it. Lack of ceremony in bringing home a bride, in contrast to the more elaborate peasant village practice, is attributed to the Rwala camel Bedouin (Musil, 1928: 228-29). Nothing is known, however, of shepherd pastoralist customs in this region in this respect.

Life-cycle Ceremonies

Birth and naming.—A woman should have her child in her husband's house. Frequently, she visits her own village and home shortly before the child is expected, but must return to her husband's village before it is born. After the child is born the mother should stay on the bed for seven days, and then, after ten days restriction to the compound she may go into the village. There was no evidence of special midwives. One woman, who was a Saraaqabii, attended the birth of a son to the other Saraaqab woman in the village. Sḥe did not do so on the occasions of other births in the village.

A newborn child is closely swaddled and the head wrapped in white cloth. Kohl is applied around its eyes and the face is covered with a thin cloth, often red chiffon. When a visitor asks to see the child the cloth is removed; the guest must remark, mashallah ("What hath God wrought!"), then praise the child, and lay a gift of money on its forehead. A gold coin is the ideal, a silver pound coin is the practice.

It was said that for the first son, first daughter, and for the next son after several daughters there is a celebration. A lamb is killed, the dabkii is danced, and the child is presented to the guests who in turn contribute gifts of money. The money collected for a daughter is used to purchase gold bracelets for her. There were no such celebrations for the several children born to villagers in Tell Ṭoqaan in the spring of 1954.

A child may be named after the day on which it is born: "Hilaal" for the day of the month in which the new moon is in the west at sunset. "Hamsii" for the fifth day of the week; "Jum^{c}a," a common name, for Friday. The name "^{c}iid" may be given a child born on a Muslim feast day, (ciid).

A child should not be named after its father or a living ascendant in his lineage as it is believed to take from the life of that person. While the father or such relatives are living, their names are living with them and should not be used. A child may, however, be named after the child of a friend; in this event the friend must provide the child with a gown.

People born in the same year are of the same jiil, "generation," and refer to one another as being jiil of each other. This relationship is remembered throughout life and appears to carry some weight of special friendly consideration. Thus, a youth requested aspirin from me for one of his jiil friends, because of his relationship to the other youth.

By the time a boy is twelve years old he usually acquires a nickname that stays with him through adulthood. Some women also are given nicknames. The names are mildly derogatory and refer to some personal trait, such as a snuffling tic or talkativeness. They are used as terms of address to their owners by friends, but only as a term of reference when a man has gained age and status. The muxtaar of the village was usually referred to by his nickname, Zukzaq, if he was not present; but if he was present he was addressed by title, by a teknonymous term, or by his own name.

Circumcision.—In March the circumciser visited Tell Ṭoqaan and circumcized six boys in the village. Boys should be circumcized between the ages of a month and seven years, but there was some evidence that circumcision may not be universally practiced. The youngest son of my host had not been circumcized and adamantly refused to be. For the villagers the brief rite is performed in the family's dwelling and is not public, though a few others may be present. It was said, however, that public celebrations for which lambs were killed were held by Shayx Nuuri in Tell Ṭoqaan and his brother in Jazraaya on the occasions of circumcision of their sons.

The one circumcision witnessed took place in the dwelling room of a foreman of one of urban landlords. The circumciser directed the laying out of a mattress and pillows and called for an older woman who was bint ^{c}amm (father's brother's daughter) to hold the child. The woman who took the child was one of the old women of the village and not a kinsman of either father or mother. Moreover, I also was asked to help hold the child. The circumciser laid out his instruments, cotton, and sulfa powder. As he operated he sang a brief verse from the Koran, and as soon as the foreskin had been cut the child's mother gave the ululation, a quavering wail, and the father beamed and shouted encouragement to his son. The foreskin was wrapped in a bit of gauze and was passed from the "bint ^{c}amm" to the child's mother and, thence, to his father, who tucked it behind the kerosene lamp on a small shelf high on the wall. The child was nursed and comforted while the wound was dressed. In following days he was dressed in a new gown.

During my stay in the village many small girls had their ear lobes and right nose flanges pierced for rings to be inserted later. A few also appeared in new gowns and kerchiefs with sequins sewn on the edges.

Marriage.—The religious teacher from Jazraaya commented on one of his visits to Tell Ṭoqaan that village life was more pleasant for a young man than city life, because he could talk freely to the girls of the village and take the one he liked best for a wife. In her discussions in Saraaqab and Afess with kinsmen on the subject of a bride for her eldest son, my host's wife remarked that he had not yet seen a girl he wanted. In both villages she inquired about girls of marriageable age and was told there was no one suitable in Afess, but that there were several in Saraaqab. She had already decided that no girls in Tell Ṭoqaan were suitable, because all those of marriageable age were of pastoralist tradition. She preferred a peasant girl. It was evident from this that a bride should meet with the approval of the mother of the household, under whose jurisdiction she would come, and that the mother may take an active part in finding a wife for her son.

From the man's point of view a girl should be known for good work, good looks, proper clothing, and good family. The bride price demanded by a girl's family was said to be some indication of this, except among the pastoralists, for whom it was "the custom" to set a high price on their daughters.

Preference for a spouse from the patrilineal kin was discussed only twice. It is not ignored, but it is taken for granted that the father's brother's son, if there is one, has first choice to marry or at least authority to permit his cousin to marry another. My host told me that he had released his cousin, the daughter of his paternal uncle, from his right to claim her for his wife. His uncle was a city man and the girl had been brought up as a city girl. But her father had first offered her to my host, a peasant farmer, because the latter was his nephew and had the right to claim her. My host said he had thought long about it and then decided that he should marry a village woman who knew village work, which his cousin did not. Such a marriage, between parallel patrilineal cousins, however, is regarded as the best. For both spouses to be of the same "blood" is good, and both families are therefore well known to each other in all respects. This cousin right was used in Tell Ṭoqaan to prevent Shayx MaHmuud's projected marriage to a Bu Layl girl in the village. Her uncle and cousin refused to give up their claim to the girl in spite of the father's willingness, and in spite of the Shayx's appeal for support to the gendarmes at Tell Sultaan. There was also talk that they wanted an exhorbitant amount of money in compensation— the most effective obstacle to the indigent man's hopes.

Two major kinds of marriage procedure are distinguished, "city" and village. City marriage procedure, after the agreement on bride price, requires a civil license and a health certificate. Fees are paid the examining doctor and the government and a tax of two and a half Syrian pounds for each 1000 pounds of the bride price is paid the government. It is evident that the prestige of a marriage a man makes increases with the amount of fees paid. After licenses are secured the announcement of the marriage is posted on the mosque door and shop doors of the bride's "side" of the village. Finally, a ceremony is conducted at the mosque by the ?imaam in which the permission and agreement of all persons concerned, including the bride, is confirmed. My host said that his second marriage followed this procedure.

But in most small villages like Tell Ṭoqaan the traditional village procedure is followed and licenses, health certificates, and mosque ceremony of the urban sequence are ignored. According to my informant, there are four steps.

When the prospective groom has decided upon a girl, the xataabii ("asking") takes place. A representative of the groom goes to the father of the girl and asks for the girl for the groom. He asks the bride price. The father, if he accepts the groom, states the price. The representative says it is too much and after talk they agree on a sum 500 pounds less than that initially asked. Thus, an asking price of 1500 pounds gets 1000 pounds, and so on.

Sometime later the sealing of the match takes place. A shayx is present with the groom and the "representative" of the bride. This person may be her father, brother, paternal uncle, uncle's son, her mother, or her guardian. Four or five witnesses are also present. The bride price may be paid or twenty-five piasters security in case of the death of one party within the year. Three times a formula of mutual acceptance of the bargain is repeated by bride's representative and groom as they clasp hands. The shayx asks and they each reply. Then the opening verse of the Koran is recited.

A day or so before the bride is brought to the groom's house, the groom purchases the customary seven items of the bride's equipment: the head dress, gamp, three gowns, belt, and mirror. A bridal chest is also included.

The final step is yawm l ^{c}aruus ("day of the bride"), when the bride is brought to her new home.

Several other practices and rules govern marriage procedures in Tell Ṭoqaan. Exchange marriages between families eliminate the bride price and only the seven pieces of bridal equipment must be supplied by the respective groom. Thus, arrangements may be made for two young men of different families to exchange their sisters; or the exchange may cross generations, for instance, a man may exchange his daughter for the sister of the man to whom he gives his daughter. In one case an exchange procedure was broken up when one man's sister refused to stay with her husband and returned home; her deserted husband then took back his daughter and refused to allow her to return to his former wife's brother until a bride price had been paid.

If a marriage has been completed, but the bride refuses to stay with her husband and returns to her family, the bride price must be refunded to the husband. The girl cannot be remarried until this is done or a satisfactory arrangement made to do so. Two young women in Tell Ṭoqaan who had left their husbands immediately after marriage refused to return to them and neither could remarry until the bride prices had been refunded. In one case, another sister was available and acceptable to the groom, but she refused to replace her sister.

In Tell Ṭoqaan and its area the bridge price is regarded as high, and the bride prices of the tribal pastoralists are the highest. The prices begin at 500 Syrian pounds for a poor man's daughter, but appear to be between 1000 to 2000 pounds for most village girls. It was said that the price for one of Shayx Nuuri's daughters is 15,000 pounds. In explanation of the high prices for girls of pastoralist background it was said that it is not only tribal custom, but that a cheap wife is not good because she does not bring back gold. Ideally, a pastoralist girl is preferred because her father uses a portion of the bride price to buy the proper clothing for her and puts all the rest into the gold coins and bracelets which are the proper accessories of a bride. Thus, in fact, a girl brings back to her husband all that he has paid for her. But a poor man keeps most of the bride price for himself and returns very little except for the necessities of clothing. One young woman commented on this latter practice, "?abuha byaakul kul," "her father eats all (of it)."

The events concerned with the one wedding which took place in Tell Ṭoqaan during the field session provide an example of the difficulty of maintaining ancient custom in the face of present economic and social conditions. It had been known for some time that a young Circassian who worked for one of the urban landlords as a tractor driver wanted to marry the daughter of a Mawali tribesman and servant of Shayx Nuuri. But the girl had previously been given by her father to another young man in the village for a bride price of a thousand pounds. On the night the marriage was to be consummated, the girl had resisted the groom, thrown him to the ground, bit his wrist, and fled to Shayx Nuuri for protection. Her refusal was allowed, but she could not marry the Circassian until the bride price was refunded. It was finally agreed that this refund was to come from the bride price that would be paid by the Circassian.

The Circassian terminated his work with the city landlord and went to work for Shayx Nuuri as chauffeur and attendant. Shayx Nuuri gave him 500 pounds advance on his work, and this was said to have been paid to the girl's father, who in turn paid the first husband. With 500 pounds still owing, the young man drove one of Shayx Nuuri's wives, to visit her father, Shayx Nawwaf es-SalaH of the Hadiidiin tribes, in the east. There he secured from Shayx Nawwaf five sheep which were paid to the girl's father. The first husband wanted money, not sheep, and so it was planned to sell the five sheep after the spring grazing. This would bring about 300 pounds. But one of the sheep was said to have become ill and just at the crucial moment the girl's father cut its throat in the proper fashion. This was considered as a lucky turn for the girl's father and would not subtract from the agreement on the refund, since the intention had been clear.

For the remaining 200 pounds, two heads of households connected with the Nuri organization pledged security if the prospective groom could not find a way to raise the money. It was expected he would be able to do so after the harvest. With one partial payment and these arrangements in advance it was then possible for the wedding to proceed.

The day before the wedding the bride, groom, and the youngest wife of Shayx Nuuri drove to Aleppo and purchased in the market there the necessary bridal clothing, bride's chest, and accessories for the bride. These were placed on display in the groom's one-roomed, domed house, which was located across the village path from the bride's house. The next day many people visited the groom's house and admired the bridal outfit. There was dancing and singing by the young girls and old women who crowded into the house. The wedding was to be rushed through that day because, it was said, the groom had to work.

Late that afternoon the bride was dressed by Shayx Nuuri's second wife, who was at the time in charge of his household in Tell Ṭoqaan. The bride sat at the back of the one room of her father's house while the Shayx's wife handed her the articles of clothing to put on. The bride's mother did not enter the room but stood close outside the door. Inside, however, a crowd of village girls gathered about the bride clapping, singing, and giving the ululation from time to time. It was said that no married women except the Shayx's wife might be present at the dressing of the bride. There was no gamp in the bridal outfit and the Shayx's wife supplied the bride with her own, and then folded and wound the headcloth in the style of a married woman on the bride's head. The bride maintained a very serious face during the dressing. The Shayx's wife splashed perfume over the bride and then went around to all those present and sprinkled them with scent. When the bride's mother came to the door of the house and asked for the key to the bridal chest, the bride's sisters began to weep and sob. The bride also began to cry, and a girl of her own age knelt down before her and remonstrated against her crying. The singing, clapping, and dancing of the young unmarried girls went on around them until the Shayx's wife who had left the room briefly, returned with a black cloak. She pulled the bride to her feet, put the cloak over her, covering her head like a cowl. A thin white cloth also covered the bride's face as a veil. All the girls left the room and stood outside the door, continuing their singing, while the Shayx's wife took the bride by the hand and led her across the short distance to the groom's house. The bride pulled back with a little show of reluctance.

In the groom's house, the bride sat down on the mattress against the far wall and a small boy (her brother) was put in her lap. There was some questioning whether or not another child should be brought rather than the brother. Again the young girls crowded into the room and Shayx Nuuri's two young sisters began to dance and sing before the bride and the child. Up to this point no older women had been present, and no youths or men. But now the old women came into the groom's house and one knelt before the bride, asked why she wept, and told her that the bride's village was now the groom's village (the phaseology was, more precisely, "your village is our village," as to a welcome guest, but a stranger!) The singing and dancing continued and the young men of the village came in from time to time and shouted their encouragement. Then the bride's mother entered and ordered all the young people out. A few older women entered and demanded to see the bride. She stood up for them to view her clothing, then sank down again on the matress. At last everyone left except the bride's mother and sisters.

Later in the evening the Shayx's wife returned to wait with the bride for the groom. Soon there was a low call outside the door and everyone left and crossed the path to the bride's father's house except the Shayx's wife. As the groom entered his house the Shayx's wife gave the quavering woman's wail and then joined the group in the bride's father's dwelling. Shortly afterward everyone, except the members of the bride's family, walked to the Nuuri threshing ground where already the dancing was in progress. Throughout the day no older men nor the bride's father had appeared in the vicinity of the two houses.

The next day the groom's house was open to visitors, and the bride's nightgown with the blood stains indicative of her virginity, was hung in a conspicuous spot under the mirror opposite the door.

For three nights many of the villagers gathered on the threshing ground after dark and danced and sang late into the night. There was not, however, a feast or distribution of food.

The bride remained in her new home for ten days; then she was free to go out into the village. The wedding took place on March 28, and in May the bride was still wearing her bridal finery; she visited around the village, spent most of her time in the Nuuri household, and engaged in very little of the work that she had been accustomed to do before marriage.

The procedure of dressing the bride and leading her to the groom's house seemed to be conducted hastily and with attention only to the important parts of customary practices. The weeping, the slight show of reluctance, the remonstrances, the child placed in the bride's lap, were performed without more than a cursory emphasis to a customary routine.

Much more elaborate marriage celebrations than this are reported from the western peasant villages, both Muslim and Christian, with an abundance of procession, contests between the young men of the two families to be linked, and many other details missing from the one in Tell Ṭoqaan. But of particular note in the Tell Ṭoqaan marriage is the part played, in benevolent feudal fashion, by the Nuuri family in financing and conducting the marriage between two persons within their economic sphere.

Death.—Two residents of Tell Ṭoqaan died and their deaths were commemorated with the three nights of Koran reading which were said to be prescribed practice. One was the wife of a local laborer; she died in the government hospital in Aleppo. The other, a household head of the Hammuud lineage, died suddenly the night of April 25, 1954, and was buried the next morning in the village cemetery. The account of the brief funeral follows.

Shortly after eight in the morning the wife of my host and I went to the compound of the deceased. The body was being prepared for burial in the court. My host's wife said I must not observe this procedure because women wash women and men, men. We sat outside the compound in the shade of the wall. All the rest of the women of the village were sitting across from the gate of the compound. There was almost no one missing, no household not represented except Shayx Nuuri's. A number of farmhands stood nearby also, and I was told that all the heads of the households were participating in the rite of washing the body of the deceased. I was told later that three white gowns were put on the body, covering it completely. Shayx MaHmuud came out of the courtyard dressed in his white gown and walked slowly up and down nearby. He had spent the night reading the Koran after the man's death.

Soon the gate opened and a door, glistening with water, was brought out and placed on the ground before the gate. Then the body, wrapped closely in a striped rug, was carried out by the men and placed on the door litter. My host, a peasant household head, was in the lead; he sang out occasionally, "La ?ila ?ill ?allah" ("There is no god but God"), and the others repeated it after him in a murmur. After the body was lowered to the litter all the bearers, as many as could stand shoulder to shoulder around the bier, stood up; they held their hands out before them, palms up, and murmured a few words; then they brushed their hands together, wiped them over their faces, and bent and lifted the bier at the signal given by the leader.

As the men lifted the bier and moved off, continuing the low chanting of La ?ila ?ill ?allah, the women began to weep and wail loudly and to follow in a group some yards behind. Leading the women in the wailing, with words which appeared to refer to the deceased, was the wife of the head of the Hammuud lineage. The bearers moved quickly through the village, but stopped five or six times. At each pause the leader half-shouted a few words.

At the south end of the cemetery the bearers stopped and placed the bier on the ground. The group of women moved to the graves on the north side of the cemetery; those who had kinsmen buried there moved to their graves, increased the intensity of their wailing, and knelt and kissed the headstones as they called on the deceased by the appropriate kin term. Others drew them away from their personal sorrowing. While the bier was resting on the ground the men stood in two ranks on the north side, facing south toward Mecca, heads bowed, while Shayx MaHmuud led the prayer. Then the bier was lifted and carried around the edge of the cemetery to the grave which had been prepared. Two girls carried buckets of water to the grave and the younger children accompanied them. The women remained seated at the north edge of the cemetery and continued wailing; the words of the leader of the mourners were taken up by the others and repeated after her. A number of the women slowly gathered around one woman at her husband's grave; he was the most recently deceased male of Tell Ṭoqaan before this. The widow had kept her gamp pulled up over her mouth most of the time.

The ceremony at the graveside could not be seen clearly; several men appeared to speak a few words. Toward the end of the rites all the children were sent to gather small stones from the nearby midden area. Two old women then carried trays of pastoralist bread and dates to the graveside. At this point the cluster of men broke up and the children were called to eat the food. The head of the deceased's lineage knelt at the head of the grave arranging the stones, then rose and appeared to be handing out something to each of the men. Then the people at the grave came slowly away; the old women brought the remains of the food to the smallest children who had remained with their mothers. Before the women rose one of them asked one of the men returning from the graveside why the grave had been dug so far off; he addressed the group to the effect that eventually everyone of them would die, and there were places for all; one here, someone else there —he cited by name the heads of households. Then everyone went his way.

No one wished to discuss or talk about the deceased or the funeral afterward. For a few days people did not walk casually over the cemetery as they were accustomed to do. The night Hammuud died, the Koran was read all night by Shayx MaHmuud, and for the two nights following, Shayx MaHmuud, the boys in his school, and the half dozen other young men in the village who were literate gathered at the home of the deceased to read.

It was said that food should again be distributed to the poor the third day after burial. An animal should be slaughtered on this occasion; the school of law adhered to by the deceased determines the kind of animal. My host said that a two-year old sheep is the Hanifite custom; a three-year old bull is the Shaafite (most of the old peasant villages west of the highway are Shaafite); and a five-year old camel is specified by the Malikite and Hanbalite schools, or all Arabs who live in tents. There were no indications of this occurring, however, after the funeral of Hammuud Hammuud.

Medicine and Magic

In Tell Ṭoqaan forms of illness and its treatments fall into three categories. My data concerning them, although fragmentary, serve to round out the picture of life in Tell Ṭoqaan. The three classes are Western or city medicine, folk medicine, and magic.

Villagers identify Western medical practices with the city. Aleppo or Idlib doctors were sought out for diagnosis and treatment. The techniques of palpation and stethoscopic examination and hypodermic injection were the most commented on and injections seemed to be regarded as a necessary part of any treatment given by such doctors. Alcohol was used liberally by everyone on cuts and tooth extractions to prevent infection. A city doctor was sought out, or the barber or circumciser, if an infection did develop. The circumciser also vaccinated for smallpox. Patent medicines, all of which except aspirin appeared to be European concocted cathartics, were in frequent use. A few people people occasionally sprayed their houses with DDT. Sickness was ascribed by two families to microbes (makruub) and cleanliness was regarded as a means to prevent disease from microbes. One woman who had borne no children was taken to a city doctor in Idlib. The chief obstacles to seeking treatment from city doctors appeared to be cost and transportation problems.

Under folk medicine and treatments are grouped those practices which did not appear to involve distinctively magical procedures, but rather to be based on experience. Wounds were treated in several ways: cauterization, applying salt, and, if infected, by bandaging a freshly cut green onion to the wound or applying a poultice of soap shavings and white of egg.

Earaches are treated by warm-water syringing or by putting a rolled-up piece of paper in the ear. The end of the paper is lighted so it glows slowly and the smoke and heat are said to make the pain "go." Herbal teas and rice soup are dietary treatments for intestinal disorders; the latter is especially prescribed for illnesses attributed to "cold." Laban, bread, and abstention from drinking water are prescribed for diarrhea. Chapped skin, especially on a baby, is treated with a preparation of dibs (raisin molasses) and milk from the noon milking for five to seven days. Muscular pain in neck and back is treated with massage by hand, by kneading the back muscles with the feet, and by "cracking" the joints by twisting and pulling head and arms. Such treatment is particularly referred to as "Arab medicine" and that given by a shayx is more effective than an ordinary man's.

In recommending the use or prescription of many remedies or treatments for specific cases of infection, success in some particular case involving a kinsman of the adviser is customarily cited as proof of its efficacy. Others, such as dietary treatments, however, are the traditional prescriptions for the condition presented.

Tattooing, whether by the Qirbaat women or by a village woman, is used therapeutically. How tattooing is believed to cure is not clear; it belongs properly with the others attributed to magic (see below). Inner sides of the wrists are tattooed with a pattern of lines and chevrons, called the Halaabiyaat, to prevent pain from work at milking. Another design, the wasm baqar, consists of three dots, one on the nose tip, one on the right cheek, and one on the chin. This is sometimes tattooed on a newborn baby which has difficulty nursing or to insure that it will nurse. A small triangle made of three dots is tattooed on the site of pain or location of illness, such as rheumatism or whooping cough (at the base of the throat). When this is done the pain or sickness allegedly goes.

Under the category of magical practices are the illnesses, conditions, and treatments which include a belief in a "supernatural" element involved in either the illness or the treatment or both. Although, as said above, tattooing belongs to this category, in the following examples the magical or supernatural element is more explicit. It was said that most of the villagers believed that sickness came from Allah but that more enlightened individuals knew that sickness came from microbes and mosquitoes. A few other "causes" however, with their prescribed treatments were noted.

Harelip in a child was said to have been caused by a pregnant woman looking at a camel's or rabbit's lip.

The "eye" of envious persons causes illness which apparently take the form of generalized aches and pains in adults and persistent discomfort and crying in small children. An envious person is one who looks at another and compliments that one for good qualities without prefixing the exclamation "mashallah" which attributes the compliment and attribute to Allah. One treatment observed for this affliction consisted of stroking and measuring a headcloth while reciting verses from the Koran, knotting the cloth, pricking the knot with a needle, and pulling the knot loose as it is held against the forehead of the sick. For another cure the afflicted person smashes an egg on which words from the Koran are written, then inhales the fumes from the burning egg shell, and recites an exorcism formula four times; this makes the illness leave, go out of the sick one. The headcloth ritual is performed by the villagers, the husband for his wife, the mother for a sick child. The egg has to be inscribed by the religious shayx

When a child (a girl about three years old) was said to be sick (feverish) from fright caused by a cat which jumped on her while she was sleeping, a cure was performed with the Koran. The mother sat down on a stool and drew the child in front of her. The reader sat on a stool facing her, opened the Koran and held it quite close to the child. He repeated the formula, Bismillaah ar RaHman ar RaHiim, as he opened the book, read silently for a moment, then he suddenly snapped the book shut, startling the child. This was repeated three times until the little girl was wailing at the top of her lungs. Later the reader said it was a very fine Koran that he used; it had everything in it, and it was "forbidden" for him to handle it as he had, snapping it shut violently. The reader was the eldest son of my host; he had learned to read in Saraaqab and was continuing Koran studies with Shayx MaHmuud.

Locally, two rituals are held in connection with sickness, the muliid and the zayaara. When a child is sick, the mother may request a muliid to be held, or she may pledge a sheep and a pilgrimage to the tomb of a saint if the child recovers. The pledge when performed, is called a zayaara. One muliid service was held for a sick child while I was in Tell Ṭoqaan.

When a muliid is to be held, the word is passed around the village and both men and women attend. It is held in the evening in the household of the sick. The Shayx reads the Koran, and food and a drink made of water, sugar, and fruit flavoring are served. The muliid held in Tell Ṭoqaan was not an occasion I could attend during the Koran reading. Upon arrival after this part of the ceremony, however, it was observed that all the household heads of the lineage, to which the sick child belonged, were present, the heads of several other families, and a number of poor men. At the other end of the room, the women's end where the food was placed on a tray, were grouped the women of the lineage. and several of the old women of the village. The mother and her sick child sat by the door.

There were no pilgrimages from the village, but one held by a party from Saraaqab at the tomb of Shayx Monsuur, halfway between Saraaqab and Tell Ṭoqaan, I attended briefly. It took place late in April, had followed from the pledge of a Saraaqab woman to perform such a pilgrimage if her sick child recovered.

(A pregnant woman may also pledge such a pilgrimage if she should bear a son —a way, perhaps of coercing the saint.) The tell on which the saint's tomb stands rises next to the main country road 7 kilometers southeast of Saraaqab. The woman, her family, and a crowd of kinsmen and friends from her "side" of the village walked to the tell in the morning. They slaughtered and cooked with rice and wheat the lamb which she had promised the saint. On our arrival to join the celebration, a circle of dancers was formed near the tomb. Inside the whitewashed domed room some of the women were clapping and singing.

Shayx Mansuur, the saint in this place, was said to be have lived to great age and to have resided in a village which was now a low ruins at the foot of the tell. Three of his sons and a daughter were also saints and had tombs in the area, at Islamiin, Shayx ᶜali (at the intersection of the Islamiin and country roads), and at Abu Xawss. Shayx Hasan, whose tomb is erected on top of the tell near Afess, was regarded as a very powerful saint. (The two shayxs buried in Tell Ṭoqaan were not thought to be powerful.) What the nature of the action of a saint may be in response to a pledge of a pilgrimage was not clear, that is, whether recovery from a sickness was believed to be owed directly to curative power of the saint which could be called into action by a pledge or whether the piety and loyalty demonstrated for a local saint brought intervention from a higher source of power, through intercession.

Accounts were given me of three famous "curing shayxs" in the area who maintain establishments to which people go for cures for various illnesses. Somewhere to the northwest a Shayx Ghiisa maintains hot spring baths where Tell Ṭoqaaniis, both men and women, have gone for treatment of joint and muscle stiffening. Shayx Riih, "near Aleppo," is reputed to have remarkable curing powers and to provide a bath into which many snakes were said to come and go through a conduit. The patients have no protection against the snakes and are greatly frightened. When the snakes leave the bath the sickness and fear leaves the patients; if the sickness does not go then, it was said, then the patient will not recover. To the west, in the village of Muntiif, Shayx Ibrahiim Xawwaas owns a spring distinguished for its curing powers. Children suffering from bone injuries or diseases and women who have no milk for their babies go there to wash in the water while the Shayx invokes Allah.

Islam

In many ways the customary beliefs and practices of Islam serve to unify and identify Tell Ṭoqaan as a Muslim village. One of the first descriptions of themselves which the villagers provided me was the formal declaration that they were Muslim farmers (muzaari^{c}aat) of the plains and distinct from Christian peasants (fallaaHiin) of the mountains. In one of the discussions of Islam it was pointed out that the prophets of the other religions were recognized and were "good," but that MuHammad succeeded and surpassed them all.

Of the "five pillars of Islam," the declaration of faith is evident, but the giving of alms has little chance of expression except from the wealthy landlords, and no examples of this were made known to me.

Two of the villagers are named with the Hajj (Hajjii, feminine) title of one who has made the pilgrimage to Mecca: Hajj Nuuri, the Circassian carpenter, and "Hajjii" Diibii, an elderly woman of the village. In neither case was it clear that the individual had actually made the pilgrimage to Mecca, but Hajj Nuuri had at least served in the Hejaz in the Turkish Army in the First World War. By virtue of this he was regularly addressed and referred to as Hajj Nuuri, was regarded as a pious man, and wore the metallic thread hair ropes of a pilgrim.

Prayer and fasting during Ramadaan remain as the chief practices by which the Tell Ṭoqaaniis give active profession of their faith and membership in the community of Islam. A number of the heads of families often pray at noon or midafternoon, on the threshing ground. One man, at least, was known to be rigorous in his observance of the five daily prayers. Two women were known to pray occasionally; they were said to have learned from Shayx MaHmuud or from watching the men.

Members of the different schools of law or rite of Sunni Islam are distinguished on the basis of practicing slightly different prayer rituals. Three of the schools, Malikite, Shaafite, and Hanafite, were said to be represented among the villagers. The members of one lineage were Malikite. Since they are also Hanaadii, their affiliation may derive from the historical background of those tribes who came into Syria from Egypt in the mid-nineteenth century. The Malikite school predominates in Upper Egypt (Gibb, 1949: 103). Most of the peasant families were Shaafite, as are most of the villages and the town of Idlib west of the Aleppo-Damascus highway. A few families were

Hanifite, as was Shayx MaHmuud, the only religious shayx in the village. There was no social factioning of the villagers along these lines. In most villages, however, homgeneity of rite prevails.

Friday services were not held regularly in the mosque. Some were held early in the year when I expressed an interest in the mosque. Twenty of the older men in the village attended. The young men did not because, I was told, they were plowing in the fields. The evening call to prayer, was given regularly and, less frequently, the noon call. Any of the older men might give the call to prayer if he were near the mosque at the proper time, but it was usually done by the head of a household whose compound and shop stood next to the mosque. He regulated his call not by observing the moment the evening sun dipped below the horizon but by his alarm clock set to the "mosque time" announced on the radio! When the alarm rang, he or another began the call.

Two "times" were recognized in the village, "Frangi" or government time, by which government schools and offices operated, and "mosque" or prayer time. In the same way, the "Frangi" or Western calendar and the Eastern calendar were both recognized and governed different activities. In the village mosque time was said to be better known than Frangi time and household and working activities followed it; that is, work began after the dawn prayer and, except during harvest, generally was finished for the day before the midafternoon prayer. Meals were eaten after the daybreak and sunset prayers.

A man's prayer ritual was usually performed individually. He might rise up from a social gathering with the muttered announcement that he was going to pray. The cleansing rituals were usually abbreviated to rinsing the mouth with a glass of water and spitting out the door. If one man decided to pray another might follow suit and stand behind the first. The individuals, as they prayed, were ignored and conversation continued around them. But an adult's gesture to tease a man while he prayed by slyly tugging his headcloth was once sharply reprimanded as Harramii, "forbidden."

One of the "images" familiar to Muslims was told me as a feature of Islam. At the time of prayer all the Muslims in the world are facing Mecca and bowing in prayer together.

"Praying" is regarded as one of the marks of an adult man, it also appears to be a requisite of responsibility for a household. It was said that even in old age there was much laxity among men. Those who were seen to pray and to observe other Muslim rules, such as the Ramadaan fast and not shaking hands with a Christian, were the heads of households and lineages. Those who failed to pray or who did not keep the rules cited were young men and boys and older men of pastoralist background or laborer status. No exclusive lines however, can be drawn.

Ramadaan, the Muslim fast month, began in 1954 at sunset on May 3. Ramadaan was described as a shahr baarakii, "blessed month." During this time one who fasts should not smoke, eat or drink from "halfway through the night" (about 2:00 A. M.) until the following sunset, although a light snack may be eaten just before daybreak. If one breaks the fast one day, this day must be made up later. Those who are working need not fast, but they ought to do so. Shayx MaHmuud did not fast because, he said, he could not talk and teach all day unless he could eat and drink. A number of others, including a few women, began the month with fasting according to rule but within a week or ten days had stopped. The heads of several peasant households were maintaining their fast up to the time the field session closed about May 20 and remained in seclusion most of the day; the other members of their households went about their daily activities as usual. In 1954 Ramadaan coincided with the beginning of harvest season and the increase in work in the fields, and fasting during a period of heavy work was commented upon as a physical hardship which only the most pious could endure.

A number of other features of Ramadaan were described. At the first of the month there should be a special meal or feast, Hasanii, "alms," "charity," but none was known to be held in Tell Ṭoqaan households. During the last ten days of Ramadaan a man should spend much time in the mosque. The last two days before ciid l ?akal or ciid iz zghiir, the feast which ends Ramadaan, are known as waqfaat. The first is called waqfit l gharaba on which there is another Hasanii. Some say, explained mu host, that this feast is for those whose fathers have died far from their own home; some say that at this time one should return to one's home if one is away.

Shayx MaHmuud was the only individual who performed some of the functions of a religious leader. He led the Friday services in the mosque, taught the Koran and Hadiith in his school, and read the Koran as required (after a death, at a ceremony for sick child. Although regarded as having greater power than an ordinary man, he did not command personal respect. I was told, and also, noted that a number of the older men in the village would not speak to him. According to the Shayx's History, the villagers had asked one household head among them, my host, to be their shayx; while he had declined, there were indications that this man did perform functions of leadership on occasion, such as announcing the beginning of harvest and directing funeral procedures.

There was no Sufi brotherhood, or religious fraternity, in Tell Ṭoqaan nor, according to my knowledge, in Saraaqab nor in the other villages east of the highway and in the Tell Ṭoqaan area. Such organizations are, however, to be found in the villages west of the highway. It was evident from conversations between the men and gendarmes that a weekly meeting of a religious fraternity was held within travel range of those who wished to attend. Without further information concerning the organization and function of the brotherhoods in the western villages, it is difficult to account for their absence east of the highway except to note that their presence probably correlates with old peasant villages and their absence with the more recently settled tribal villages.

In summary, the condition of supernatural beliefs and religious organization in Tell Ṭoqaan seems weak in comparison the persistence and strength of ritual observances reported for the peasant area to the west and depicted by French writers working in Syria during the Mandate Period. Once more, the cultural heterogeneity of the village and the predominance of tribal peoples in the society sets the local conditions for this lower intensity of expression, particularly in communal ways. Pastoralists have never been distinguished for their orthodoxy, except in times of conquest movements, and in their daily life the practice of religious rituals is a family matter and indeed, primarily a father's, with his sons. The role of the religious shayx in Tell Ṭoqaan was scarcely more than that of the specialist in literacy and the sacred text, and purveyor of the magical power of the inscribed paper, egg, or stone; he had no property and no visible personal power in the village. His nationalism was not particularly harkened to by the important men of the village and the young men who were his companions carried no weight in the community. From the national level, the successful separation of Syria from French control and the development of a secular, parlimentary state left behind in Tell Ṭoqaan only a memory of the political significance of religious differences within their own society. Nor, at the time of my residence had militant religious unity become a useful tool in the eastern rural areas of any national political faction. These conditions surely contributed also to the impression that the Tell Ṭoqaaniis were far from being fanatical or devout Muslims. Rather, they expected to survive in life by hard work at the right times, thrift, shrewd business deals, and luck — and for this last a man thanked Allah. There was no profit in exceptional display of piety, but for poor peasants and landless men it was one of the few means to community notice and respect.

XV

CONCLUSION

Tell Ṭoqaan: The Local Factors

WHEN ITS CULTURAL CHARACTERISTICS are taken into consideration, Tell Ṭoqaan does not emerge as a fair representative of a traditional peasant village of the Levant area. But the particular can appear as a type or kind by virtue of the historical approach which seeks to characterize uniqueness, in this case, the uniqueness of Tell Ṭoqaan as a Syrian Village. Although the pattern of culture is unlike that of any other peasant village, Tell Ṭoqaan combines traits and forms to be found elsewhere in the Levant.

Four factors contribute fundamentally to the specific cultural situation in Tell Ṭoqaan: local-habitat features, ethnographic location, and land-tenure and ethnic histories.

Its environmental situation provides the bases for a more differentiated agriculture and husbandry than is true of other villages in the immediate area. Tell Ṭoqaan land has more water to use for irrigation, though not enough for extensive or expanding development by peasant technology. In addition, the marsh border, streamside, uncultivated tell slopes, and limestone ridges furnish natural pasturage, which is more widespread and richer in forage than is common in the vicinity. Consequently, irrigated cotton fields and vegetable gardens and property in local flocks give a diversity to the subsistence pattern which is not duplicated in villages of the surrounding countryside. Elsewhere thereabouts dry cereal farming prevails as the regional specialization and vegetables are only grown for household needs.

Present land usage, however, is not the same as that of the past. Before the local disturbances of the early Mandate Period, the lands of Tell Ṭoqaan appear to have been exploited by typical traditional peasant techniques and organization. There were irrigated gardens and fruit orchards along the stream; cereal farming on the surrounding divisions of land; marshside and sown-pasturage grazing of cattle and other work animals; and contract arrangements with nomadic shepherds of long acquaintance for fallow grazing and care of villagers' property in flocks of sheep and goats.

The ethnogeographical location of Tell Ṭoqaan is especially pertinent to its history and present status as a village community. Because it lies within a zone of recent competition between cultivation and nomadic pastoralism, peoples representing both systems or subcultures have sought control of it and of its well-watered lands. From its founding in the third quarter of the nineteenth century until the early years of the Mandate Period, a village community held the site, and its security was owed to an astute landholder who combined the advantages of military status in the Ottoman army with diplomatic dealings with local Arab tribal leaders. But, following the wars and destruction of the early Mandate Period, people of the pastoral system and tradition took over the dominant position in the area and in Tell Ṭoqaan. As a result, the most distinctive fact concerning Tell Ṭoqaan, now, is the presence in the village of two subcultures: what remains of nomadic shepherd pastoral tradition in a sedentary community and what remains of agricultural peasant tradition in a culturally heterogeneous community. Both have been modified by the gradual introduction of industrial equipment.

Changes in landholding and tenure contribute to the present fabric of Tell Ṭoqaan. At, and for some time after its founding, Tell Ṭoqaan lands were apparently divided among a larger number of peasant freehold and tenant plots than they are today. But during the period of widespread local disturbance and rebellion against the Mandate government in Syria, from 1920 on, the area of Tell Ṭoqaan was among those where fighting took place; many of the peasant freehold or tenant farmers abandoned their lands and tenures, left Tell Ṭoqaan, and the city and tribal elite took control. Remaining peasant freehold tenures were reduced and most of the land is now concentrated in the hands of the elite. Hence, while the traditional open-field and two-field rotation systems are still followed, the present holdings occur in large enough blocs so that it is efficient and profitable to use the equipment of industrial agriculture. The few and small peasant freeholdings or subtenures, and the large plots of the group of landholders of the elite class have not been fragmented into tiny plots by sale or inheritance processes. Nor were they earlier regrouped by the Mandate survey and the agrarian-reform program. Thus in size they have been open to exploitation by mechanized agriculture, but have retained the traditional arrangements of dispersed divisions further sectioned into plots.

With respect to ethnic history, the peopling of Tell Ṭoqaan has resulted in a small and diverse population; ethnic diversity is expressed in residents of Turkish, Kurdish, Circassian, and Arab background. While nearly all the population are Sunni Muslims, the two women from the Alowite mountains may represent a religious difference.

In local representation the Sunni Muslims, moreover, are divided among three of the four schools of law and ritual of that branch of Islamic faith. Finally, local distinctions are made between people of various tribal affiliations, and people of peasant lineages.

It is these local and particular expressions of the general environmental condition, sociocultural organization, and history in the Levant which together form the matrix of the specific cultural situation in Tell Ṭoqaan.

Culture Patterns in Tell Ṭoqaan

Tell Ṭoqaan is essentially a small community of Muslim cultivators and shepherds of varied backgrounds, whether of occupation or of social origin and affiliation. Cultural patterns in Tell Ṭoqaan are, therefore, mixed. Present in the community and interacting with each other are elements of tribal shepherd pastoralist tradition, local peasant agricultural tradition, and practices of industrial agriculture.

The peasant core of the population consists of a few families and lineages, most of whom have been associated with each other as residents of the village over several generations. On the whole, these families pursue economic activities of peasant tradition. They produce the major part of their own subsistence and maintenance requirements, and a surplus for market or tenure obligations. Uniformity in style of living is displayed in house and compound design, furnishings, and clothing. Differentials in signs of affluence are few, and as soon as one family acquires a gasoline lamp or adds a new room to the compound, another does also. Economic differences exist and are to be explained only in part by age, accumulation of property, status in lineage, or status as freeholder or tenant farmer. It is true that many have lost economic status as traditional tenants or as foremen of landlords' properties in consequence of the introduction of industrial machinery and reduction of tenures. But, in general it is the members of this group which maintain the peasant village tradition; they provide the succession of village muxtaars, furnish the necessary entertainment for officials, and make decisions of local village concern. A Muslim religious functionary is associated with them as religious shayx and teacher. Most of these peasants are not literate, but with them rests the knowledge of peasant cultivating techniques, annual calendar of agricultural events, folklore, and the practice of the rites of Islam.

The shepherd pastoralist tradition is manifested in two ways: in the prevailing preference for clothing of pastoral style and design and in substitution of the properties in flocks of sheep and goats, since land is not available, and in local practices concerned in maintaining them. In the population also are some families whose manner of living includes more elements of the pastoral tradition than of a peasant tradition: their diet is pastoralist; their household furnishings include articles found in the pastoralist's tent; their women and girls are more extensively tattooed than peasant women. Although some of the peasant households now depend extensively on properties in sheep and goats and have acquired pastoralist practices, for professional help in handling their animals they turn to people of shepherd background.

In its class relation to the landholding elite there is a marked division between the village population and the locally resident household of Shayx Nuuri and the absentee urban landlords. The Nuuri family has acquired some of the traits of urban elite. They have an urban residence as well as the village dwelling complex, use urban goods and furnishings, and sons and one daughter are urban educated as well as the head of the family. There is also a close unity and social connection between the men of the Nuuri family and the urban landlords. Much more contact, however, and cultural continuity exists between the Nuuri family and the villagers than between the urban elite and the villagers. In clothing styles, food, language habits, manners, and interests the local aristocracy follows though, at more luxurious level, the same pattern as the villagers. But between urban elite and villager the class distinction is far more sharply marked in material and intellectual elements; the urban elite are Western-clothed and educated men.

Finally, the introduction of industrial agricultural machinery has brought in its wake associated patterns of large-scale exploitation, rapidity of work operations, and requirements of knowledge of machine operation which are not found in peasant technology. Men who were peasants or shepherds have become landless rural laborers.

Such are the cultural patterns in Tell Ṭoqaan. Together with social heterogeneity they characterize the community as a mixed village of peasants, shepherd people, rural proletariat, and landed gentry.

Tell Ṭoqaan and the Urban System

Since much of the culture in Tell Ṭoqaan is traditional, the relationships with the pastoral and urban systems are likewise. It is particularly in its relations to the urban system that the cultural situation in Tell Ṭoqaan provides the basis for two suggestions that I would like to make in regard to the character of Levant peasant village society and culture and the mechanisms of culture change. The first is that the Levant peasant society, of the plains area at least, is considerably urbanized, insofar as many activities and traits within it are commerical and characteristic of the traditional Levant urban center.[1] Operations of some Tell Ṭoqaan residents as end or connecting points of the urban entrepreneurial system, that is, shopkeepers, peddlers, middlemen, and employees, or clients of urban patrons, in dicate that ties between the two are close. The rural subordination to urban control in the commercial field as well as in landholding is well known and well documented in Latron (1936), but the point I wish to stress here has to do with the implications of such extensive relations in village society.

Redfield (1953: 32-34) has suggested that in peasant communities the impersonal "urban" relations of commercial activities are not a part of the local community life, of the relations of peasants with each other, but are included in its relationships with outsiders: "The peasant village maintains its local solidarity, its folklike inward-facingness, but now qualifies the sharp exclusiveness of the primitive settlement with institutionalized forms for admitting strangers." Among the strangers he memtions, one is the shopkeeper. If commercial traits are as extensive in other, more typical Levant villages as they are in Tell Ṭoqaan, if local shopkeepers are not "strangers " but are members of the village society, for example, then this aspect of urban society in the Levant does extend to the peasant village societies. In Tell Ṭoqaan, it will be recalled, the most prominent and successful shopkeepers and middlemen are members of the core of peasant lineages. Moreover, commercial and contract relations, as in the case of clients of peasant farmers, exist between villagers of the same community.[2] Sjoberg (1952, 1955) remarked that commercial organization is poorly developed in feudal society or the preindustrial city. However, it would appear that in the Levant type of feudal society and culture, commercial enterprise is characteristically so developed. While technological system remains preindustrial, commerce is found within Levant peasant village society as well as extending to it as part of the urban system of relationships.

1. Commercial relationships may be seen as a means developed by the urban center to secure goods from the hinterland on which it depends. Money and trinkets are the media of exchange. Gilmore (1953: 19-20) distinguishes two types of urban centers, the commercial city and the exploitive city. The latter type adds to commercial activities, predatory activities, that is, conquest and seizure of the surplus producing hinterland. Both of these types of urban-rural relationships seem characteristic of the Levant urban system.

2. These features, peasant shopkeepers and client relationships in Tell Ṭoqaan, are distinguished from the commercial basis of labor among households in the village. The people themselves recognized that buying and selling labor among themselves was atypical of traditional village life.

In the Levant, the density of population in the plains agricultural zone and density of rural settlement, contribute to conditions which facilitate communication, contact, and circulation. Spatial isolation of villages in relation to one another is not a characteristic of the Levant, with the possible exception of frontiers of agricultural expansion into pastoral zones. The prevalence of contract relationships, particularly as a means of interlocking the three socioeconomic systems, the economic and social exclusiveness of kin or lineage segments within both village and urban centers, and economic competition between all social groupings indicate that Levant peasant culture and society is extensively "urbanized". Commercial relationships hold between the local kinship units of the village society as well as between other spheres of the society.

My suggestion is, secondly, that owing to the extensive commercial exploitation of the rural areas, two lines of diffusion of Western industrial civilization to the rural areas are observable in Tell Ṭoqaan. Both move outward from the urban center. Urban traders carry light consumer goods, many of industrial origin, to the rural areas. Industrial agriculture, moreover, is also spreading by the entrepreneurial system. In the Tell Ṭoqaan area, for example, the use of tractors for plowing first came about through this system, to be followed later by investment in machinery by the elite landholders.

Thus, it is by way of the urban elite and the mechanisms of the urban system in the Levant that diffusion of industrial civilization is taking place, but the line is a double one. The elite control the dissemination of new goods and tools (Sjoberg, 1952), but the urban elite in the Levant appear to be composed of two different parts, merchants and entrepreneurs on the one hand and landholders on the other. In Tell Ṭoqaan and its area, the marketing of milk products and animals, eggs, and other produce, and the stocking of shops and peddlers' kits connects with the commercial entrepreneurial system; the elite landholders are now chiefly in control of industrial agricultural techniques and the extent of their use.

Nature and Direction of Cultural Change

The characteristics of the mixed social structure, the cultural patterns and the incidents that illustrated the conflict and competition between them, are ample indications that culture change is taking place in Tell Ṭoqaan. In a general sense, it is in two directions, one of which may be intracultural, local, that is, a consequence of local conditions, and not a part of the second general direction of change, that connected with the diffusion of industrial goods and technology.

This first movement is spurred by the competition between shepherd pastoralist and agricultural village tradition. If other factors are not considered, two issues are involved. One is whether nomadic pastoral tradition in content and custom can survive in a sedentary agricultural situation, the other whether Tell Ṭoqaan will become a tribal village of pastoral derivation or remain primarily a peasant community.

Evidence of the competition between pastoral and peasant "styles" appears in specific items and customs. The linguistic dichotomy between village and pastoralist Arabic is noted locally, but no overt expression is made that one has more prestige than the other. More of the population, however, speak the village form of Arabic than the pastoralist one, although the majority and the aristocracy of the population, including members of long sedentarized pastoralist tribes, are of shepherd origin. Peasant village bread has greater prestige than pastoralist bread, and there is some indication that girls of village tradition or who know a village woman's skills are preferred as wives to girls of pastoralist background. Household interiors of pastoral people are furnished and decorated, when possible, in village style. Moreover, the building of houses and compounds by families who have lived in tents at the edge of the village is considered a step upward in social status.

It is only within the year-round village population, however, that peasant village tradition triumphs over pastoral tradition. Once families of pastoral background have settled in an agricultural village, conformity to the local standard of living is bound to hasten the loss or replacement of certain of their own traits. But it is interesting to note that in the case of Tell Ṭoqaan and its area, pastoral clothing styles, emphasis on sheep as property, the lack of a sufi or religious fraternity, and a persistence of tribal law indicate that elements of the pastoral system predominate and show stability even though agriculture prevails.

The second issue in Tell Ṭoqaan, in terms of local historical trends, is whether or not the village will become a tribal or "one-ᶜashiirii" village, another full member of the Bu Layl enclave.

The two local village types found in the Tell Ṭoqaan area are distinguished chiefly on the basis of social organization. They are the tribal and peasant (fallaaHiin) village. The tribal village is composed of families and lineages which are regarded as sharing a common genealogical descent and affiliation with each other in the whole community. It is a section of a tribe, is named after a supposed progenitor, and is headed by a shayx, who is the leader of the most powerful family in terms of wealth, male descendants or kin, and clients. A section is affiliated, again by genealogical repute, with other villages of equal status into a tribal enclave. The enclave likewise bears a name and is led by a paramount shayx, he is head of one of the sections, but also holds his position by strength. The Bu Layl villages are the local enclave in the Tell Ṭoqaan area.

The peasant village, is composed of a number of "segments" or lineages. The lineages are similar in structure to each other, but are not necessarily considered to be of common descent. Each occupies a discrete settlement quarter in the village. Kafer Aamiin is the example in the area of a small peasant village without dual division. Saraaqab and Afess are large villages, apparently of this structure but are further divided into two factions, or "sides." How villages of this type are linked to others is not known in detail for this area. Saraaqab and Afess are connected with each other by marriages and Afess is regarded as a satellite or "daughter" of Saraaqab. Information from Tell Ṭoqaan also suggests that marriage and links of kinship are important elements of intervillage solidarity. Most of the villages west of the highway are of the Shaafite sect of Islam; there are also a few Shiite villages, but the extent of religious solidarity within one of these groups as compared to the other is not known to me.

The difference in social structure between the local tribal and peasant villages may also be expressed in terms of the location of the elite. The tribal village, to judge from the Bu Layl enclave and one Bu Shab^{c}an village observed, includes local residence of the elite as tribal or section shayxs who compose a local landed gentry or aristocracy. These marry within their "class", hold a major share of the land, and employ landless men as farmhands or as tenants. On the other hand, absentee urban landlords seem to be characteristic of the peasant villages.

In Tell Ṭoqaan opinion is divided as to the present character of their village organization. Some people say they have the solidarity of a typical small peasant village, and are semiautonomous in the administration of local custom, although under the ultimate control of the elite and the gendarmes of the national state system. Some say, however, that a dual division has taken place in the village, and that the two systems represent two factions in one community, like a large peasant village or one that is expanding in size. None but the local Bu Layl themselves look upon Tell Ṭoqaan as a Bu Layl village. As long as the elite of each system retain their landholdings in Tell Ṭoqaan the peasant village direction of development seems the more likely, provided no other factors interfere.

The second trend is in the direction of large-scale economic organization production and industrialization of agriculture and ultimate incorporation into a national economy and a national state political structure. Increase in scale is not necessarily wholly connected with the introduction of industrial agricultural machinery and, in fact, in Syria if not on the local scene, it may precede. The recent development of large landed estates throughout the Levant, and particularly in northern Syria, seems to be an aspect of the economic expansion which began slowly in the eighteenth century and which has increased in tempo up to the present.

In Tell Ṭoqaan and its area an example of this is seen in the extension of the entrepreneurial system to the marketing of milk products. Milk is bought in quantity, much of it processed on the spot into cheese and clarified butter, and transported by truck or bus to an urban center. The enterprise is initiated and financed by an urban merchant. For local consumption the villagers still manufacture dairy products on a household scale, but the availability of a market for surplus increases the value of local property in flocks of product animals.

One change seen in particular in Tell Ṭoqaan is the reduction in the village organization of peasant freehold and tenant cultivation, and a corresponding increase in farmhand wage labor. The peasant village system of cultivation is a small-scale enterprise with the division of land into plots which can be worked by extended family units, simple equipment, and unpaid personnel. In the traditional collective village system, cultivation is organized and controlled by the village in terms of such family units, and uniformity of planting and village synchronization of operations follows a traditional, local pattern.

In Tell Ṭoqaan, village control of cultivation and associated activities remains only in a few concerns: in the choice of herdsman, in the agreement on planting popcorn, in the two-field rotation, and, possibly, in the role of one recognized person to signal the time to begin the summer sequence of harvest operations.Connected with village solidarity in economic activities there remain some social customs and practices which also function to maintain whole-village cohesiveness: the funeral ritual, the village celebration of a wedding, and communal hyena hunt, and the luncheons for the gendarmes and visiting dignitaries. But village control of the cultivation practices in Tell Ṭoqaan is gradually disappearing. The peasant equipment is being replaced by industrial machinery which only the wealthy elite can afford. Much of the arable land is cultivated in large units by wage labor; much of it is plowed, planted, and harvested with machines. As a corallary to the reduction in land cultivated by peasant tenure or freehold, much of the agricultural production is now destined for market and less is held back for local needs. Industrial crops, such as cotton, become more important, when the national market is favorable, than the food staple crops. This amounts to loss of security in the subsistence "income" to the peasants of the village society and a transference of income to the elite landholders. Consequently, as the economic gap widens between the classes, it becomes impossible, as my informants pointed out, to keep up the expenses of traditional peasant life.

Incidents which occured in Tell Ṭoqaan in 1954 illustrate the tension thus set up between the traditional village system, with its emphasis on local organization and solidarity, and the expanding large-scale economy and the nationalization of sociopolitical controls. For example, there was the occasion on which a woman who lived in Tell Ṭoqaan as a consequence of marriage but who was a member of the Bu Shab^{c}an tribe and had come from Saraaqab, visited a Bu Shab^{c}an village. She identified herself by her present village of post-marital residence; it would have been expected that she would have claimed genealogical kinship as a Bu Shab^{c}anii, or at least to have said that she was from Saraaqab. Her action suggests, as does Shayx Nuuri's use of the national legal system to prosecute thieves, that the traditional significance of local, semiautonomous, sociopolitical organization characteristic of rural areas has been much reduced. Throughout the village society, in fact, tribal membership appeared to have little function outside of the aura of localized sociopolitical solidarity of the Bu Layl tribal villages and the economic co-operation in grazing arrangements between local nomadic and sedentary sections of the Bu Layl tribe.

The Tell Ṭoqaaniis are explicitly aware of the conflict between traditional tribal, kinship, and local village loyalties and the larger context of national control and citizenship. The local feud, which may be seen both as clash between competing groups and as a unifier of the local group, appears to be inactive at present, and national control through the gendarmes and courts is superceding such local processes. But kinship rights can still be effective, for one man in Tell Ṭoqaan was prevented from making a marriage he desired by the refusal of the girl's patrilineal uncle and cousin to release her from her traditional obligation.

The extensiveness of commercial relations among its families distinguishes Tell Ṭoqaan from other villages in its area. Traditional village customs of mutual aid in housebuilding, bride-price accumulation, and welfare remain only in memory and talk, except for a rare case of pledges by two men to help a young man with part of his bride price. Exchange of labor or co-operation between families is generally avoided except on a restricted basis which links no more than two families. When the labor force of the family is insufficient for the work at hand, other villagers will only agree to work if they are paid, preferably in money. Economic insecurity is seen in the turnover in personnel filling the local employment posts; the presence of numbers of vagrants and unemployed; the frequency with which men leave the village to seek work elsewhere, temporarily or permanently; the failure of shops. All these certify to the extent to which the traditional village system is disappearing as machinery and large-scale production replace the organization of human and animal labor in extended household units.

One of the results, and at the same time a further contributing factor, in this situation is the make-up of Tell Ṭoqaan society. There are more small families and broken families, many of recent immigration, which subsist on wage labor for the landlords than there are large lineages or extended families living on freehold and tenant farming. Here, again, competition between small-scale economy and that of large scale industrial farming has helped bring on a partial reduction of traditional village social structure based on the peasant system. In the complex of competing and coexistent systems and traits that is Tell Ṭoqaan, the peasant system is the local, traditional, small-scale one which operates within the dimensions of extended family, village, or local area. All of these are closely connected with each other and tend to "face inward" against neighbors or against the larger system of nation, national economy, and state tradition. Peasant or folk medicine is based on experience and believed is efficacious by the people who use it; city medicine derives from the wider context of professional institutional training. Peasant fuel is locally collected and made by traditional practices and in local design; kerosene, alcohol, and Primus stoves belong to the national economy of import.

Except in the areas of transportation and cultivating techniques, it is difficult to draw any distinction between industrial and traditional urban systems as they affect Tell Ṭoqaan. Industrial agricultural machinery and techniques are replacing peasant agricultural technology and reducing traditional areas of pastoral grazing to such a degree that the change can be observed and at least estimated in quantitative terms. The same can be said of the substitution of motor transport for camel transport in terms of cost and time. In both respects, change in Tell Ṭoqaan is extensive and revolutionary insofar as the peasant village community type is disappearing.

Otherwise, however, the products of industrial civilization are trickling down to the rural areas by the traditional urban system of itinerant merchants and traders and rural village markets. Brought by such avenues are tools, materials, articles of clothing which are not of traditional design but which are still not too dissimilar to be unacceptable. Some of these serve as functional replacements because they are, as in the cases of matches and cigarette lighters,

Primus stoves, kerosene lamps, rubber boots, and flashlights, improvements in terms of efficiency and comfort which do not tax the peasant technology and economy. A few others, such as shoehorns and city shoes and wrist watches, are items of prestige and fashion. A multiplicity of small notions are absorbed easily into traditional life. But this acceptance can also be seen as an increasing dependence on a world market of factory-made goods and as an accompaniment to the more fundamental change in cultivation technology.

Sjoberg (1952: 239) predicted the following course of events for the industrial-urbanization of feudal societies: "However, instead of encompassing the whole society (which is now almost the case in the United States), in the feudal order the industrial-urbanized society will in all probility be imposed upon the existing structure with the latter remaining to some degree intact." The bifurcation of society between elite and peasants will persist, he says, there will remain two coexistent societies; there will be modification rather than destruction. But this I question. It appears, to me, from this study of Tell Ṭoqaan, that it is the characteristics of peasant culture and village organization which are disappearing with the industrialization of its economy; that it is the typical traditional cultural patterns of the peasant household in a peasant village, if not the social bifurcation, which are in process of destruction. Regardless of how familiar and traditional are the means by which new things are received into an ancient and resilient culture, or how closely they are controlled by the usual rulers, a machine which replaces a peasant destroys a tradition.

APPENDIX A

In transcribing the Arabic terms into the system used here, it has not been possible to achieve consistency. The rendering of various terms, especially geographical or tribal names which have already appeared in the literature, has usually been in an established form. I have tried to transcribe, however, words I heard used in Tell Ṭoqaan in the symbols listed in Table XII (below), and thus to give as accurately as I could record it the Tell Ṭoqaaniis' pronunciation.

This table is an adaptation to typescript of the system in current usage by linguists for the transcription of Arabic in the Roman alphabet. In speech a and aa are backed when preceded or followed by velarized stops (ṭ, ḍ) and by g, gh, H, q, ṣ, and r; a and aa are fronted when preceded or followed by the rest of the consonants. Stress is on the first long-voweled syllable from the end of the word: da-jaa'-jii; yaa'-bis.

TABLE XII

PHONEMIC SYMBOLS USED IN TRANSCRIPTION OF ARABIC WORDS

Examples are taken from Tell Ṭoqaan (Tall Ṭawgaan) Arabic.

Symbol	Arabic Script	Example	English or Phonetic Equivalent
a		dajaajii, hen	debt
		ḍab^c, hyena	dull
aa		shabaab, young men	slab
		Haarr, hot	arm
aw		yawm, day	owe
ay		bayt, house	bait
b	ب	bayt, house	bait
c	ع	^caraab, Arabian	(Voiced pharyngeal fricative)
ch	ك	chaθiir, many	church
d	د	darj, drawer	dart

TABLE XII (Cont'd)

Symbol	Arabic Script	Example	English or Phonetic Equivalent
ḍ	ض	ḍabc, hyena	velarized d
đ	ذ	đurah, corn	thus
f	ف	faar, mouse	far
g	ڨ	gubgaab, clogs	gun
gh	غ	ghanam, sheep	(Voiced velar fricative)
h	ه	hawa, air	here
H	ح	Haarr, hot	(Unvoiced pharyngeal fricative)
i		jisr, bridge	gist
ii		ṭaHiin, flour	seen
j	ج	jisr, bridge	jump
k	ك	ktiir, many	king
l	ل	libis, clothing	list
m	م	maa^{c}iz, goat	mock
n	ن	naar, fire	near
q	ق	qubbii, dome	velarized k
r	ر	raas, head	rock
s	س	sinii, year	sin
ṣ	ص	ṣaar, became	velarized s
sh	ش	shabb, young man	shine
t	ت	tannuura, oven	tack

TABLE XII (Cont'd)

Symbol	Arabic Script	Example	English or Phonetic Equivalent
ṭ	ط	ṭaHiin, flour	velarized t
u		ṣuxn, warm	put
uu		zaytuun, olive	soon
w	و	waja, face	wall
x	خ	xubz, bread	(German, hoch)
y	ي	yaabis, dry	yam
?	أ	?ism name	(glottal stop)
Θ	ث	ΘalaaΘa, three	think (pastoralist form) tick (village form)

APPENDIX B

FAMILIES AND INDIVIDUALS OF TELL ṬOQAAN

The 55 families resident in Tell Ṭoqaan in 1954 are listed and described in Table XIII. Information basic to an understanding of the social organization of the village is also included, as is also census data. Census figures represent the number of persons living in each residence between January 4 and May 20, 1954; they do not indicate size of original family, because daughters leave the household upon marriage and sons bring wives from other families.

At the end of Table XIII the families in the Nuuri household are given. Individuals without family, lineage, or ethnic afflication are listed with pertinent data in Table XIV.

Families 1-17, 24, 25 comprise those "old" families and lineages of Tell Ṭoqaan; to these, however, may be added the families of remnant lineages, Nos. 18-23, which were once larger groups. Families 26, 33, 34, 40, 42, and 44 are regarded as acceptable families and close to the "old" category but ones whose heads are not second-generation residents. The heads of their households came to the village as very young men and have been long and firmly established in the village society. All the rest rank as newcomers and are regarded of little consequence by the members of the old group. The adults in these new families comprise immigrants to Tell Ṭoqaan, and most of them came within the last 10 or 15 years. Few hold any property, animals, or subtenures or are higher in economic status than laborers.

The incipient dual organization of the village might be expected to follow the division between old residents and newcomers. To some extent this is true: the Bu Layl families and several other new families (Nos. 27, 48, 49, 50, 52) are all associated with Shayx Nuuri, whose "side" is already distinguished in the village from that of the urban landlords. Other newcomers, however, are associated with the urban landlords (35, 36). The pastoralist-peasant dichotomy does not follow the Nuuri-urban landlord division, nor do the tribal and ethnic categories follow it.

TABLE XIII

RESIDENT FAMILIES OF TELL TOQAAN

Key No.	Lineage Name	House Name	With Local Lineage	Family Type	Tribal or Ethnic Affiliation	Social Status	Economic Status of Head of Household	Census	
								Male	Female
1.	SalaaH ad Diin	YaHya ᶜaarif	Yes	Nuclear	Turkish	Head of house; peasant	Peasant landholder (2 faddaan)	4	1
2.	Hammuud	Abdullah Hammuud	Yes	Extended	Bu Shayx	Lineage head; peasant	Peasant shareholder; client of Shayx Nuuri	9	2
3.	Hammuud	Hassan Hammuud	Yes	Nuclear	Bu Shayx	Head of house; peasant	Mason; laborer for Shayx Nuuri	4	3
4.	Hammuud	Hammuud Hammuud	Yes	Nuclear	Bu Shayz	Head of house; peasant	Dependent of No. 2 (deceased 4-25-54)	1	1
5.	Tell Haanii	AHmad Ibraahiim	Yes	Extended	Peasant	Lineage head; Muxtaar; peasant	Peasant shareholder (3 faddaan), Mazhar Effendii	3	3
6.	Tell Haanii	Xaliil Hassuun	Yes	Extended	Peasant	Head of house; peasant	Peasant shareholder (2 faddaan, Shanaasii Agha)	6	2
7.	Tell Haanii	Husayn Xaliil	Yes	Nuclear	Peasant	Son of No. 6; peasant	Peasant shopkeeper	2	2
8.	Tell Haanii	Hammuud Hassuun	Yes	Nuclear	Peasant	Head of house	Peasant shareholder (1 faddaan, YaHya Agha)	3	2

TABLE XIII (Cont'd)

Key No.	Lineage Name	House Name	With Local Lineage	Family Type	Tribal or Ethnic Affiliation	Social Status	Economic Status of Head of Household	Census	
								Male	Female
9.	Tell Haanii	Ibraahiim Naayif	Yes	Nuclear	Peasant	Peasant	Works for uncle (No. 5)	4	2
10.	Tell Haanii	MHammad Jum^c^a	Yes	Nuclear	Peasant	Peasant	Works for uncle (No. 5)	2	2
11.	Mabruuk	MHammad Salli^c^	Yes	Nuclear	Hanaadii	Head of house; peasant	Peasant shopkeeper	2	4
12.	Mabruuk	Jum^c^a Mabruuk	Yes	Nuclear	Hanaadii	Peasant	Laborer (chauffeur, YaHya Agha)	1	2
13.	Mabruuk	Jum^c^a Alaawii	Yes	Nuclear	Hanaadii	Peasant	Laborer (farmhand, Bayt Sharqii, Effendiin)	2	3
14.	Darwiish	MHammad ^c^iid	Yes	Extended	Kurd	Head of house; peasant	Former peasant share-holder; laborer (farmhand)	5	6
15.	Darwiish	Ibraahiim Darwiish	Yes	Nuclear	Kurd	Peasant	Laborer (farmhand), Bayt Sharqii	1	5
16.	Hawraanii	Abd RaHman	Yes	Nuclear	Peasant	Head of house	Former peasant foreman	3	1
17.	Hawraanii	AHmad Hawraanii	Yes	Nuclear	Peasant	Son of No. 16	Laborer for Shayx Nuuri	2	1
18.	None	^c^Ali Sariyya	Remnant	Nuclear	Peasant	Peasant	Laborer foreman, YaHya Agha	4	2

19.	None	Shahuud	Remnant	Nuclear	Mawali	Old pastoralist	Former shepherd; servant and client of Shayx Nuuri	2	5
20.	Jaddaan	MHammad Jaddaan	Remnant	Extended	Mawali-dollih	Old pastoralist	Laborer (farmhand, Shayx Nuuri)	5	2
21.	None	Husayn ^{c}ali	Remnant	Extended	Peasant	Peasant	Laborer (farmhand, Shanaasii Agha)	1	2
22.	DaHduu^c	Osman DaHduu^c	Remnant	Nuclear	Turkish	Peasant	Laborer (day)	2	2
23.	None	AHmad Bagg	Remnant	Nuclear	Hanaadii	Peasant	Laborer foreman, Shanaasii Agha	4	3
24.	Halabii	Ta^{c}lib	Yes	Extended	Peasant (urban origin)	Peasant	Peasant and laborer (1 faddaan)	3	4
25.	Ibn Kawwaam	Ghazzii	Yes	Extended	Sa^{c}ab	Peasant	Laborer (farmhand), YaHya Agha	4	2
26	None	Hassan Baṭṭa?	No	Extended	Hadiidiin	Pastoralist	Laborer (farmhand, Shayx Nuuri)	2	4
27.	Harbawwii	Harbawwii	No	Extended	Bu Harb	Pastoralist	Laborer (farmhand, Shayx Nuuri)	3	4
28.	None	MHammad Alaywii a) Fatuuma b) Hrayba	No	Poly-gynous	Bu Layl	Pastoralist	Partner in Sheep, Shayx Nuuri	a) 2 b) 2	1 5

TABLE XIII (Cont'd)

Key No.	Lineage Name	House Name	With Local Lineage	Family Type	Tribal or Ethnic Affiliation	Social Status	Economic Status of Head of Household	Census Male	Census Female
29.	None	Amuuna Jemma (widow)	No	Nuclear	Bu Layl	Pastoralist	Laborer (farmhand, Shayx Nuuri)	6	2
30.	None	Amiina (widow)	No	Nuclear	Bu Layl	Pastoralist	Laborer (day)	1	2
31.	None	Hamaadii	No	Nuclear	Bu Layl	Pastoralist	Laborer (farmhand, Shayx Nuuri)	2	3
32.	None	Sallah ᶜAluush	No	Nuclear	Bu Layl	Pastoralist	Camel transport	2	2
33.	Darfash	Darfash a) Subha b) Seriira	No	Poly-gynous	Harraam-shii	"Old" pastoralist	Laborer (day); property in sheep; client of Nuuri	a) 2 b) 1	2 1
34.	Darfash	Abid Jumᶜa	No	Nuclear	Harraam-shii	"Old" pastoralist	Laborer (farmhand, Shayx Nuuri)	2	1
35.	Sarawwii	Jumᶜa Sarawwii	No	Extended	Bu Saraw-wii	Pastoralist	Shareholder (3 faddaan, YaHya Agha)	1	3
36.	Sarawwii	Jaasim Zahiyya	No	Extended	Bu Saraw-wii	Pastoralist	Laborer (farmhand, Shanaasii Agha)	2	2
37.	None	Shawwax	No	Nuclear	Baggara	Pastoralist	Laborer (gardener, Shanaasii Agha); client of YaHya ᶜaarif	2	-

38.	None	Hilaal	No	Nuclear	Baggara	Pastoralist	Gardener, Shayx Nuuri	3	1
39.	None	Mustafa Sa^c^tuuf	No	Nuclear	Bu Chamal	Peasant	Laborer; dependent on No. 2	2	3
40.	None	MHammad Frayj a) Amun b) Fatuuma	No	Poly-gynous	Hadiidiin-Bu Slayb	Head of house; "Old" pastoralist	Property in sheep	a) 4 b) 2	6 3
41.	None	Ibrahiim ?id-Diik	No	Extended	Peasant	Head of house; peasant	Peasant-shopkeeper	3	6
42.	None	AHmad Adwaan	No	Nuclear	Mawali-Dollih	Head of house; "Old" pastoralist	Client of YaHya ^c^aarif; shop (closed); laborer for cheese agent at Rasaafa	2	3
43.	None	Abu ?Umar	No	Nuclear	Peasant	Peasant	Peasant-gardener and laborer (day), YaHya Agha; property in sheep	2	2
44.	None	Hajj Nuuri	No	Nuclear	Circassian	Head of house	Peasant-carpenter	4	3
45.	None	Fajjar	No	Nuclear	Mawali-Aswad	Pastoralist	Village herdsman	3	3
46.	None	Yussuf as Skayf	No	Nuclear	Peasant	Peasant	Peasant; shoe repairman	2	-

TABLE XIII (Cont'd)

Key No.	Lineage Name	House Name	With Local Lineage	Family Type	Tribal or Ethnic Affiliation	Social Status	Economic Status of Head of Household	Census	
								Male	Female
47.	None	Abu Xaalid	No	Extended	Bu Harb	Pastoralist	Laborer (day)	2	2
48.	None	Hammad	No	Nuclear	Sarayya	Pastoralist	Laborer (day); client of Nuuri	4	4
49.	None	Husayn the Circassian	No	Nuclear	Circassian	Peasant	Laborer foreman, Shayx Nuuri	1	2
50.	None	Amiin the Circassian	No	Nuclear	Circassian	Peasant	Laborer (chauffeur); client of Nuuri	1	1
51.	None	Hammuudii	No	Nuclear	Mawali	Pastoralist	Laborer (day); client of YaHya ᶜaarif	2	2
52.	None	Shahaada	No	Nuclear	Dlim	Pastoralist	Laborer (day); client of Nuuri; property in sheep	2	2
53.	None	?Umm Mustafa	No	Nuclear	Peasant	Peasant	Husband worked in another village	-	2
54.	None	Turkii Raxiil	No	Nuclear	Hadiidiin	Pastoralist	Laborer (day)	1	1
55.	None	Mussah	No	Nuclear	Bu Shabᶜan	Pastoralist	Laborer foreman, Bayt Sharqii	4	3

56.	Bu Layl	Nuuri a) Ayuush b) Sakkra c) Fawzii	No	Poly-gynous	Bu Layl	Tribal shayx	Tribal shayx and landlord	4	11
							CENSUS TOTALS	160	152
								312	

TABLE XIV

INDIVIDUALS LIVING IN TELL ṬOQAAN

No.	Name	Status	Employer or Affiliation	Census	
				Male	Female
1	Shayx MaHmuud Chawlak	Teacher ?imaam, client	Villagers YaHya ^{c}aarif	1	
2	^{c}Ali Sa^{c}iid	"Slave"	Shayx Nuuri	1	
3	Xlayf	Shepherd	Shayx Nuuri	1	
4	Ibrahiim ?urdinii	Farmhand	Shayx Nuuri	1	
5	Abdullah Ma^{c}aatii	Farmhand	Shayx Nuuri	1	
6	AHmad	Farmhand	AHmad Ibrahiim (Bayt Tell Haanii)	1	
7	Hakmat	Farmhand	AHmad Ibrahiim (Bayt Tell Haanii)	1	
8	?Abu Shariif	Farmhand	AHmad Ibrahiim (Bayt Tell Haanii)	1	
9	Shariif	Farmhand	AHmad Ibrahiim (Bayt Tell Haanii)	1	
10	Brother of No. 7	Farmhand	Jum^{c}a Saraawwii	1	
11	AHmad "Shayx" ^{c}awwii	Client	YaHya ^{c}aarif	1	
12	"Umm filfil"	Negress*	*		1
13	Son of No. 12	Infant		1	
14	Wada	(Irrational)	"Village ward"		1
			CENSUS	12	2
			TOTALS	14	

*Because of her ambiguous position this woman and her child have not been included in family data and analysis. She was proposed as wife of Hamuudii (see Table XIII, Family No. 51, finally nominally under Nuuri protection.

APPENDIX C

LAND DIVISIONS OF TELL ṬOQAAN

The thirty-two divisions of land are listed with names and rotation position in the spring of 1954 in Table XV. "Cultivated" in the table indicates the division was sown in winter crops at that time; "fallow" that the division had been left unplanted or was in preparation for summer crops. Divisions 1-16, and 30 are west and north sectors of the lands. Together they are called the "west" side and comprise "one field" of the two-field rotation system; 17-32 (except 30) comprise the "east" side. The key numbers correspond to those on the map (Fig. 3) which shows where each division is approximately located.

TABLE XV

LAND DIVISIONS OF TELL ṬOQAAN

Key No.	Name of Division	Meaning of Name	Rotation Position
1	gharbii ḍ ḍay^{c}a	"west of the village"	Cultivated
2	darb ShuuHa	"ShuuHa path"	Cultivated
3	mit?arriḍ	"abundant producer"	Cultivated
4	sahim jabas	"watermelon part"	Cultivated
5	?ard zuruura	"stony land"(?)	Cultivated
6	?arḍ jurn	"stone-trough land"	Cultivated
7	?arḍ jirwa kbiira	"big pomegranate (tree) land"	Cultivated
8	?ȧrḍ jirwa zghiira	"little pomegranate (tree) land"	Cultivated
9	^{c}abd l Qadduur	Proper name	Cultivated
10	?iṭ ṭawiil	"the long one"	Cultivated

TABLE XV (Cont'd)

Key No.	Name of Division	Meaning of Name	Rotation Position
11	wasṭaanii	"middle"	Cultivated
12	rub^{c}a kbiir	"big square"	Cultivated
13	rubca zghiir	"little square"	Cultivated
14	shmaalii xuurbii	"north of the ruin"	Cultivated
15	sahim mafazdii	Meaning unknown	Cultivated
16	shmaalii tall	"north of tell"	Cultivated
17	?arḍ s saqii	"watering land"	Inundated
18	tall zghiir	"little tell"	Fallow
19	tall kbiir	"big tell"	Fallow
20	darb ?usmaniyya	"Osmaniyya path"	Cultivated
21	tall ?it traajab	Meaning unknown	Fallow
22	ṭariiq Jazraaya	"Jazraaya road"	Fallow
23	mushmaat kbiir	Meaning unknown	Fallow
24	mushmaat zghiir	Meaning unknown	Fallow
25	ba?ṣaṣa	Meaning unknown	Fallow
26	?illukarr	Meaning unknown	Fallow
27	?abu AHmad	Proper name	Fallow
28	?arḍ shiyyaH	"old field" (?)	Fallow
29	baakir	Proper name?	Fallow
30	shuqf ma^{c}issra ṭariiq ?ajlass	? piece on Ajlass road	Cultivated
31	shuqf qubblii tall	"piece south of tell"	Partly cultivated
32	sahim shmaaliyyaat	Meaning unknown	Fallow

BIBLIOGRAPHY

Ashkenazi, T.
1938 Tribus semi-nomades de la Palestine du Nord. Paris.

Bacon, E.
1946 A Preliminary Attempt to Determine the Culture Areas of Asia. Southwest. Journ. Anthropol., 2:117-32.
1954 Types of Pastoral Nomadism in Central and Southwest Asia. *Ibid.*, 10:44-68.

Baldensperger, P. J.
1894 Orders of Holy Men in Palestine. Palestine Exploration Fund Quarterly Statement, pp. 22-38.

Barth, F.
1953 Principles of Social Organization in Southern Kurdistan. Universitets Etnografiske, Bull. No. 7. Oslo.
1954 Father's Brother's Daughter Marriage in Kurdistan. Southwest. Journ. Anthropol., 10:164-71.

Bergheim, S.
1894 Land Tenure in Palestine. Palestine Exploration Fund Quarterly Statement, pp. 191-95.

Blanchard, R.
1929 Asie occidentale. Geographie universelle, 8:1-234. Paris.

Bodenheimer, F. S.
1935 Animal Life in Palestine. Jerusalem.

Bonné, A.
1955 State and Economics in the Middle East. 2d ed., rev.; London.

Bowen-Jones, H.
1950 Notes on a Distinction between Peasantry and Small Farming. Advancement of Science (British), 7:68-72.

Burckhardt, J. L.
1822 Travels in Syria and the Holy Land. London.

Coon, Carleton S.
1951 Caravan: The story of the Middle East. New York.

Crist, R. E.
1953 The Mountain Village of Dahr, Lebanon. Smithsonian Instit. Ann. Rept. 1953, pp 407-23.

Davies, R. P.
1949 Syrian Arabic Kinship Terms. Southwest. Journ. Anthropol., 5:244-52.

Davis, K.
1955 The Origin and Growth of Urbanization in the World. Amer. Journ. Sociol., 60:429-37.

De Boucheman, A.
1934 Note sur la rivalité de deux tribus moutonnieres de Syrie: les "Mawali" et les "Hadidiyn." Revue des études Islamiques, 1:11-58.
1935 Material de la vie bedouine. Documents d'études orientales, No. 3. Damascus: L'Institute Français de Damas.
1937 Une petite cité caravanière: Soukhné. *Ibid.*, No. 6. Damascus: L'Institute Français de Damas.

Delegation generale de la France Combattante au Levant, inspection de mouvances bedouines de l'état de Syrie.
1943 Les tribus nomades de l'état de Syrie. Damascus.

Dubertret, L., and J. Weulersse
1940 Manuel de géographie. Syrie, Liban et Proche Orient 1: La peninsule arabique. Beirut.

Du Buisson, Du M.
1932 Instruments agricoles de Syrie. L'Ethnographie, 25:110-15.

Dunn, R. P., Jr.
1952 Cotton in the Middle East. Memphis.

Eberhard, W.
1953 Nomads and Farmers in Southeastern Turkey. Oriens, 6:32-49.

Fevret, M.
1949 La sericulture au Liban. Révue de géographie de Lyon, 24:247-60, 341-62.
1950 Un village du Liban: El Mtaine. *Ibid.*, 25:267-87.

Firth, R.
1952 Elements of Social Organization. London.

Fisher, W. B.
1950 The Middle East: A Physical, Social, and Regional Geography. London.

Gibb, H. A. R.
1949 Mohammedanism: An Historical Survey. London.

Gibb, H. A. R., and H. Bowen
1951 Islamic Society and the West: A Study of the Impact of Western Civilization in Moslem Culture in the Near East. Vol. 1: Islamic Society in the Eighteenth Century. Oxford.

Gibert, A.
1949 L'irrigation de la plaine de Homs et ses problems. Révue de géographie de Lyon, 24:151-58.

Gilmore, H. W.
1953 Transportation and the Growth of Cities. Glencoe, Illinois.

Granqvist, H.
1931 Marriage Conditions in a Palestinian Village. Part 1. Societas Scientiarum Fennica, Commentationes Humanarum Litterarum, Volume 3, No. 8. Helsingfors.
1935 Marriage Conditions in a Palestinian Village. Part 2. *Ibid.*, Vol. 6, No.8 Helsingfors.

Granott, A.
1952 The Land System in Palestine. (tr. by M. Simon) London.

Gulick, J. A.
1953 The Lebanese Village: An Introduction. Amer. Anthropol., 55:367-72.
1955 Social Structure and Culture Change in a Lebanese Village. Wenner-Gren Found. Anthropol. Res., Viking Fund Publ. Anthropol., No. 21. New York.

Hakim, G.
1953 Economic Development in the Middle East. *In:* Economic Problems of Underdeveloped Countries in Asia, ed. B. K. Madan, pp. 113-23. New Delhi.

Harrison, P. W.
1924 The Arabs at Home. New York.

Hazen, N. W.
1937 Agriculture in Palestine and the Development of Jewish Colonization. Foreign Agric., 1:119-48.

Hitti, P.
1951*a* History of the Arabs. 5th ed., rev; New York.
1951*b* History of Syria. New York.

Hourani, A. H.
1954 Syria and Lebanon: A Political Essay. Third Impression. Oxford.

Ibn Jubayr.
1952 The Travels of Ibn Jubayr. (tr. by R.J.C. Broadhurst). London.

Jaussen, P. A.
1948 Coutumes des Arabes au pays de Moab. Paris. (Reprint of edition of 1907.)

Jouin, J.
1934 La coutume féminine dans l'Islam Syro-Palestinian. Révue des études Islamiques, 4:481-505.

Keen, B. A.
1946 The Agricultural Development of the Middle East. London.

Latron, A.
1936 La vie rurale en Syrie et au Liban. Beirut.

Leach, E. R.
1940 Social and Economic Structure of the Rowanduz Kurds. London. School Econ. and Pol. Sci., Monogr. Soc. Anthropol., No. 3. London.

Lewis, N. N.
1949 Malaria, Irrigation, and Soil Erosion in Central Syria. Geog. Rev. 39:278-90.
1955 The Frontier of Settlement in Syria: 1800-1950. Internat. Affairs, 31:48-60.

Mouterde, R., and A. Poidebard
1943 Les limes de Chalcis. Paris.

Naaman, A.
1950 Précisions sur la structure agraire dans la région de Homs-Hama (Syrie). Bull. de l'Association de géographes Français. 206-07:53-59.

Olivier, G. A.
1807 Voyage dans l'empire Othoman, l'Egypte et la Perse. Vol. 4. Paris.

Patai, R.
1951 Nomadism: Middle Eastern and Central Asian. Southwest. Journ. Anthropol., 7:401-14.
1952 The Middle East as a Culture Area. Middle East Journ., 6:1-21.
1955 Cousin-right Marriage in Middle Eastern Marriage. Southwest. Journ. Anthropol., 11:371-90.

Poliak, A. N.
1935 Le charactère colonial de l'état mamelouk dans ses rapports avec la horde d'or. Revue des études Islamiques, 9:231-48.

Preston, H. G.
1903 Rural Conditions in the Kingdom of Jerusalem during the Twelfth and Thirteenth centuries. Philadelphia.

Proux, Mlle.
1938 Les Tcherkesses. La France Mediteranéenne et Africaine, 1:43-87.

Redfield, R.
1953 The Primitive world and Its Transformations. Ithaca.
1956 Peasant Society and Culture. Chicago.

Reich, S.
1937 Études sur les villages Araméens de l'Anti-Liban. Documents d'etudes orientales, 7. Damascus: L'Institute Français de Damas.

Reifenberg, A.
1938 The Soils of Palestine. (tr. by C. L. Whittles). London.

Royal Institute of International Affairs
1950 The Middle East: A Political and Economic Survey. London and New York.

Salamé, M.
1955 L'élevage au Liban. Révue de géographie de Lyon, 30:81-101.

Sjoberg, G.
1952 Folk and Feudal Society. Amer. Journ. Sociol., 58:231-39.
1955 The Pre-industrial City. *Ibid.*, 60:438-45.

Tannous, A. I.
1943 The Arab Village Community of the Middle East. Smithsonian Instit. Ann. Rept., pp. 523-43.
1955 Dilemma of the Elite in Arab Society. Human Organization, 14:11-15.

Tadmor, G.
1952 The Syrian Scene. Middle Eastern Affairs, 3:106-13.

Thoumin, R. L.
1936 Géographie humaine de la Syrie centrale. Paris.

Von Oppenheim, M. F.
1939 Die Beduinen. Vol. 1. Leipzig.

Weulersse, J.
1938 La primauté des cités dans l'économie Syrienne. 15th International Georgraphical Congress. Comptes rendu 2. Travaux 3:235-39. Amsterdam.
1940 Le Pays des Alouites. Two volumes. Tours.
1946 Paysans de Syrie et du proche-orient. 8th ed.; Paris.

Widmer, R.
1936 Population. Chap. *In:* Economic Organization of Syria, ed. S. Himadeh. Beirut.

Wolf, E. R.
1955 Types of Latin American Peasantry: A Preliminary Discussion. Amer. Anthropol., 57:452-71.

Worthington, E. B.
1946 Middle East Science. London.

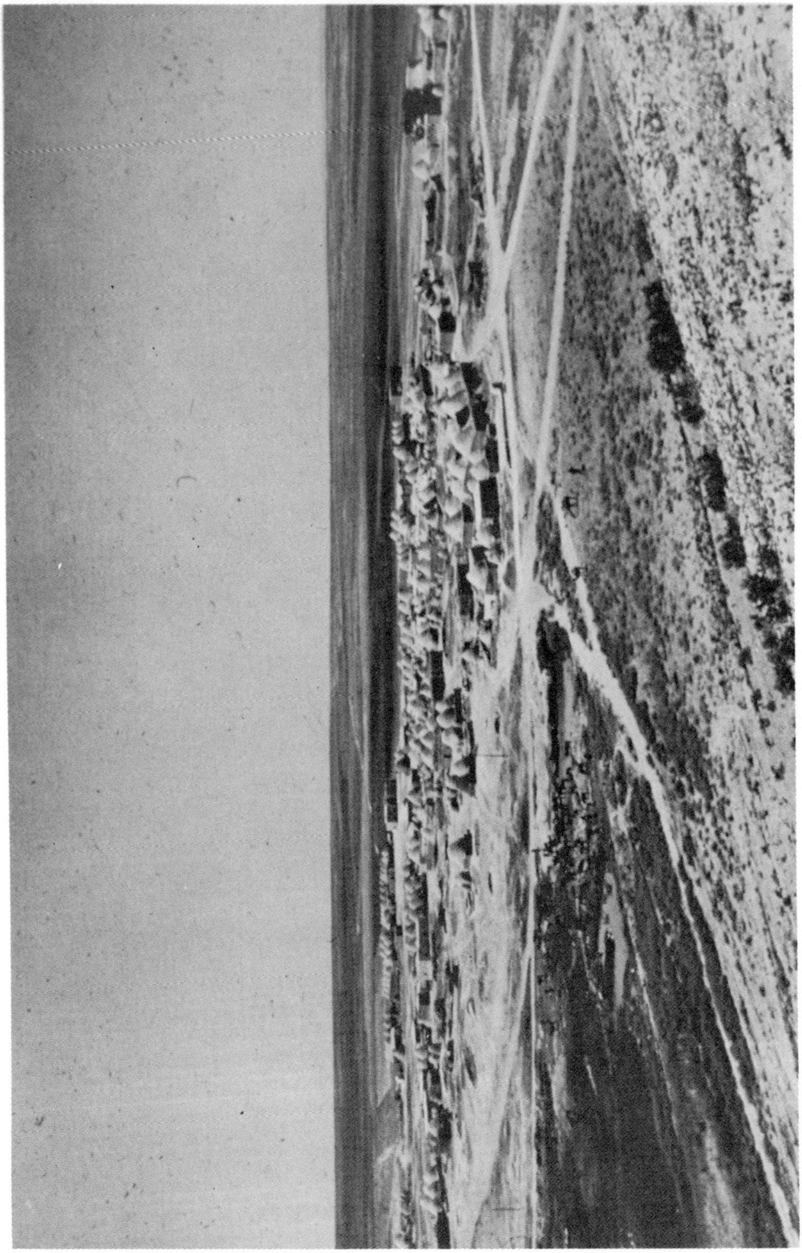

Fig. 6. Tell Ṭoqaan.

Fig. 7. Shayx Nuuri's house and stable compound.

Fig. 8. Cemetery and Camping Ground.

Fig. 9. Shepherd family following flocks to spring grazing.

Fig. 10. Qirbaat (Gypsy) Tents.

Fig. 11. Boy with hedgehog.

Fig. 12. Young men playing ball.

Fig. 13. Young men and hunting dogs.

Fig. 14. Market Day at Ma^{c}aret Mishriin.

Fig. 15. Plowing.

Fig. 16. Plowshare used in stony soil.

Fig. 17. Peasant's seedling bed.

Fig. 18. Young woman planting cotton with seed tube.

Fig. 19. Irrigation wheel.

Fig. 20. Irrigating garden beds.

Fig. 21. Jilbaan (vetch) harvest.

Fig. 22. The Haylaan (threshing machine).

Fig. 23. Excavating on the village midden.

Fig. 24. A shayx's tomb in Tell Ṭoqaan.

Fig. 25. Milking sheep.

Fig. 26. Selling milk to cheese agent.

Fig. 27. Mixing mud for bricks.

Fig. 28. Making mud bricks.

Fig. 29. Mason laying mud brick wall.

Fig. 30. Constructing an arch.

Fig. 31. Building a domed room.

Fig. 32. Women building a storage bin.

Fig. 33. Interior: grain storage bin in rear.

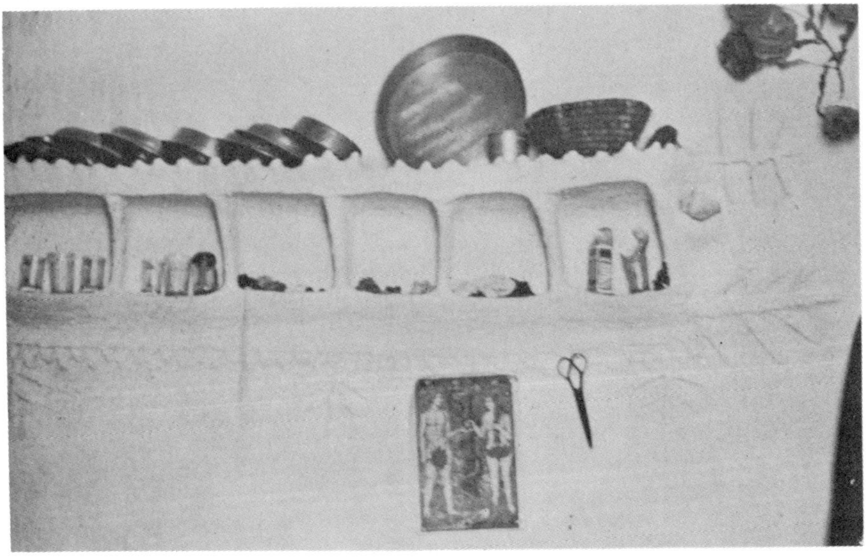

Fig. 34. Interior: molded shelf.

Fig. 35. Burden carrying.

Fig. 36. Girls drawing water.

Fig. 37. Tools and utensils.

Fig. 38. Making winter fuel.

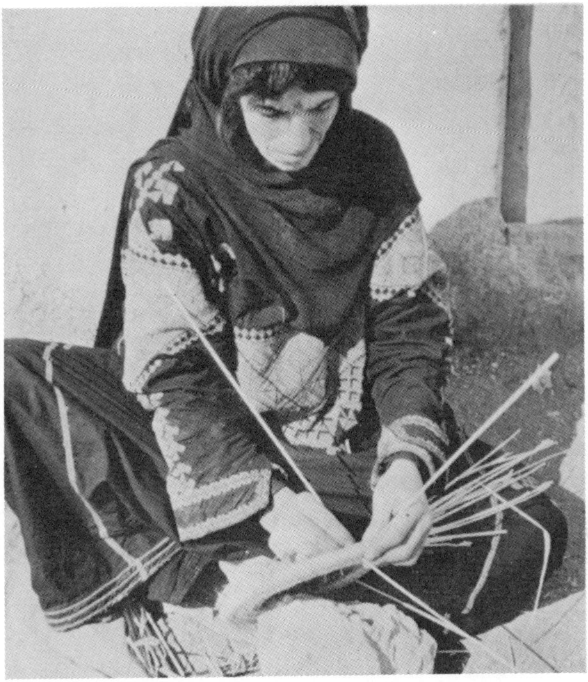

Fig. 39. Making a tray of wheat straw.

Fig. 40. Washing pots and pans.

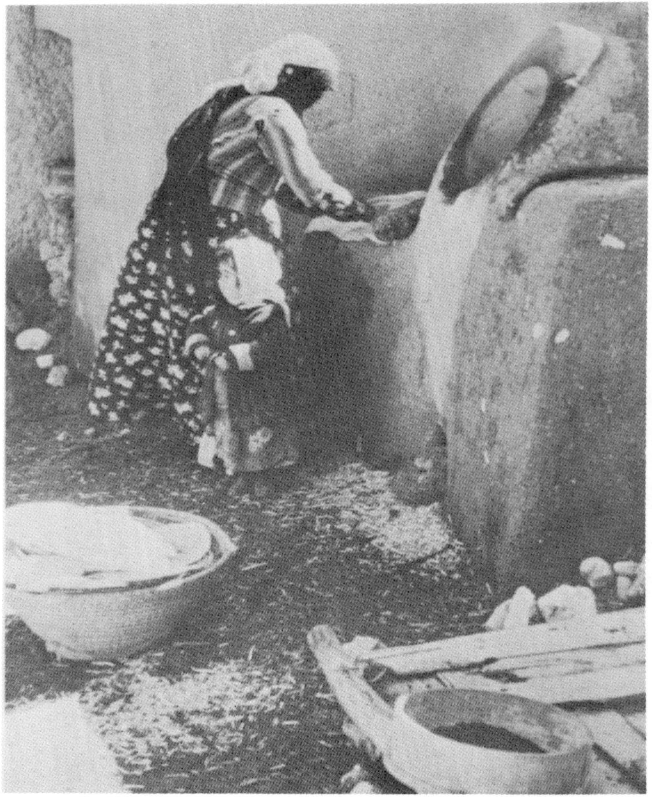

Fig. 41. Baking village bread.

Fig. 42. Portable fireplace.

Fig. 43. Stationary fireplace.

Fig. 44. Mother and children.

Fig. 45. Pounding wheat at Shayx Nuuri's.

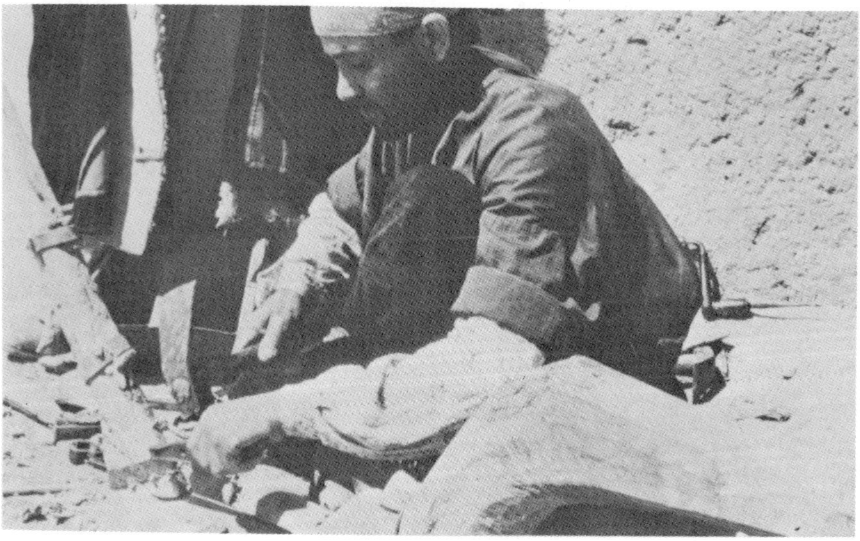

Fig. 46. Carpenter repairing plow.

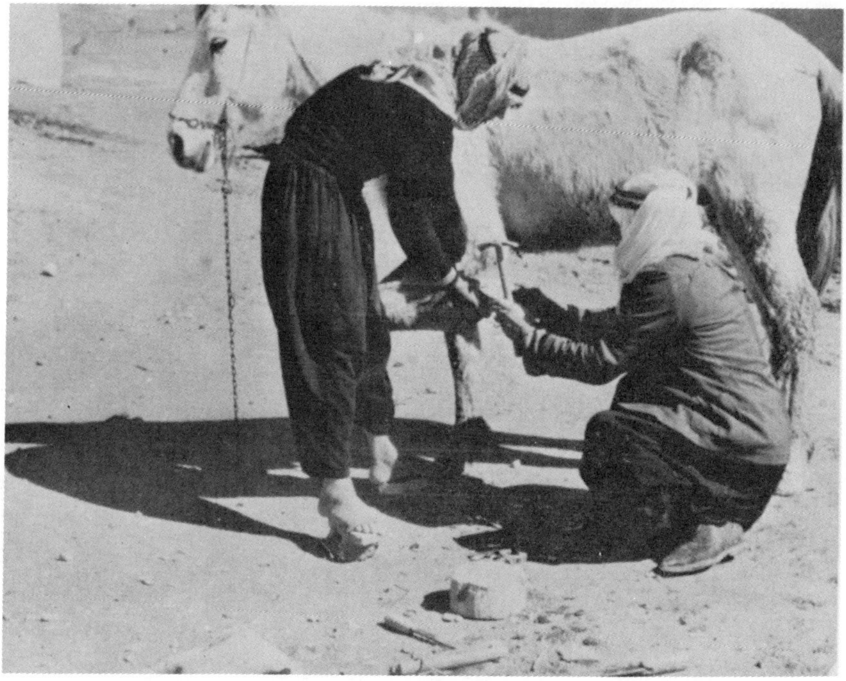

Fig. 47. Horseshoeing.

Fig. 48. Seed tubes mounted on tractor.

Fig. 49. Women's clothing: Pastoralist.

Fig. 50. A recent bride.

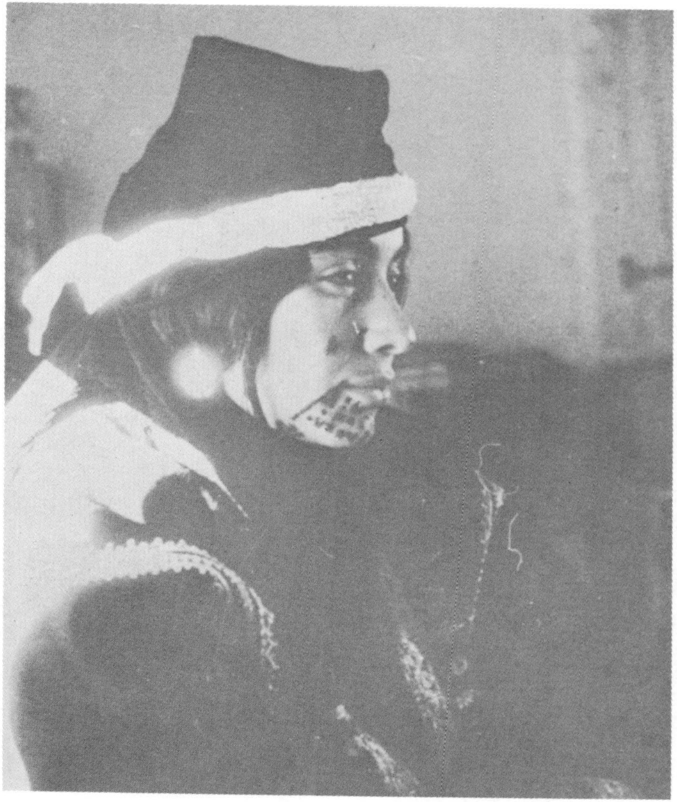

Fig. 51. Facial tattoos.

Fig. 52. Forearm tattoos.

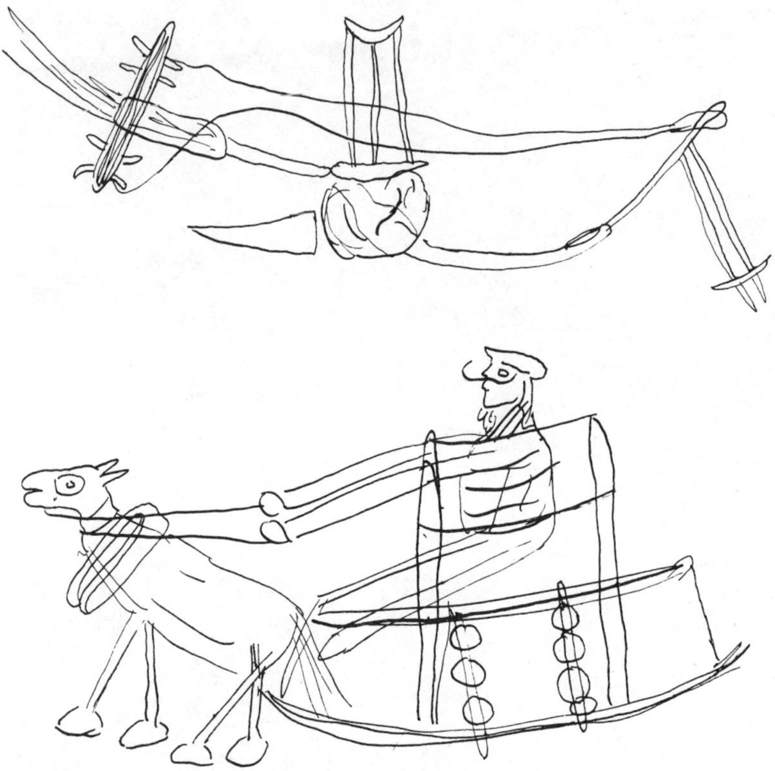

Fig. 53. Plow and threshing machine. Drawings by villager.

Fig. 54. Man smoking water pipe. Three persons contributed to the original drawing.